ISLE WIGHT

www.philips-maps.co.uk
First published in 2004 by Philip's,
a division of Octopus Publishing Group Ltd
www.octopusbooks.co.uk
Endeavour House, 189 Shaftesbury Avenue
London WC2H 8JY
An Hachette UK Company
www.hachette.co.uk

Second edition 2010
First impression 2010
IIOWBA

978-1-84907-080 5 (Red Books)

© Philip's 2010

This product includes mapping data licensed from
Ordnance Survey® with the permission of the
Controller of Her Majesty's Stationery Office.
© Crown copyright 2010. All rights reserved.
Licence number 100011710.

Photographic acknowledgements:
title page Shellyrolo/iStockphoto.com
XII top left matphoto/iStockphoto.com
XII top right Amanda Lewis/iStockphoto.com
XII centre Chris Moncrief/Dreamstime.com
XII bottom rest/iStockphoto.com
XIII left Steve Stone/iStockphoto.com
XIII right Amanda Lewis/iStockphoto.com
XIV Biginfocus/Dreamstime.com
XV top Epphoto/Dreamstime.com
XV bottom Chris Steer/iStockphoto.com

Printed in China

Contents

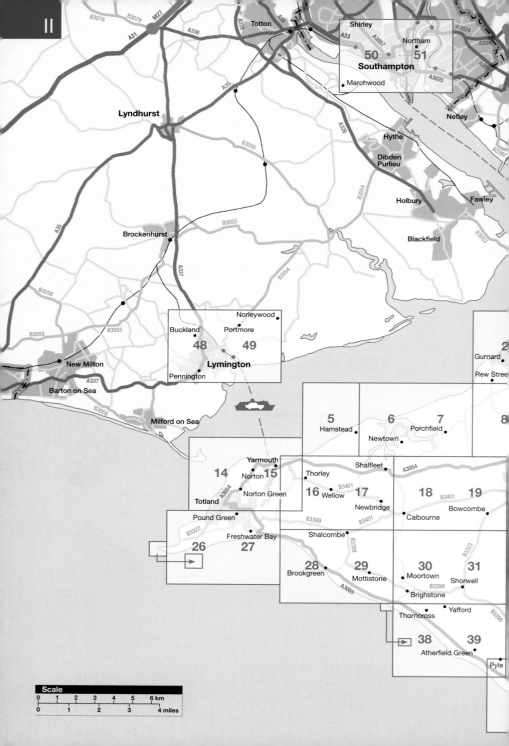

II

B3078　B3079　M27

B3079

A31

A336　Totton

A326

A31

A336

A31

A35

Lyndhurst

B3056

A326

Southampton
Shirley
A33　A3057　Northam
50 — 51
Marchwood

A3024

A334

A3025

Netley

Hythe

Dibden
Purlieu

A3051

A3056

B3056

B3054

Holbury

Fawley

B3055

Brockenhurst

B3055

Blackfield

B3053

A35

A337

B3054

B3058

B3055

New Milton

B3055　B3055

Norleywood

Buckland　Portmore

48　49

Lymington

Pennington

Gurnard　2

Rew Stree

A337

Barton on Sea

B3058

Milford on Sea

5
Hamstead

6
Newtown

7
Porchfield

8

B3058

14

Yarmouth
Norton　15
Norton Green

Totland

Pound Green

Thorley

Shalfleet　A3054

16　17
Wellow　B3401
Newbridge

18　B3401　19
Calbourne　Bowcombe

B3322

26　27
Freshwater Bay

B3399

Shalcombe

B3399　B3401

B3323

28　29
Brookgreen　Mottistone

30　31
Moortown　Shorwell
B3399
Brighstone

Thorncross　Yafford

38　39
Atherfield Green

A3055

Pyle

B3399

Scale
0　1　2　3　4　5　6 km
0　1　2　3　4 miles

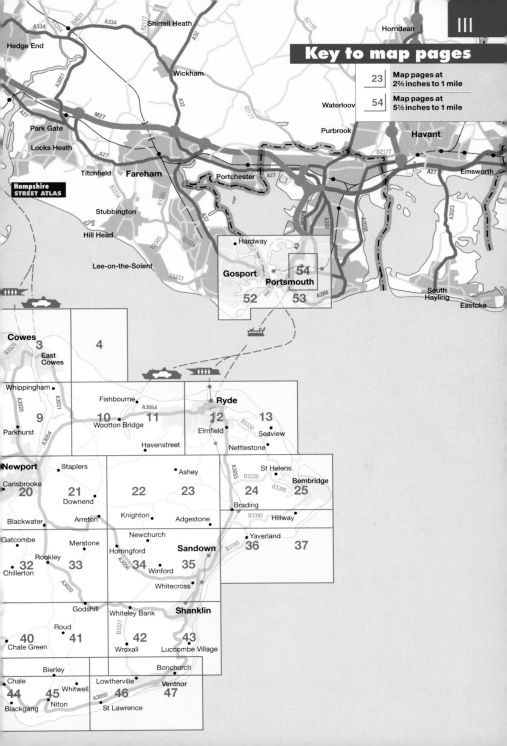

III

Key to map pages

| 23 | Map pages at 2⅔ inches to 1 mile |
| 54 | Map pages at 5⅓ inches to 1 mile |

Horndean

Shirrell Heath

Hedge End

A334   B3035   A334   Wickham   B2150

Waterloov

Park Gate   M27   Purbrook   Havant

Locks Heath   A27   Portchester   Emsworth

Titchfield   **Fareham**   A27

Hampshire STREET ATLAS

Stubbington

Hill Head

Hardway

Lee-on-the-Solent

Gosport   **Portsmouth**   South Hayling

52   **53**   Eastoke

Cowes

3   **4**

East Cowes

Whippingham

Fishbourne   **Ryde**

9   **10**   **11**   **12**   **13**

Parkhurst   Wootton Bridge   Elmfield   Seaview

Havenstreet   Nettlestone

Newport   Staplers   Ashey   St Helens

Carisbrooke   **21**   **22**   **23**   **24**   Bembridge

20   Downend   **25**

Blackwater   Arreton   Knighton   Adgestone   Brading   Hillway

Gatcombe   Newchurch   Yaverland

Merstone   Horringford   **Sandown**   **36**   **37**

32   **33**   **34**   Winford   **35**

Rookley   Whitecross

Chillerton

Godshill   **Shanklin**

Whiteley Bank

Roud   **42**   **43**

40   **41**   Wroxall   Luccombe Village

Chale Green

Bierley   Bonchurch

Chale   Lowtherville   Ventnor

44   **45**   Whitwell   **46**   **47**

Blackgang   Niton   St Lawrence

Tourist information

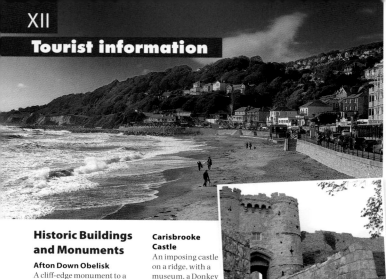

▲ Bembridge Windmill
◄ Ventnor
► St Catharine's Oratory
►► St Boniface Church
◄ Carisbrook Castle
▼ Tennyson monument

Historic Buildings and Monuments

Afton Down Obelisk
A cliff-edge monument to a 15-year-old who fell to his death here in 1846, built as a warning to visitors. **Afton Down 27 E6**

Appuldurcombe House
A partially restored Baroque house built in the 18th century, with 11-acre grounds, including gardens designed by Capability Brown, a nature trail, and an Owl and Falconry Centre with daily flying displays. Special events include plays and military re-enactments. **Wroxall, near Ventnor** ✆ **01983 852484 • www.appuldurcombe.co.uk 42 A4**

Ashey Sea Mark
A solid white sea-mark constructed for sailors in 1735. **Ashey Down Summit 23 A4**

Bembridge Fort
An abandoned 1860s land fort. Guided tours only. **Between Culver Cliff and Brading • www.nationaltrust.org.uk 24 E1**

Bembridge Windmill
The only surviving windmill on the island, built c.1700 and retaining its original wooden machinery. **Mill Road, Bembridge • www.nationaltrust.org.uk** ✆ **01983 873945 25 B3**

Brading Roman Villa
A 1st-century AD Roman villa excavated in the 1880s, with important 4th-century mosaics. Visitor centre and exhibition. **Morton Old Road, Brading •www.bradingromanvilla.org.uk** ✆ **01983 406223 23 F1**

Carisbrooke Castle
An imposing castle on a ridge, with a museum, a Donkey Centre, an 800-year-old Great Hall, a wellhouse with a treadwheel, and excellent views. **Carisbrooke, Newport** ✆ **01983 522107 • www.english-heritage.org.uk 20 B4**

Grays Monument
A memorial to a 9-year-old chimney sweep killed by his employer in 1822. **Church Litten, Newport 20 E6**

Hoy Monument
A tall stone column topped by a large finial sphere, erected in 1814 by local merchant Michael Hoy to commemorate a visit to Britain by Tsar Alexander I. **St Catherine's Down (near Blackgang) 44 F8**

Long Stone
Neolithic barrow (large grave) marker situated on tumuli and dated 3000–2000BC. **Mottistone Down, near Brighstone 29 D5**

Morton Manor
A manor house first built in 1249, augmented by a Tudor longhouse and largely rebuilt in 1680, with Georgian interiors and splendid gardens with rhododendrons, azaleas, magnolias and more. **Yarbridge, near Brading** ✆ **01983 406168 36 A7**

Needles Old Battery
A dramatically sited 1862 coastal fort built to prevent invasion by the French, with an exhibition, the original gun barrels, a restored laboratory, searchlight position and posi-tion-finding cells, children's information boards and activity packs, and a 65m tunnel leading to a splendid viewpoint over the Needles (famous chalk pinnacles) and a tearoom. **West High Down, Alum Bay** ✆ **01983 754772 • www.nationaltrust.org.uk 26 B4**

Newport Roman Villa
The remains of a Roman farmhouse built c. AD280, with part of a bath and a hypocaust system, recreations of everyday scenes (and re-enactment days), and a Roman herb garden. **Cypress Road, Newport** ✆ **01983 529720 •www.iow.gov.uk 20 E6**

Nunwell House and Gardens
A handsome family residence built in 1522, with the Parlour Chamber where Sir John Oglander played host to Charles I on his last night of freedom. There are displays on the family's military connections, an Old Kitchen exhibition, and 5 acres of grounds, including a walled garden with views across the Solent. **Coach Lane, Brading** ✆ **01983 407240 • www.islandbreaks. co.uk 23 F3**

Old Town Hall, Newtown
A 17th-century hall, now containing an exhibition on local history, including 'Ferguson's Gang' of anonymous benefactors. **Newtown** ✆ **01983 531785 •www.nationaltrust.org.uk 6 E2**

Osborne House
Queen Victoria's imposing three-storey seaside retreat and the place where she died, built in 1848, given to the nation by Edward VII and managed by English Heritage. Interior highlights include the Indian Room, Victoria's bedroom and closet, and the royal nursery. The grounds include a late 18th-century walled kitchen garden and pleasure grounds that survived from the previous estate on the site, and the parterre gardens and terraces have been restored to their Victorian layout. **East Cowes** ✆ **01983 200022 • www.english-heritage.org.uk 3 F2**

St Catherine's Oratory (Pepper Pot)
An octagonal tower, built in 1328 as a penance for stealing property from a wreck. It is said to have been used as a lighthouse. **St Catherine's Down, Chale • www.english-heritage.org.uk 44 E5**

Tennyson Monument
A marble Maltese cross erected in memory of Alfred Lord Tennyson after his death in 1892; the poet had

Ventnor Botanic Garden
A 22-acre botanic garden founded in 1970, with plants from around the world, a Visitor Centre with exhibitions and library, a coastal path, a picnic area and a playground. **Undercliff Drive, Ventnor** ☎01983 855397 ·www.botanic.co.uk **46 D4**

Wayside Herbs and Flowers
A small herb and wildflower garden with Kune Kune pigs and Shetland and Jacob sheep, plus a programme of summer events. **Bamfurlung Chine Lane, Yafford** ·www.waysideherbs.co.uk ☎01983 740787 **38 H8**

settled at Farringford in 1853. **Tennyson Down, Freshwater Bay·** www. isleofwightattractions.co.uk ☎01983 280111 **26 H5**

Yarmouth Castle
A Tudor castle, Henry VIII's last fortress, with exhibitions of local paintings and photographs of old Yarmouth, fine views over the Solent from its battlements and good picnic spots on its rampart lawns. **Yarmouth** · www.english-heritage.org.uk ☎01983 760678 **15 C6**

Gardens and Parks

See also Appuldurcombe House, Morton Manor and Nunwell House and Gardens (Historic Buildings)

Afton Park Beautifully sited 7-acre gardens with an orchard, a wildflower meadow, a plant nursery, farm shop and a café. **Newport Road, Freshwater** ☎01983 755774 · www.aftonpark.co.uk **27 D8**

Mottistone Manor Garden
A terraced garden with borders and a kitchen garden surrounding a medieval/Elizabethan manor house in a wooded valley with views of the Channel. **Hoxall Lane, Mottistone** ☎01983 741302 · www.nationaltrust.org.uk **29 D4**

Old Smithy Gardens
Landscaped gardens set around a former blacksmith's forge (now a retail complex), with a Model Village of local places of interest, an aviary, grottoes, and a cottage garden with unusual herbs. **High Street, Godshill** ☎01983 840364 ·www.theoldsmithy.com **41 D8**

Places of Worship

All Saints (Church of the Lily Cross) A church on a 950-year-old site of Christian worship; the present (4th) church was built in the early 14th century, with two naves separated by a wooden screen, one for parishioners, the other for manorial workers. The 'Lily Cross' wall-painting was uncovered in the 19th century. **Godshill 41 D8**

Church of the Holy Cross
Originally a Norman church retaining its old doorway with a sculpted grotesque, a 13th-century chancel, and a 15th-century bell thought to have come from nearby Quarr Abbey, now housed in a 1925 bellcote. The churchyard contains the tomb of Samuel Giant, said to have been the biggest man in the world, who died in 1844. **Binstead 11 F6**

St Andrew An isolated ancient church overlooking a treacherous stretch of coast, built in the 12th century but altered and enlarged several times, with a 15th-century tower. **Chale 44 C6**

St Boniface The island's second-smallest church, on a place of worship dating back as far as the Saxon occupation and dedicated to a Saxon saint. **Bonchurch 47 D7**

St George, Arreton A church on the site of a private chapel of the lords of the manor of Arreton, first recorded in AD901: the present building is mainly 11th century, with some late Saxon or early Norman elements and a 13th-century

tower. The churchyard contains the tomb of Elizabeth Wallbridge, heroine of bestselling story 'The Dairyman's Daughter.' **Arreton 21 E2**

St Mary the Virgin, Brading
A church with a Norman nave containing a simple Jacobian table serving as an altar, beneath which Saxon remains were discovered, and a memorial to Reverend Leight Richmond, author of 'Annals of the Poor'. **24 B3**

St Mildred Built in the 1850s, this fanciful Gothic-inspired church was used by Queen Victoria when at Osborne House. As well as royal memorials and the queen's pew, it contains a beautiful bronze screen by Alfred Gilbert in the chancel arcade. **Beatrice Avenue, Whippingham 9 E8**

St Peter Originally a Norman building, the current grade-1 Perpendicular church mostly dates from the 15th century. It has an unusual layout, a pulpit that is entered through one of the piers. Jacobean benches and a 14th-century mural of St Christopher. **Shorwell 31 B2**

Museums and Galleries

See also Carisbrooke Castle

Bembridge Heritage Centre
An exhibition of village life past and present, in a former Victorian school building. **Church Road, Bembridge** ☎01983 873606 **25 C5**

Brighstone Village Museum
A small museum on Victorian

life. **North Street, Brighstone** ☎01983 740689 ·www.nationaltrust. org.uk **30 B2**

Calbourne Water Mill and Rural Museum
A working water mill first mentioned in the Domesday Book, with various small museums (including an old fire station and bakery), displays on renewable energy, punts and children's activities, and surrounded by ancient oak woodland providing a habitat for badgers, red squirrels and more. **Newport Rd, Calbourne** · www.calbournewatermill.co.uk ☎01983 521227 **17 E2**

Classic Boat Museum
A collection of restored sailing and motor boats and boating memorabilia. **The Quay, Newport** ·www.classicboatmuseum.co.uk ☎01983 583493 **20 E8**

Cowes Maritime Museum
A small exhibition tracing local maritime history through models and paintings. **Library, Beckford Road, Cowes** ☎01983 823433 ·www.iwight.com **3 B4**

Dimbola Lodge
A photography museum and gallery in the one-time home of 19th-century photographer Julia Margeret Cameron, with displays of antique cameras and exhibitions of Cameron's and others' images, including contemporary work. **Terrace Lane, Freshwater Bay** ☎ 01983 756814 **27 C6**

East Cowes Heritage Centre
Small museum on the history of East Cowes in permanent and temporary exhibits. **8 Clarence Road, East Cowes** ☎01983 280310 ·www.eastcowesheritagecentre.org.uk **3 C3**

Fort Victoria Model Railway

The world's largest computer-controlled model railway. **Fort Victoria Country Park** ☎01983 761553 • www.fortvictoriamodelrailway.co.uk **14 F6**

Island Planetarium

An astronomy centre and planetarium theatre hosting multimedia shows, stargazing evenings and lectures. **Fort Victoria Country Park, near Yarmouth** • www.islandastronomy.co.uk ☎01983 761555 **14 F6**

Isle of Wight Bus Museum

A collection of island buses and coaches, plus an early-1900s Ryde Pier tram car, in a former grain warehouse. **The Quay, Newport** ☎01983 533352 • www.iowbusmuseum.org.uk **20 E8**

Isle of Wight Military Museum A good selection of

World War 2 and postwar armoured vehicles and other equipment, guided tours. Regular displays in summer includr rides round the tank course. **490 Newport Road, Cowes** www.isleofwight.com/militarymuseum ☎ 01983 527491 **9 A6**

Isle of Wight Model Railway

A miniature-railway centre with history displays, antique sets and track layouts. **The Parade, Cowes** ☎01983 280111 **3 B5**

Lilliput Antique Doll and Toy Museum

More than 2000 dolls and playthings dating from c.2000BC to 1945. **High Street, Brading** • www.lilliputmuseum.org.uk ☎01983 407231 **24 B3**

Museum of Island History

A museum charting the island's history from prehistoric times, with interactive exhibits, quizzes, games and more. **Guildhall, High Street, Newport** • www.iwight.com ☎01983 823433 **20 E7**

Quay Arts Centre

An art gallery and live events venue in a 19th-century brewery warehouse. **Sea Street, Newport Harbour** ☎01983 82249 **20 E7**

Shipwreck Centre and Maritime Museum

Local maritime heritage displays, including items recovered from shipwrecks, diving equipment, ships' models, and exhibits about the lifeboat services. **Arreton Barns Craft Village, Arreton** ☎01983 533709 **21 E2**

Smuggling Museum

An exhibition on smuggling history and methods from the 13th century onward. **Ventnor Botanic Garden (see xiii)** ☎01983 853677 **46 D4**

Nature and Animals

See also Appuldurcombe House and Carisbrooke Castle

Amazon World

A simulated rainforest with a large Jurassic-themed adventure park, exotic animals, falconry displays and talks by the keepers. **Watery Lane, Newchurch, near Arreton** www.amazonworld.co.uk ☎01983 867122 **34 C5**

Brickfields Horse Country

An equestrian attraction with shire horses, miniature Shetland ponies, a farm corner, a museum, a blacksmith's forge, a riding school, a play area and special events. **Newnham Road, Binstead, Ryde** ☎01983 566801 • www.brickfields.net **11 E3**

Butterfly and Fountain World

Indoor landscaped gardens (a Japanese garden with koi carp, a tropical garden and an Italian garden) with freeflying butterflies, fountain displays and more. **Staplers Road, Wootton** • www.butterfly-world-iow.co.uk ☎01983 883430 **10 B2**

Coastal Visitors Centre

The point of contact for those interested in or concerned about the island's coastline, the longest stretch in the UK, with themed rooms on different aspects of the coast and its management, from plant and animal life to marine archaeology, aquarium tanks and a children's touch pool. Guided walks, children's activities and talks. **Isle of Wight Centre for the Coastal Environment, Dudley Road, Ventnor** ☎01983 857220 • www.coastalwight. gov.uk/coastalcentre.htm **47 A5**

Colemans Animal Farm

A family farm with feeding and petting sessions, milking, pony rides, a tractor fun park, sand pits, an adventure play and picnic areas and daily activities. **Colemans Lane, Porchfield** • www.colemansfarmpark.co.uk ☎01983 522831 **7 E1**

Dinosaur Farm Museum

A conservation facility for and museum of locally discovered dinosaur remains, with a fossil identification service, children's activities and a tearoom. **Military Road (A3055), nr Brighstone** • www. isleofwight.com/dinosaurfarmmuseum ☎01983 74084 **38 G6**

Dinosaur Isle

A purpose-built attraction with life-sized models of some of the Isle's dinosaur types in a recreated landscape, interactive exhibits, and the opportunity to see volunteers working on new fossil finds. **Culver Parade, Sandown** ☎01983 404344 • www.dinosaurisle.com **36 B4**

Donkey Sanctuary

A donkey-rescue charity housing more than 200 donkeys and other animals over 50 acres, and offering an 'Adopt a Donkey' scheme. **Lower Winstone Farm, Whiteley Bank, Wroxall** www.iwdonkeysanctuary.co.uk ☎01983 852693 **42 B7**

Flamingo Park Wildlife Encounter

Animal park with flamingos, pelicans, penguins, owls, wallabies, meerkats, Asian otters, beavers, red squirrels, an aviary, a Discovery Zone, feeding sessions and landscaped gardens overlooking the Solent. **Springvale, Seaview** ☎01983 612153 • www.flamingopark.com **13 B4**

The Needles Rocks and Lighthouse

Fort Victoria Marine Aquarium and Sunken History Exhibition

An aquarium largely devoted to local sea fish and invertebrates, set in the remains of a Victorian fort with a tropical reef section and an exhibition on marine archaeology around the world. **Fort Victoria Country Park, near Yarmouth** •www.fortvictoria.co.uk/aquarium/marine–aquarium.htm ✆ 01983 760283 **14 F6**

Isle of Wight Zoo

Incorporating the Tiger and Big Cat Sanctuary – a collection of rare and endangered big cats. The zoo also features lemurs and monkeys, spiders, reptiles and amphibians, plus a children's play area and pets' corner. **Seafront, Yaverland, Sandown** • www.isleofwightzoo.com ✆ 01983 403883 **36 B4**

Natural History Centre

A 17th-century squire's cottage housing collections of shells, minerals, insects and birds, plus aquaria, a pond with koi carp and ornamental fountains, and a replica set of the Crown Jewels used during a rehearsal for the Queen's coronation. **High St, Godshill** • www.shellmuseum.co.uk ✆ 01983 840333 **41 D8**

Shanklin Chine An historic gorge, once the haunt of smugglers, with waterfalls, nature trails (with the chance of red squirrels), nature hide, rare plants, a Heritage Centre with exhibitions, and a Victorian tea garden. It is part of The Chines, a special coastal feature (see also Blackgang Chine xv). **Old Village, Shanklin** ✆ 01983 866432 www.shanklinchine.co.uk **43 C7**

Activities

Adgestone Vineyard

A vineyard and winery offering tastings and cellar tours. **Adgestone** ✆ 01983 402503 • www.adgestonevineyard.co.uk **23 F2**

Bembridge Trail

A 10-mile walking trail from the middle of the island to its eastern tip, over downland and past marshes, historic houses and the village of Brading. **From Newport to Bembridge 22 E2**

Blackgang Chine

Dramatic 40-acre landscaped clifftop gardens with a range of family attractions, including Wild West Town, a roller coaster, Dinosaurland, a shipwreck collection and a maze. **Chale, near Ventnor** ✆ 01983 730330 •www.blackgangchine.com **44 C4**

Cowes Week

The world's most famous sailing regatta, held annually in early August since 1826. There are 8 or 9 days of racing involving about 900 craft, and a host of social events, including balls and a fireworks finale. **Cowes** ✆ 01983 296621 •www.cowesweek.co.uk

Fort Victoria Country Park

A country park with seashore and woodland walks, a nature trail, ranger tours, and fine views over the Solent, and containing an aquarium (see xiv), a planetarium (see xiii) and a model railway (see xiii). **Fort Victoria, near Yarmouth** ✆ 01983 823893 • www.fortvictoria.co.uk **14 F6**

Freshwater Golf Club

One of two 18-hole courses on the island, with panoramic views of the Solent and English Channel, and Neolithic and Bronze Age burial mounds forming natural 'hazards', set on a Site of Special Scientific Interest with many rare and endangered plant and animal species. **Afton Down, Freshwater** • www.freshwaterbaygolfclub.co.uk ✆ 01983 752966 **27 E6**

Hamstead Trail A 7-mile walking trail crossing the island from north to south, passing saltwater marshes and ancient burial grounds, including the Long Stone (see xii). At the south coast a the remains of a fossil forest can be seen at low tide. **From Hamstead to Brook 16 F3**

Island Brass Rubbing Centre

A craft centre with reproduction medieval brasses depicting chivalrous scenes; tuition is provided. **Arreton Barns Craft Village, Arreton** ✆ 01983 528353 **21 E2**

Island Sailing Club

A friendly family yachting club with excellent facilities. **70 High Street, Cowes** www.islandsc.org.uk ✆01983 296911 **3 B5**

Island Speedway

Motorcycle speedway races. **Smallbrook Stadium, Ashey Road, Ryde** • www.islandspeedway.co.uk ✆ 01983 811180 **12 C1**

Isle of Wight Steam Railway

5-mile country trips in restored Victorian and Edwardian steam trains, plus a museum, woodland walk and play area. **Railway Station, Havenstreet** • www.iwsteamrailway.co.uk ✆ 01983 882204 **22 E8**

The Needles Park

A park offering views of the spectacular Needles Rocks and lighthouse. Features a chairlift to the beach with its coloured sand, children's attractions, a pier with shopping arcade, glass manufactory, sand shop, Jurassic golf, junior driver and boat trips, as well as summer fireworks displays. **Alum Bay** ✆ 01983 752401 • www.theneedles.co.uk **26 D5**

Robin Hill Countryside Adventure Park

A country park with activities for all ages, including a Countryside Centre with a sensory zone, a play village, a wooden maze, a toboggan run, woodland walks and a treetop trail. **Downend, Arreton** ✆ 01983 730052 • www.robin-hill.com **21 F4**

Rosemary Vineyard One of

Britain's biggest vineyards, with both guided walks and self-guided trails, and free tastings. **Smallbrook Lane, Ryde** ✆ 01983 811084 •www.rosemaryvineyard.co.uk **12 C3**

Round the Island Cycling Route

A route taking in dedicated cycleways, disused

▲ Isle of Wight SteamRailway

railway lines, bridleways and quiet country lanes. Maps are available from tourist centres. ✆ 01983 813818

St Helens Beach

One of the island's 13 award-winning beaches, adjoining some National Trust land that is home to a variety of interesting wildlife. A calm spot with wonderful views over Bembridge Harbour, it is excellent for swimming. **St Helens 25 B7**

Solent and Wight Line cruises

Half-hour Cowes Harbour sight-seeing trips, cruises taking in Cowes, Yarmouth and the Needles, full-day trips to Portsmouth and more. **66 Newnham Road, Binstead, Ryde** ✆ 01983 564602

Tennyson Trail

A 12½-mile walk across the downs and through forests, passing ancient burial sites and the Tennyson Monument, and affording excellent views. **From Carisbrooke Castle to the Needles 20 A3**

Walking Festival

The UK's biggest walking festival, held each May, with more than 130 volunteer-led walks, including castles, the Red Squirrel Safari, storytime walks, lanternlit strolls, ghost walks, a pram walk and a 70-mile 24-hour walk around the island. ✆ 01983 813818

Waltzing Waters An indoor

synchronised water, light and music show. **Westridge, Ryde** ✆ 01983 811333 •www.waltzingwaters.co.uk **12 F1**

Worsley Trail A 12½-mile walk

past pine forests and farm buildings, over chalk downlands, fields and a disused railway line. **From Mottistone Down to Old Shanklin 30 C5**

Coastal Path

Major administrative and Postcode boundaries

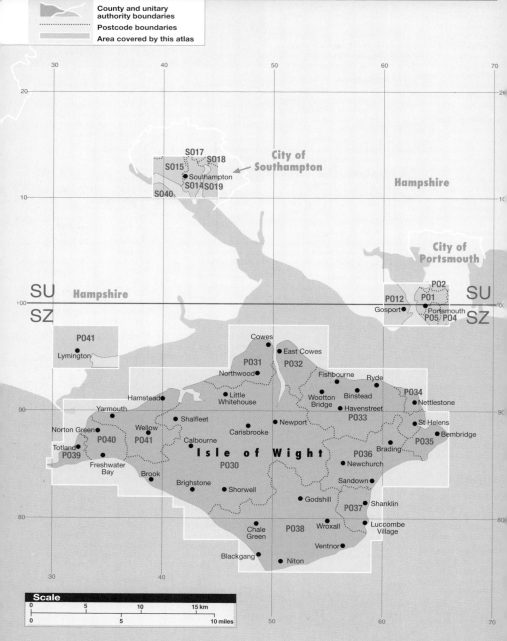

County and unitary authority boundaries
Postcode boundaries
Area covered by this atlas

Key to map symbols

⟨22⟩	Motorway with junction number
	Primary route – dual/single carriageway
	A road – dual/single carriageway
	B road – dual/single carriageway
	Minor road – dual/single carriageway
	Other minor road – dual/single carriageway
	Road under construction
	Tunnel, covered road
30	Speed cameras – single, multiple
	Rural track, private road or narrow road in urban area
	Gate or obstruction to traffic – restrictions may not apply at all times or to all vehicles
	Path, bridleway, byway open to all traffic, restricted byway
	Pedestrianised area
BS22	Postcode boundaries
	County or unitary authority boundaries
	Railway with station
	Tunnel
	Railway under construction
	Metro station
	Private railway station
	Miniature railway
	Tramway, tramway under construction
	Tram stop, tram stop under construction
	Bus, coach station

◆	Ambulance station
◆	Coastguard station
◆	Fire station
◆	Police station
✚	Accident and Emergency entrance to hospital
H	Hospital
+	Place of worship
i	Information centre – open all year
P	Shopping centre, parking
P&R	Park and Ride, Post Office
Ⓧ	Camping site, caravan site
▶ ✕	Golf course, picnic site
Church ROMAN FORT	Non-Roman antiquity, Roman antiquity
Univ	Important buildings, schools, colleges, universities and hospitals
	Woods, built-up area
River Medway	Water name
	River, weir
	Stream
	Canal, lock, tunnel
	Water
	Tidal water

 Adjoining page indicators and overlap bands – the colour of the arrow and band indicates the scale of the adjoining or overlapping page (see scales below)

The dark grey border on the inside edge of some pages indicates that the mapping does not continue onto the adjacent page

The small numbers around the edges of the maps identify the 1-kilometre National Grid lines

Abbreviations

Acad	Academy	Meml	Memorial
Allot Gdns	Allotments	Mon	Monument
Cemy	Cemetery	Mus	Museum
C Ctr	Civic centre	Obsy	Observatory
CH	Club house	Pal	Royal palace
Coll	College	PH	Public house
Crem	Crematorium	Recn Gd	Recreation ground
Ent	Enterprise	Resr	Reservoir
Ex H	Exhibition hall	Ret Pk	Retail park
Ind Est	Industrial Estate	Sch	School
IRB Sta	Inshore rescue boat station	Sh Ctr	Shopping centre
Inst	Institute	TH	Town hall / house
Ct	Law court	Trad Est	Trading estate
L Ctr	Leisure centre	Univ	University
LC	Level crossing	W Twr	Water tower
Liby	Library	Wks	Works
Mkt	Market	YH	Youth hostel

Enlarged maps only

Railway or bus station building

Place of interest

Parkland

The map scale on the pages numbered in blue is 2⅔ inches to 1 mile
4.2 cm to 1 km • 1:23 810

0 — ¼ mile — ½ mile — ¾ mile — 1 mile
0 — 250m — 500m — 750m — 1km

The map scale on the pages numbered in red is 5⅓ inches to 1 mile
8.4 cm to 1 km • 1:11 900

0 — 220yds — 440yds — 660yds — ½ mile
0 — 125m — 250m — 375m — 500m

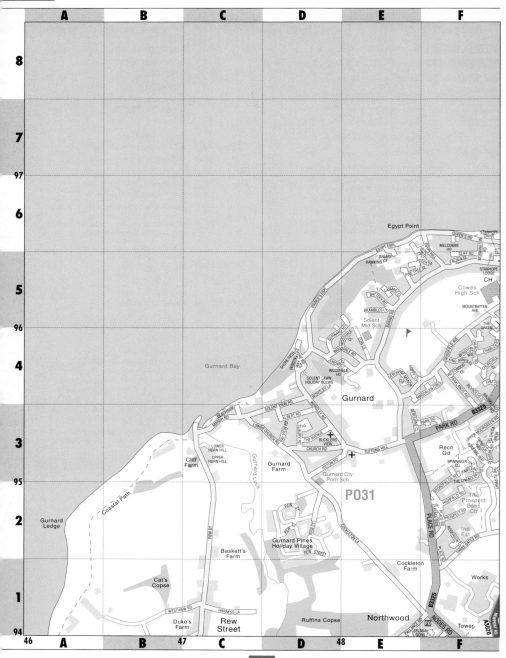

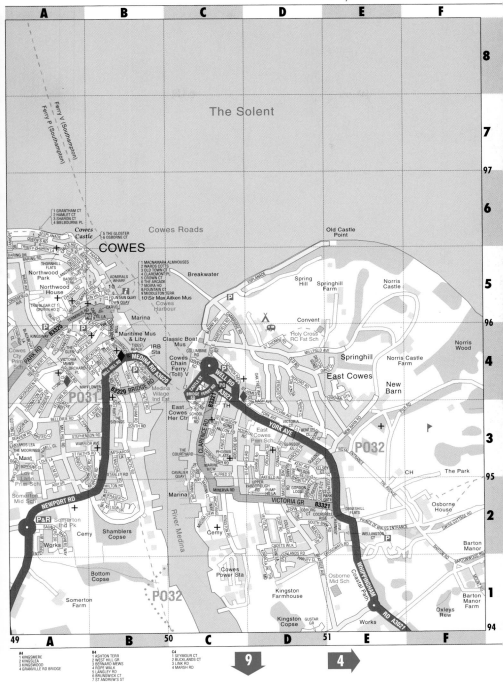

The Solent

Cowes Roads

Old Castle Point

Cowes Castle

COWES

Breakwater

Spring Hill

Springhill Farm

Norris Castle

Northwood Park

Northwood House

Convent

Holy Cross RC Fst Sch

Norris Wood

Springhill

East Cowes

Norris Castle Farm

New Barn

Cowes City Prim Sch

Maritime Mus & Liby

Classic Boat Mus

PO31

Cowes Chain Ferry (Toll)

Medina Village Ind Est

East Cowes Her Ctr

East Cowes Prim Sch

PO32

Mast

Love Lane Prim Sch

Somerton Mid Sch

The Courtyard

Marina

CH

The Park

Osborne House

NEWPORT RD

P&R

Cemy

Shamblers Copse

Cemy

VICTORIA GR

Daneshill Flats

Swiss Cottage Rd

Barton Manor

Bottom Copse

Cowes Power Sta

PO32

Kingston Farmhouse

Osborne Mid Sch

Barton Manor Farm

Somerton Farm

Kingston Copse

Kingston Copse GUSTAR GR

Works

Oxleys Rew

Barton Manor Farm

Whippingham Coastal Path

RD A3021

A4
1 KINGSMERE
2 KINGSLEA
3 KINGSWOOD
4 GRANVILLE RD BRIDGE

B4
1 ASHTON TERR
2 WEST HILL GR
3 BERNARD MEWS
4 ROPE WALK
5 LANGLEY RD
6 BRUNSWICK CT
7 ST ANDREW'S ST

C4
1 SEYMOUR CT
2 BUCKLANDS CT
3 LINK RD
4 MARSH RD

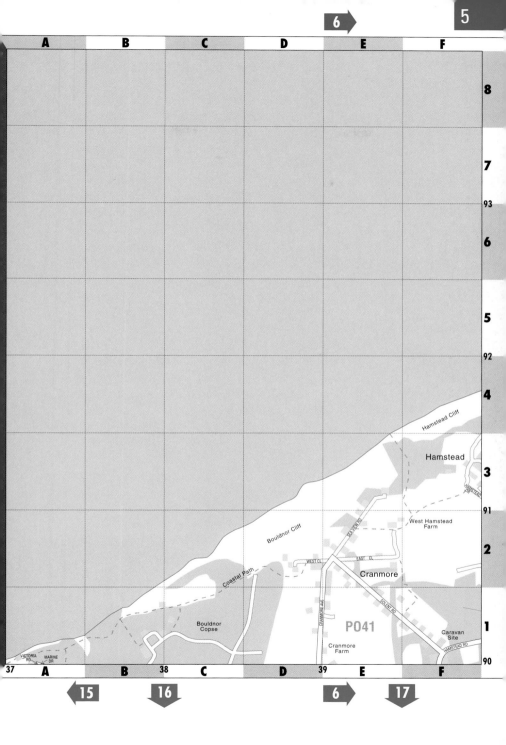

A   B   C   D   E   F

8

7

93

6

5

92

4

Hamstead Cliff

Hamstead

3

91

West Hamstead
Farm

Bouldnor Cliff

SEA VIEW RD

HAMSTEAD

2

WEST CL   EAST CL

Coastal Path

Cranmore

SOLENT RD

Bouldnor
Copse

CRANMORE AVE

P041

Caravan
Site

1

Cranmore
Farm

HAMSTEAD RD

VICTORIA
RD   MARINE
DR

90

37   A   B   38   C   D   39   E   F

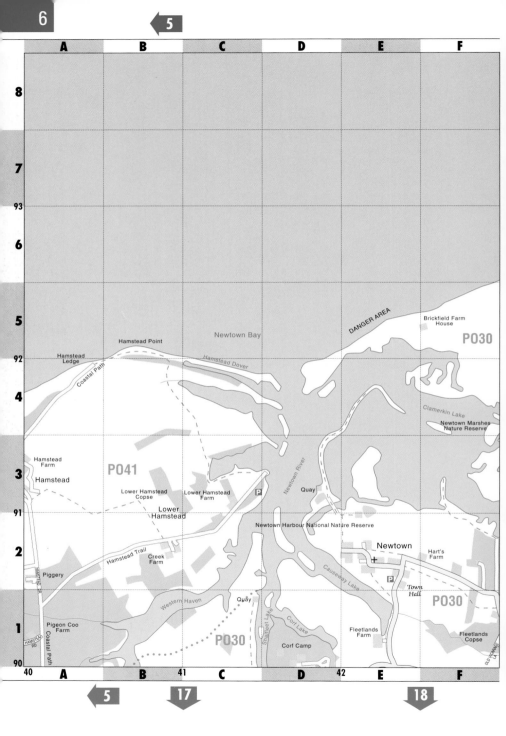

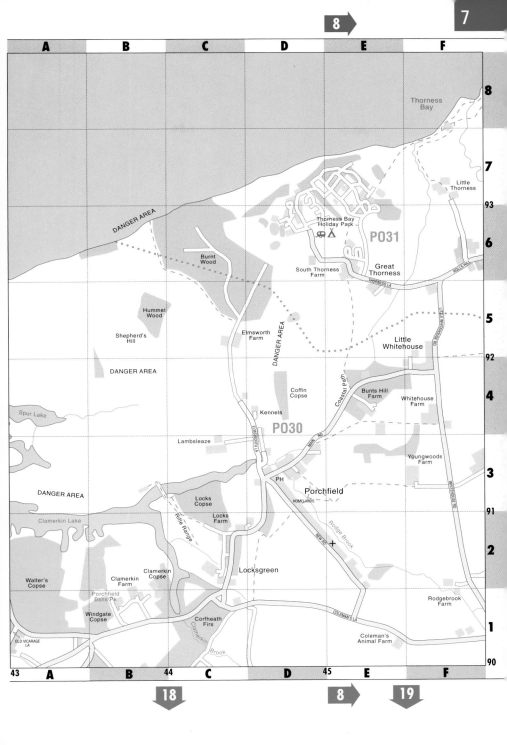

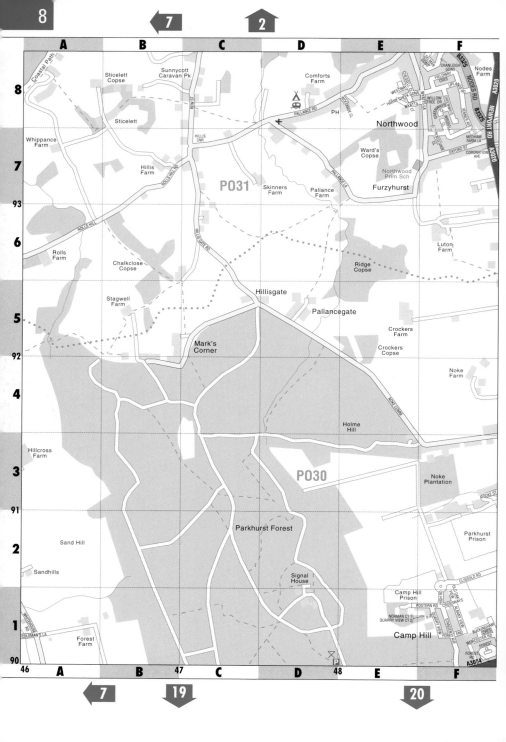

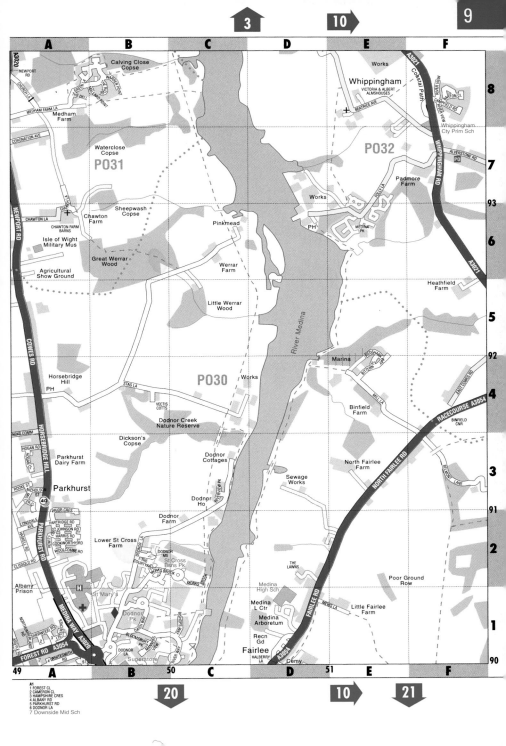

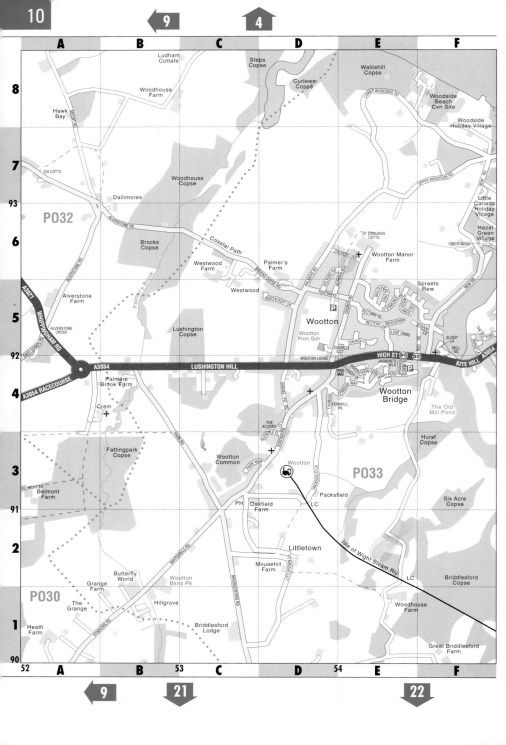

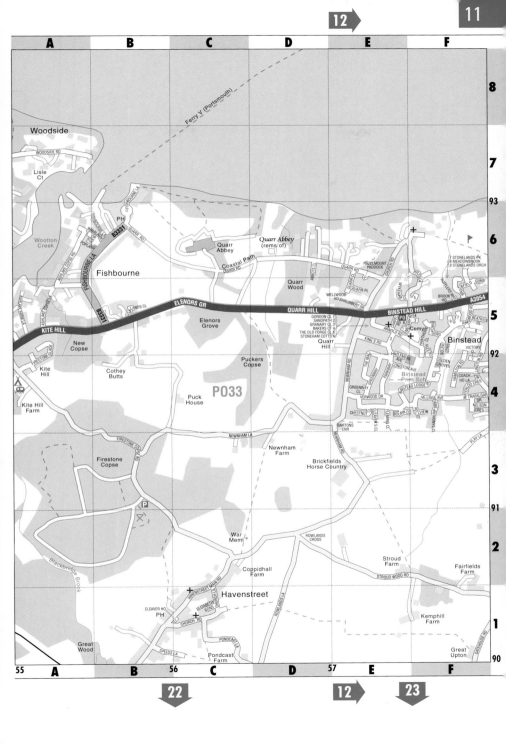

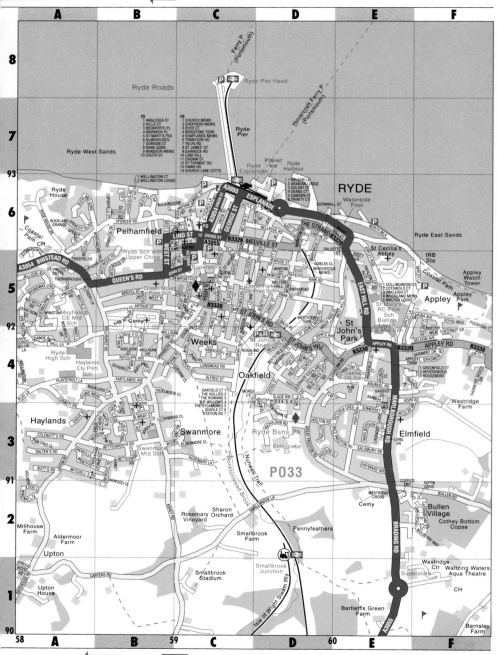

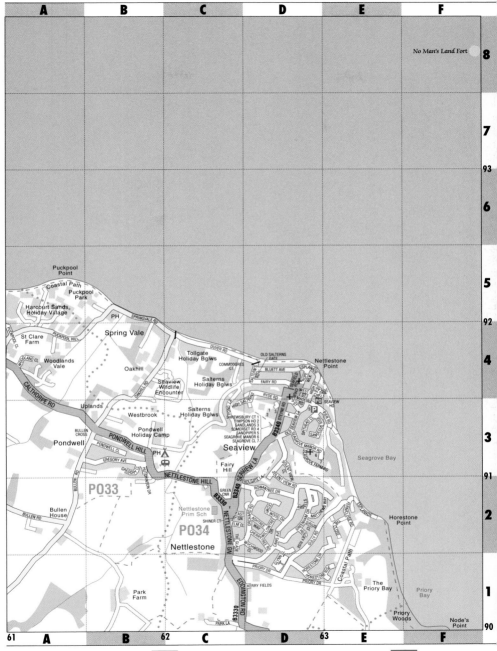

No Man's Land Fort

8

7

93

6

5

92

4

Puckpool
Point

Coastal Path
Puckpool
Park

Harcourt Sands,
Holiday Village

St Clare
Farm

Woodlands
Vale

PH

SPRINGVALE RD

Spring Vale

Oakhill

DUVER RD

Tollgate
Holiday Bglws

COMMODORES
CT

OLD SALTERNS
GATE

BLUETT AVE

Nettlestone
Point

PUCKPOOL HILL

ORMELL RD

Seaview
Wildlife
Encounter

Salterns
Holiday Bglws

FAIRY RD

RYDE RD

ESPLANADE

WEST
ST

SEAVIEW
HO

CALTHORPE RD

Uplands

Westbrook

Salterns
Holiday Bglws

HIGH SALTERNS

SHREWSBURY CT 1
TIMPSON HO 2
SANDLANDS 3
SOMERSET RD 4
SANDPIPER 5
SEAGROVE MANOR 6
SEAGROVE CL 7

SPITHEAD

B3340

P

SEAVIEW LA

Seagrove Bay

3

BULLEN
CROSS

Pondwell

POND WELL HILL

PONDWELL CL

PH

Pondwell
Holiday Camp

Seaview

GROVE MANOR RD

GREGORY AVE

GREGORY

HILTON RD

NETTLESTONE HILL

Fairy
Hill

SEAVIEW LA

SOLENT VIEW RD

91

PO33

Bullen
House

BULLEN RD

BULLEN RD

B3330

Nettlestone
Prim Sch

SHINER CT

GREEN
CNR

B3340

HOLGATE LA

EAST
GN

ROWAN TREE DR

W WOOD CL

MELTINGHAM
CL

Horestone
Point

2

PO34

Nettlestone

NETTLESTONE GN

THE QUAE

PRIORY DR

KERRY FIELDS

HORESTONE RISE

HORESTONE RD

PRIORY DR

Coastal Path

FERNCLIFFE PROMENADE

The
Priory Bay

1

Park
Farm

EDDINGTON RD

B3330

PARK LA

Priory
Woods

Priory
Bay

Node's
Point

90

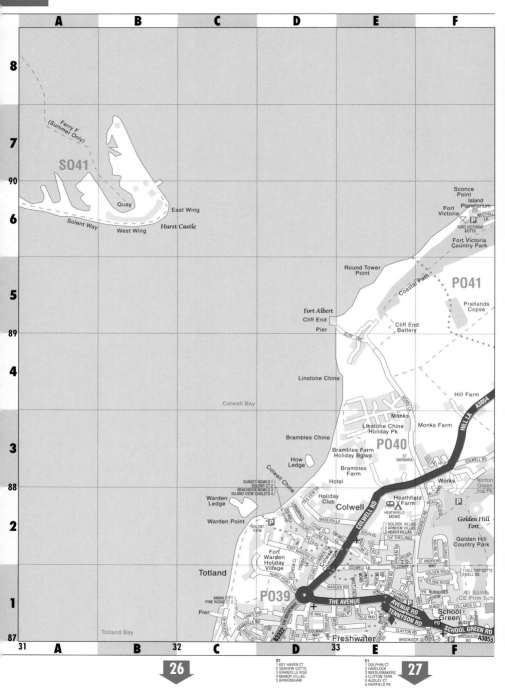

S041

Ferry F (Summer Only)

Quay

East Wing

Solent Way

West Wing

Hurst Castle

Sconce Point

Fort Victoria

Island Planetarium

WESTHILL LA

P

FORT VICTORIA COTTS

Fort Victoria Country Park

Round Tower Point

Coastal Path

P041

Pratlands Copse

Fort Albert

Cliff End

Pier

CLIFF END

Cliff End Battery

Linstone Chine

Hill Farm

Colwell Bay

Monks

Linstone Chine Holiday Pk

Monks Farm

HILL LA

A3054

Brambles Chine

P040

Brambles Farm Holiday Bglws

ST BARBARA

COLWELL RD

How Ledge

Colwell Chine

Brambles Farm

Hotel

Works

Norton Green Ind Pk

SUNSET BGWLS 1
SOLENT CT 2
BEACHSIDE BGWLS 3
ISLAND VIEW CHALETS 4

Warden Ledge

Holiday Club

Colwell

Heathfield Farm

HEATHFIELD MDWS

1 GOLDEN VILLAS
2 ARNHEM VILLAS
3 HEATH VILLAS

Golden Hill Fort

Warden Point

SOLENT VIEW

P

MADEIRA LA

COLWELL RD

BIRCH CL

THE SHEILINGS

Golden Hill Country Park

Fort Warden Holiday Village

Totland

HURST POINT

COLWELL RD

COLWELL RD

WARDEN RD

ST ANDREWS WAY

GOLDEN RIDGE

1 HILL TOP COTTS
2 DELL SQ

THE NURSERIES

All Saints CE Prim Sch

P039

AMAN CT 1
PINE RIDGE CT 2

Pier

THE AVENUE

THE MALL

AVENUE RD

TENNYSON RD

P

SUNSET

COLLARDS CL

School Green

Lby

Totland Bay

LANES END

HILL

CLAYTON RD

Freshwater

BROOKSIDE CL

BROOKSIDE RD

SCHOOL GREEN RD

A3055

26

27

D1
1 KEY HAVEN CT
2 SEAVIEW COTTS
3 GRANVILLE RISE
4 MANOR VILLAS
5 BIRKENSHAW

E1
1 DOLPHIN CT
2 HAVELOCK
3 NEEDLEMAKERS
4 CLIFTON TERR
5 AUDLEY CT
6 FAIRFIELD PK

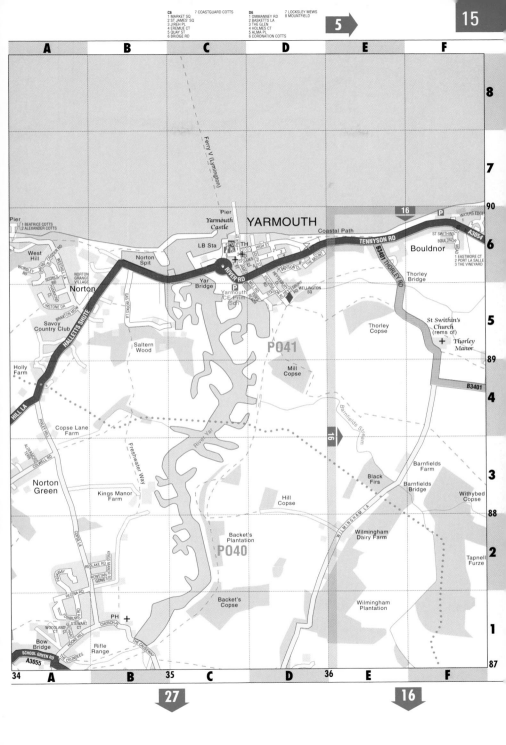

5

A   B   C   D   E   F

8

7

90

16

YARMOUTH

Pier
Yarmouth
Castle

Coastal Path

WATERS EDGE

ST SWITHINS

Bouldnor

1 EASTMORE CT
2 PORT LA SALLE
3 THE VINEYARD

6

Pier

1 BEATRICE COTTS
2 ALEXANDER COTTS

West
Hill

LB Sta

TH   HIGH ST

Norton
Spit

TENNYSON RD

B3401 THORLEY RD

BOULDNOR

A3054

RIVER RD

Yar
Bridge

Thorley
Bridge

NORTON
GRANGE
VILLAGE

Norton

Yarmouth
CE Prim
Sch

WELLINGTON
SQ

St Swithin's
Church
(rems of)
Thorley
Manor

5

Savoy
Country Club

HALLETTS SHUTE

GAS WORKS LA

Saltern
Wood

P041

Thorley
Copse

89

Holly
Farm

Mill
Copse

B3401

4

HILL LA

PIXLEY HILL

Copse Lane
Farm

Freshwater Way

River Yar

16

Barnfields Stream

Black
Firs

Barnfields
Farm

3

Norton
Green

COLWELL RD

Kings Manor
Farm

Hill
Copse

Barnfields
Bridge

Withybed
Copse

88

COPSE LA

Backet's
Plantation

P040

WILMINGHAM LA

Wilmingham
Dairy Farm

Tapnell
Furze

2

REDLAKE RD

KINGS MANOR RD

REGINA RD

Backet's
Copse

Wilmingham
Plantation

1

PH

CHURCH LA

Bow
Bridge

Rifle
Range

THE CAUSEWAY

87

SCHOOL GREEN RD

A3055

34   A   B   35   C   D   36   E   F

27

16

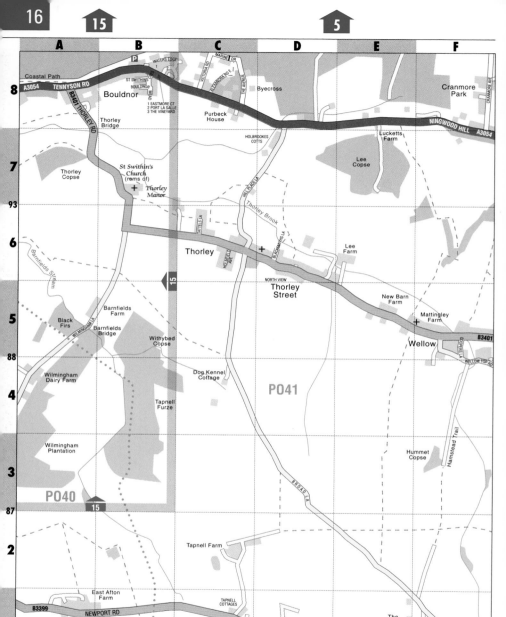

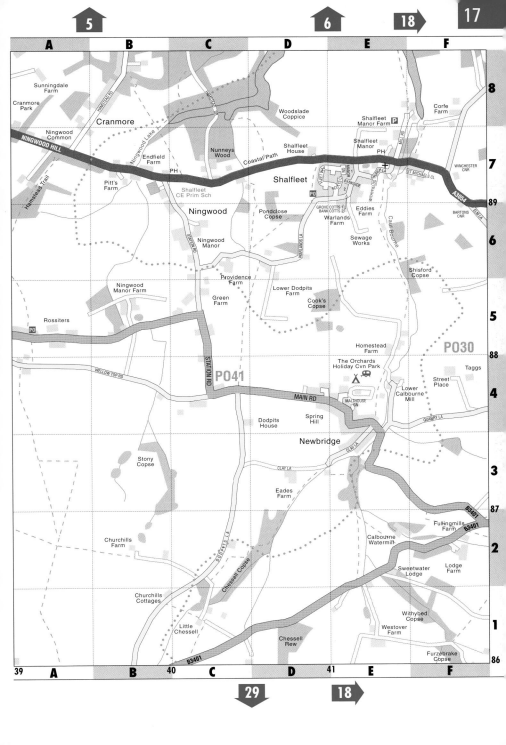

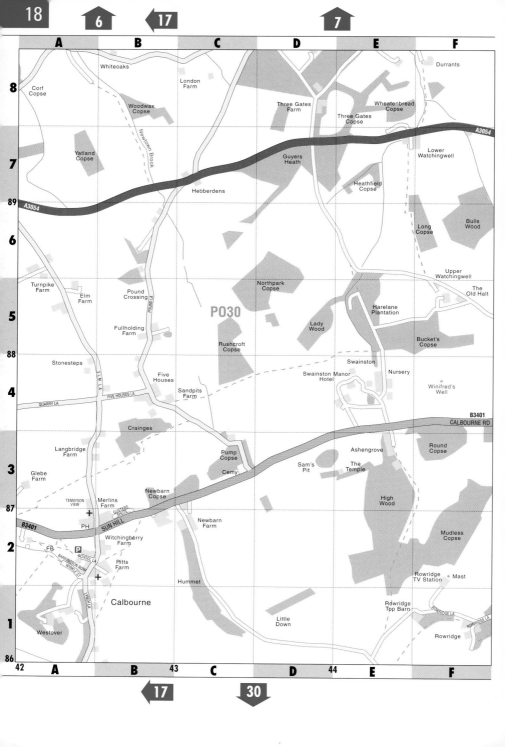

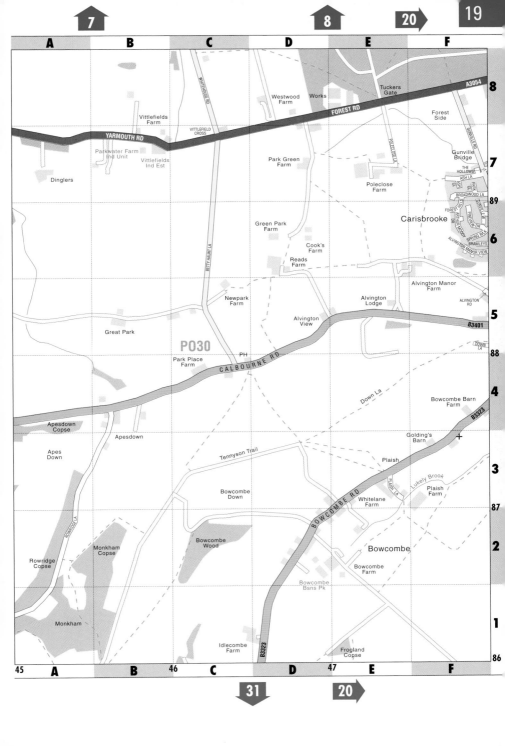

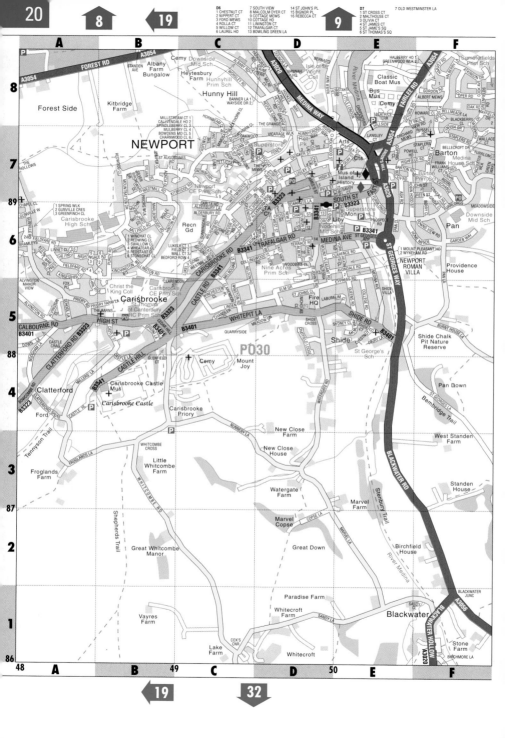

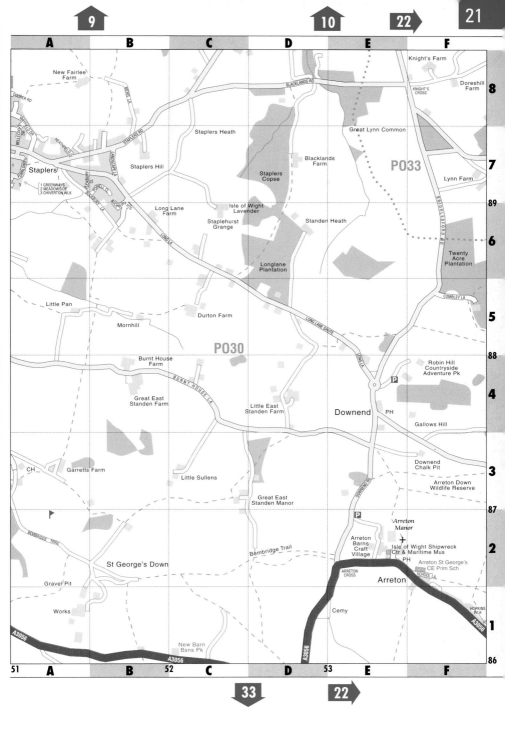

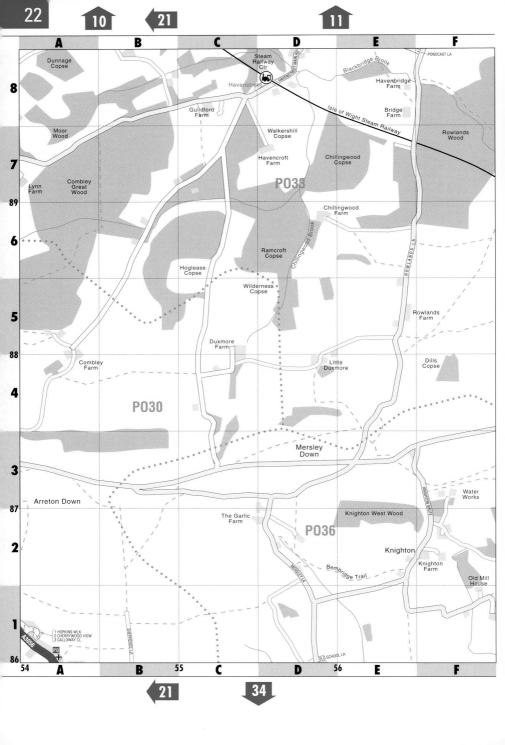

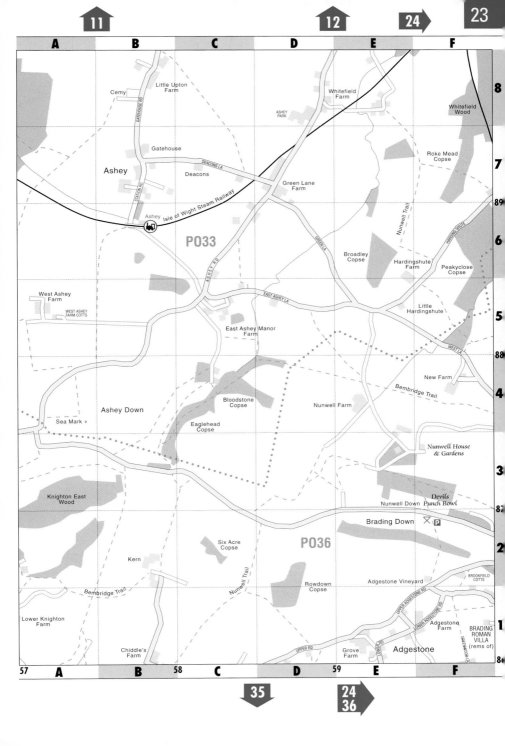

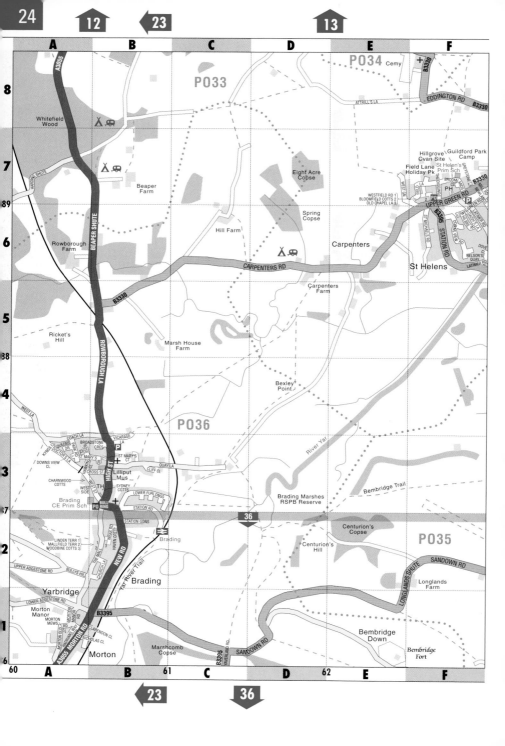

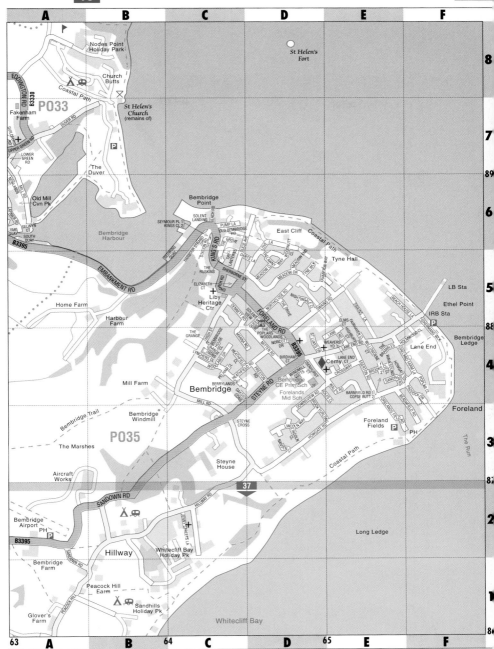

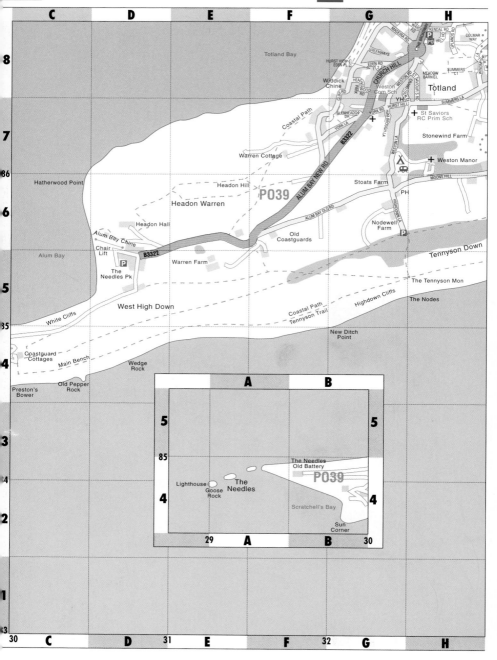

C   D   E   F   G   H

8   Totland Bay

Widdick
Chine

Weston
Com Sch
Totland

YH

Coastal Path

7   Warren Cottage

Stonewind Farm

St Saviors
RC Prim Sch

Weston Manor

86   Hatherwood Point

Headon Hill

Stoats Farm

PH

6   Headon Warren

Headon Hall

Nodewell
Farm

Alum Bay Chine

Old
Coastguards

Chair
Lift

B3322

Alum Bay   Warren Farm

Tennyson Down

The
Needles Pk

5   West High Down

The Tennyson Mon

The Nodes

White Cliffs

85   Coastal Path
Tennyson Trail

Highdown Cliffs

New Ditch
Point

4   Coastguard
Cottages

Main Bench

Wedge
Rock

Preston's
Bower

Old Pepper
Rock

A   B

5   5

85   The Needles
Old Battery

P039

4   Lighthouse   The
Needles

4

Goose
Rock

Scratchell's Bay

Sun
Corner

29   A   B   30

30   C   D   31   E   F   32   G   H

Headon Hill

P039

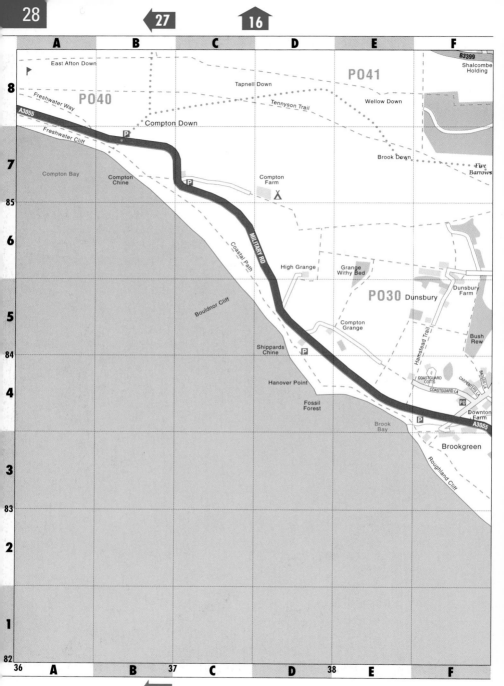

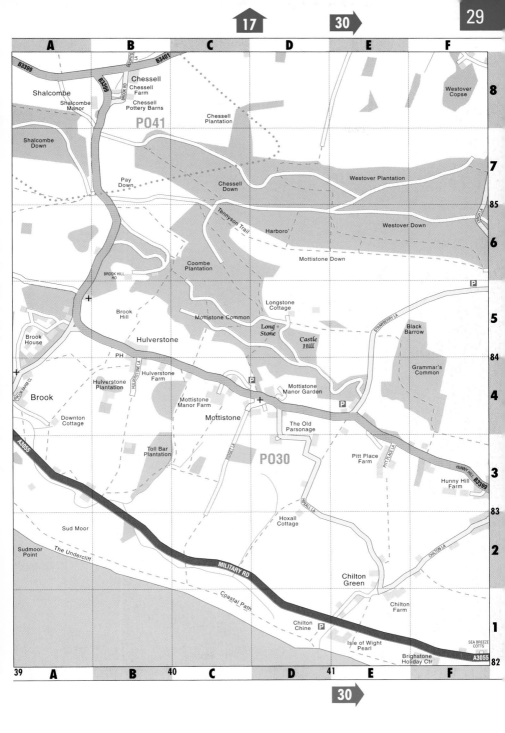

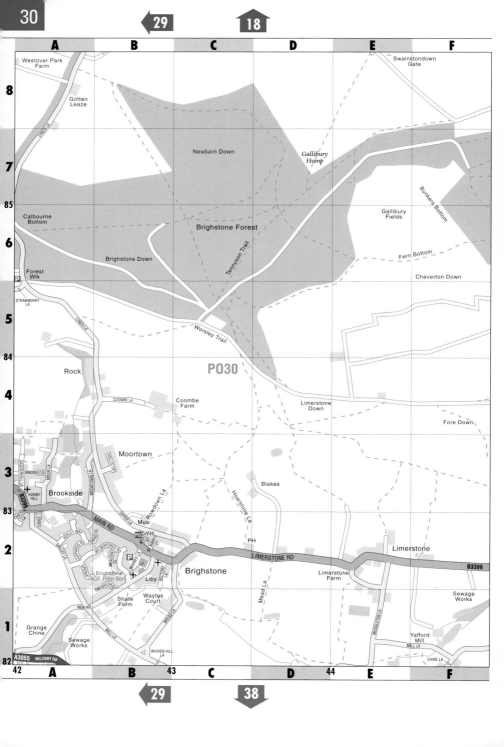

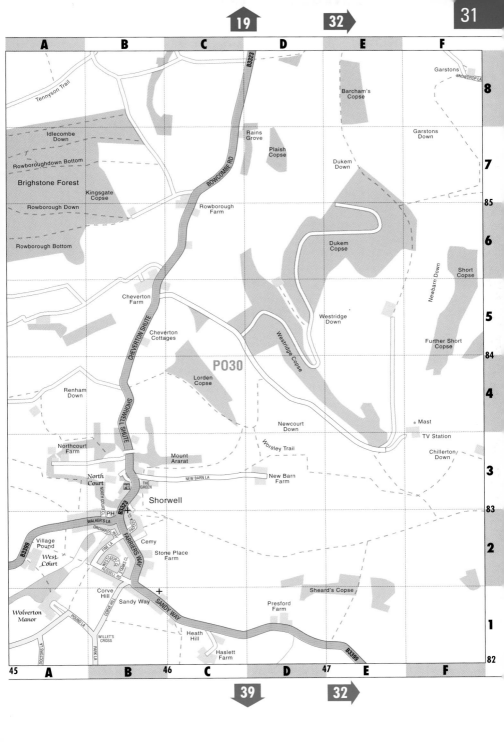

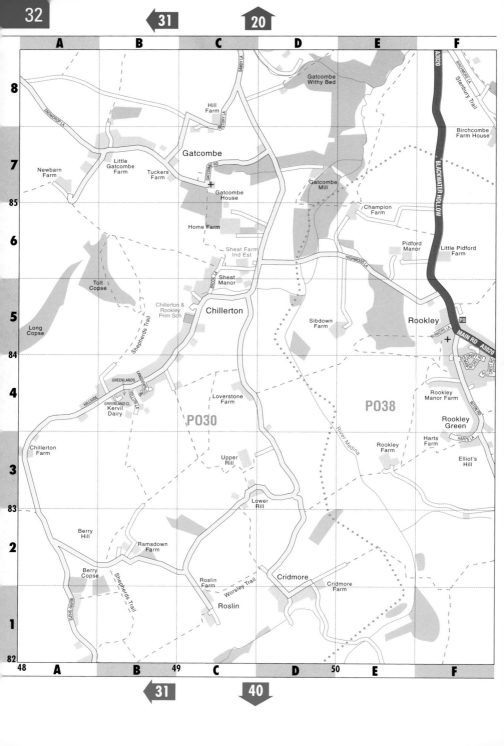

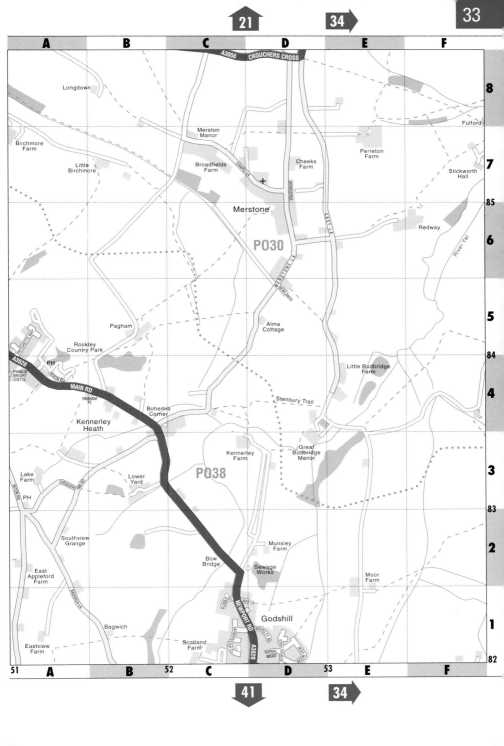

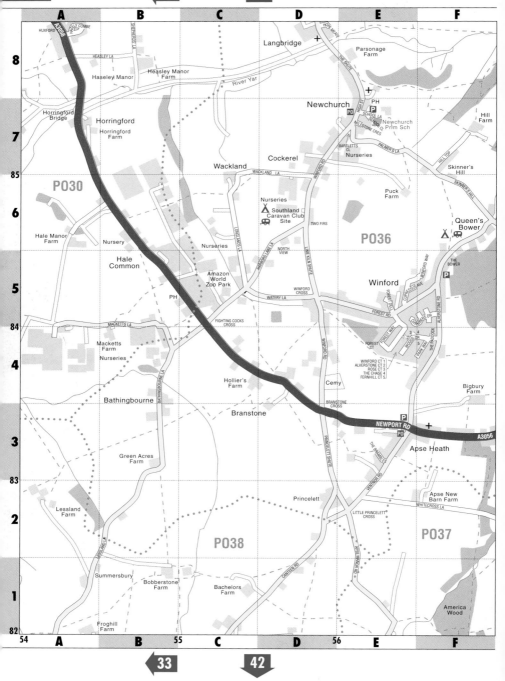

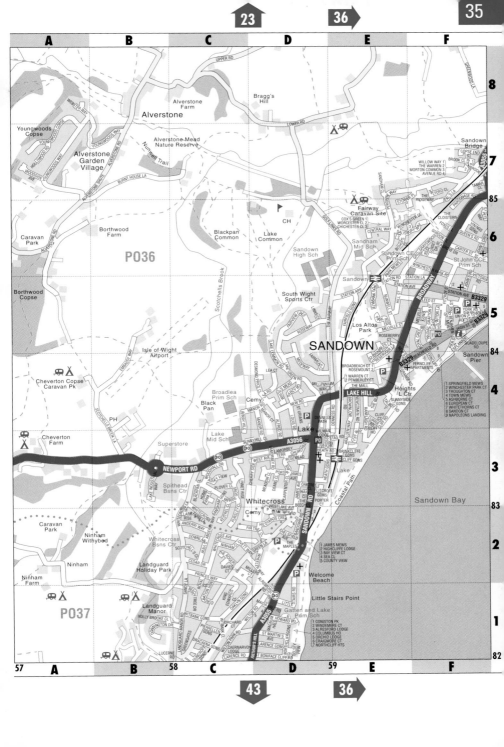

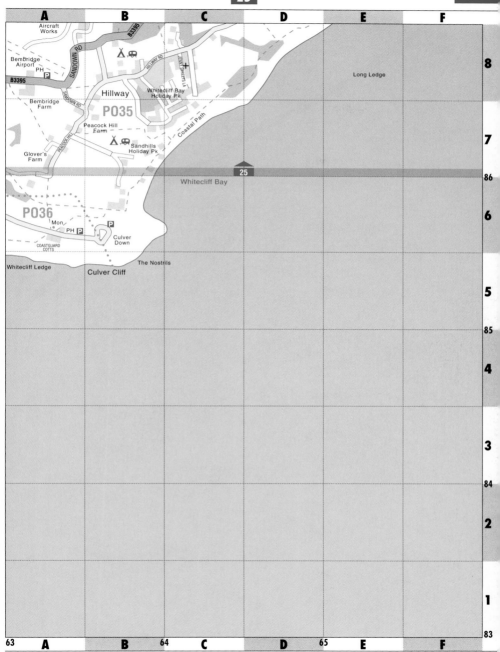

Aircraft
Works

Bembridge
Airport PH
P

B3395

SANDOWN RD

B3395

Hillway

HILLWAY RD

KNIGHTSTREETS LA

Whitecliff Bay
Holiday Pk

PO35

Peacock Hill
Farm

Bembridge
Farm

PEACOCK HILL

Glover's
Farm

Sandhills
Holiday Pk

Coastal Path

Long Ledge

25

Whitecliff Bay

PO36

Mon
PH P
P

COASTGUARD
COTTS

Culver
Down

Whitecliff Ledge

Culver Cliff

The Nostrils

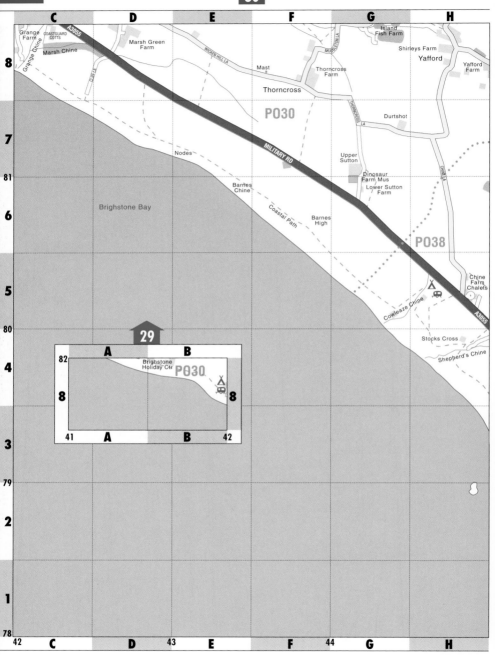

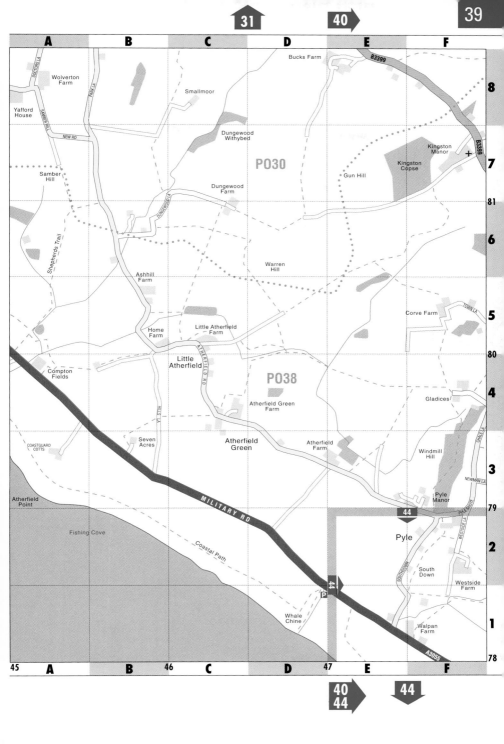

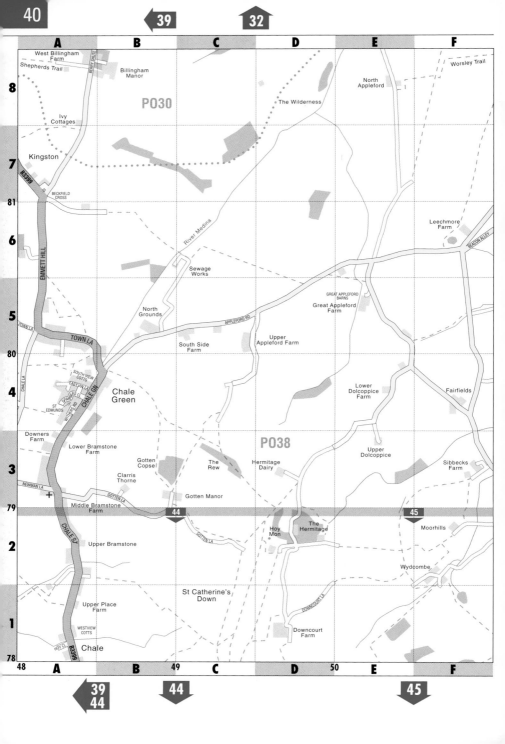

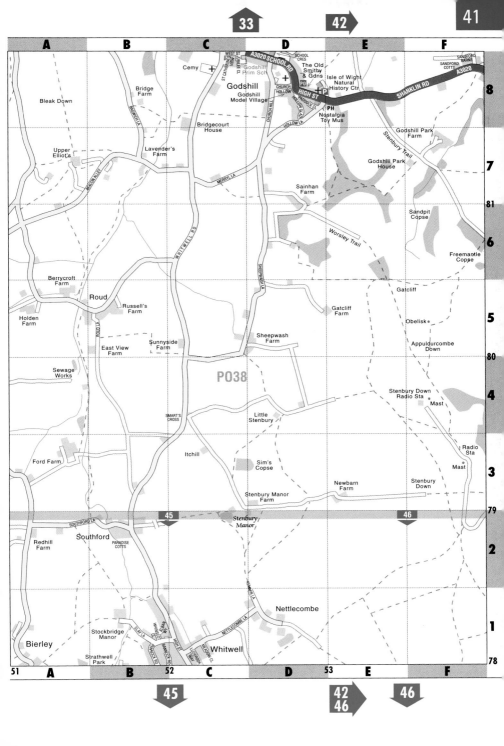

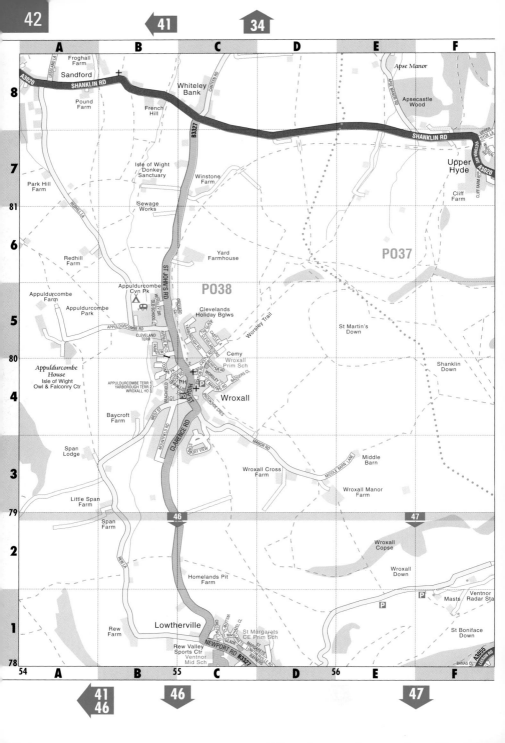

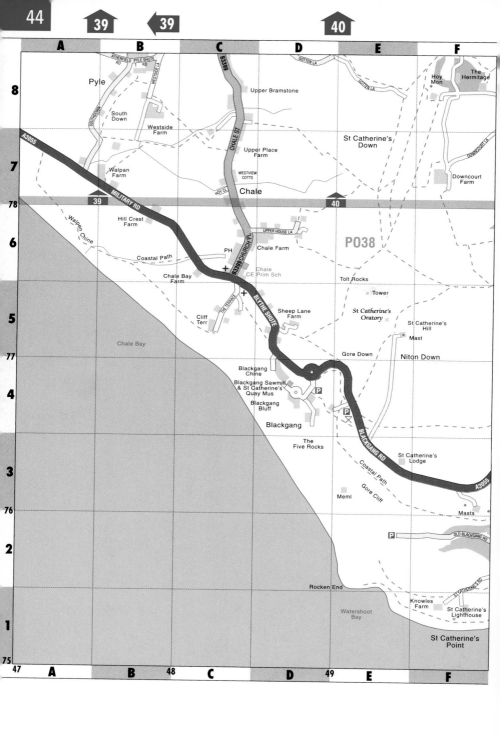

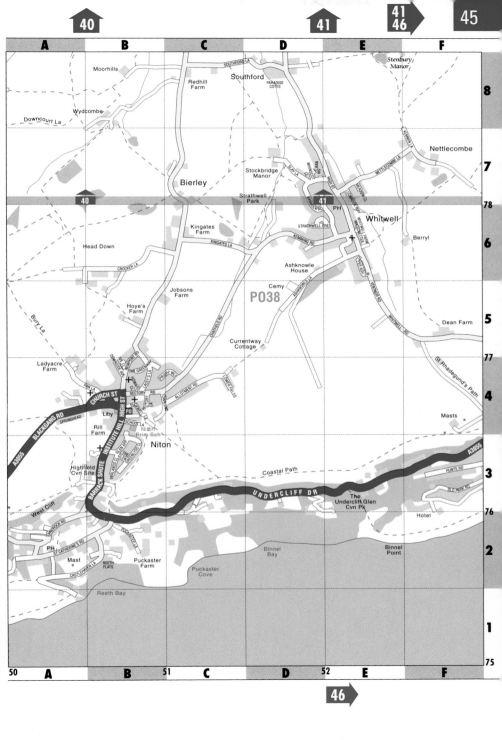

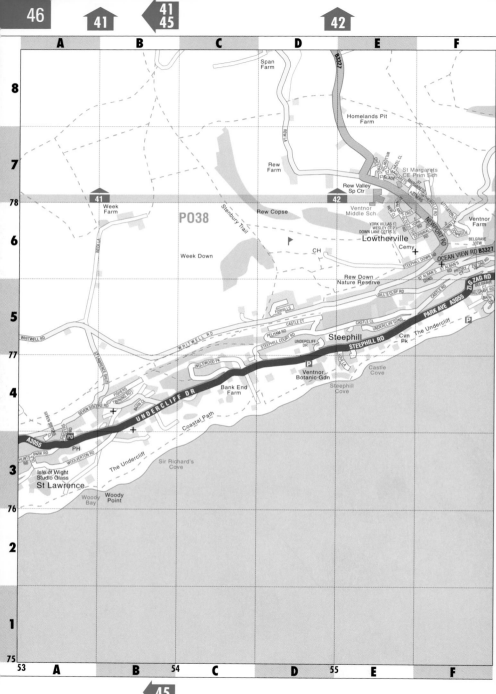

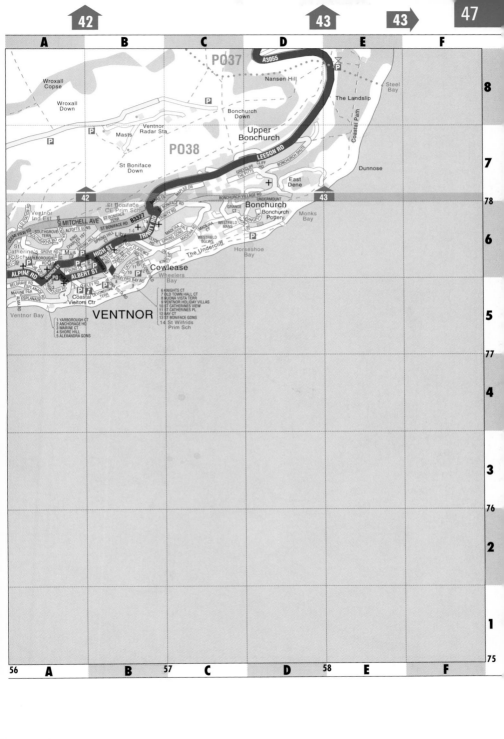

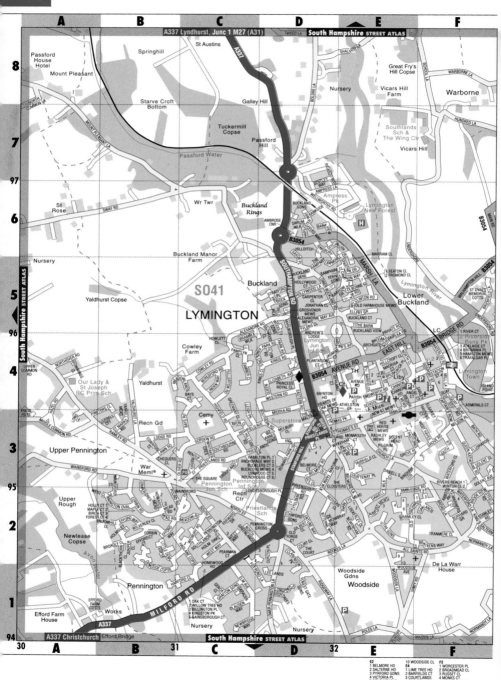

S041

LYMINGTON

Buckland Rings

Buckland

Lower Buckland

Passford House Hotel

Mount Pleasant

Springhill

St Austins

Galley Hill

Starve Croft Bottom

Tuckermill Copse

Passford Water

Passford Hill

St Rose

Sway Rd

Wr Twr

Buckland Manor Farm

Nursery

Yaldhurst Copse

Cowley Farm

Our Lady & St Joseph RC Prim Sch

Yaldhurst

Upper Common Rd

Upper Pennington

Upper Rough

Newlease Copse

Pennington

Efford Farm House

Works

Nursery

War Meml

Pennington Jun Sch

Recn Ctr

Priestlands Sch

Pennington Cross

Great Fry's Hill Copse

Warborne

Nursery

Vicars Hill Farm

Vicars Hill

Southlands Sch & The Wing Ctr

Ampress

Lymington New Forest

Southampton Rd

Lymington Jun & Inf Sch

Superstore

Cemy

Recn Gd

Avenue Rd

East Hill

Bridge Rd

Lib

Mus

Lymington Town

Woodside Gdns

Woodside

De La Warr House

Milford Rd

E2	10 WOODSIDE CL	F2
1 BELMORE HO	E4	1 WORCESTER PL
2 SALTERNE HO	1 LIME TREE HO	2 BROADMEAD CL
3 PYRFORD GDNS	2 BARFIELDS CT	3 RUSSET CT
4 VICTORIA PL	3 COURTLANDS	4 MONKS CT
5 GOLD MEAD CL	4 CARLTON HO	5 CONFERENCE PL
6 PEARTREE DR	5 MOSBACH PL	
7 PEARTREE CT	6 KEEL GDNS	
8 PIPPIN CL	7 UNION PL	
9 CHURCH MEAD		

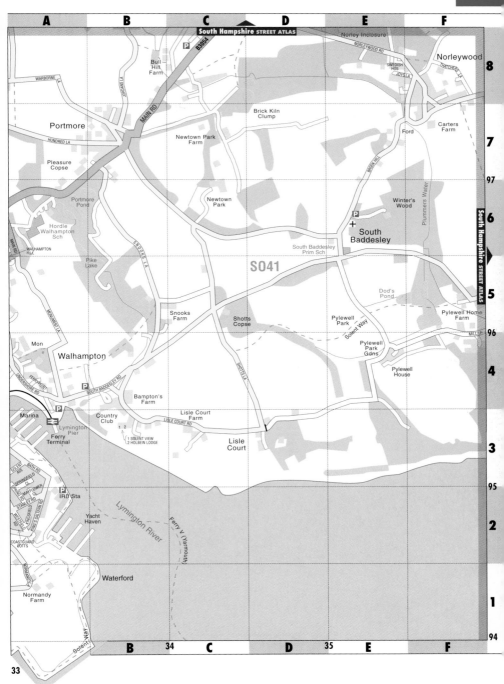

South Hampshire STREET ATLAS

A **B** **C** **D** **E** **F**

B3054

Norley Inclosure

NORLEYWOOD RD

Norleywood

SWEDISH
HOS
BOYS LA

THATCHERS LA

Bull
Hill
Farm

8

WARBORNE LA

PUNSHILL LA

Brick Kiln
Clump

Ford

Carters
Farm

7

Portmore

MAIN RD

HUNDRED LA

Newtown Park
Farm

BROCK HILL

97

Pleasure
Copse

Plummers Water

Winter's
Wood

Newtown
Park

6

Portmore
Pond

P

South
Baddesley

MAIN RD

Hordle
Walhampton
Sch

WALHAMPTON
HILL

S BEAULIEU LA

South Baddesley
Prim Sch

SO41

5

Pike
Lake

Dod's
Pond

Snooks
Farm

Shotts
Copse

Pylewell
Park

Solent Way

Pylewell Home
Farm

MILL LA

96

Mon

Walhampton

NEWBRIDGE LA

Pylewell
Park
Gdns

4

FERRY POINT
RD

UNDERSHORE RD

P

SOUTH BADDESLEY RD

Bampton's
Farm

SHOTTS LA

Pylewell
House

P

Marina

Lymington
Pier

Country
Club

1 2

Lisle Court
Farm

LISLE COURT RD

1 SOLENT VIEW
2 HOLBEIN LODGE

Lisle
Court

3

Ferry
Terminal

SO FTH
AVE

BATH RD

SPRINGFIELD
CL

MAYFLOWER

STANLEY RD

PRIESTLANDS
RD

WESTFIELD RD

P

IRB Sta

COASTGUARD
COTTS

Yacht
Haven

Lymington River

Ferry v (Yarmouth)

95

2

Waterford

1

Normandy
Farm

NEW LA

Solent

94

33

B 34 **C** **D** 35 **E** **F**

South Hampshire STREET ATLAS

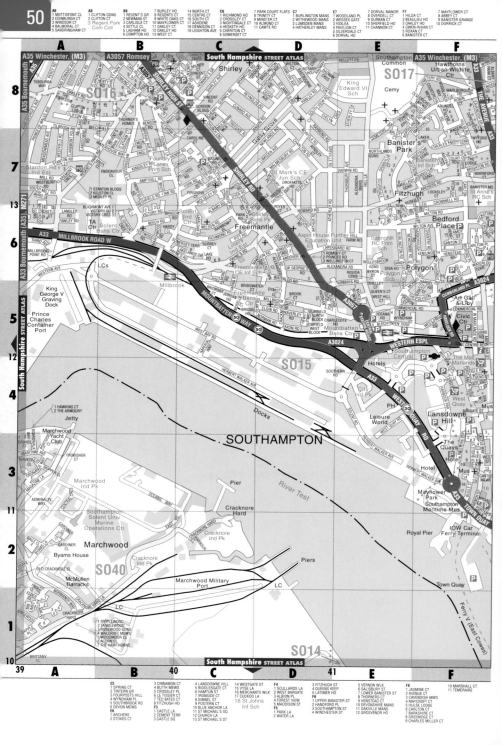

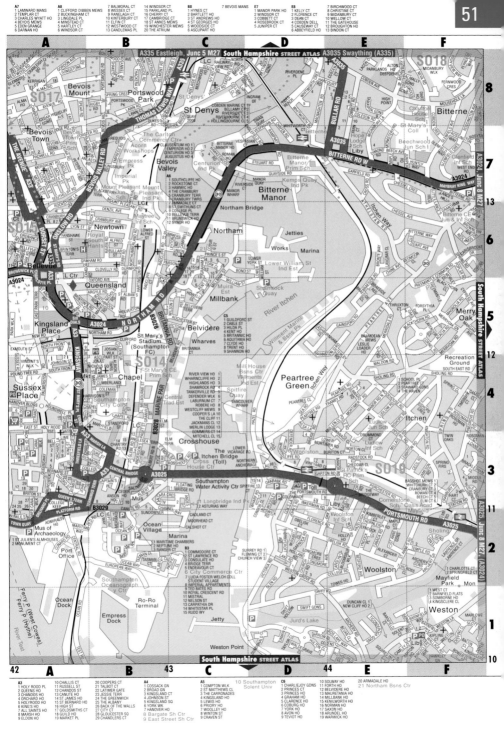

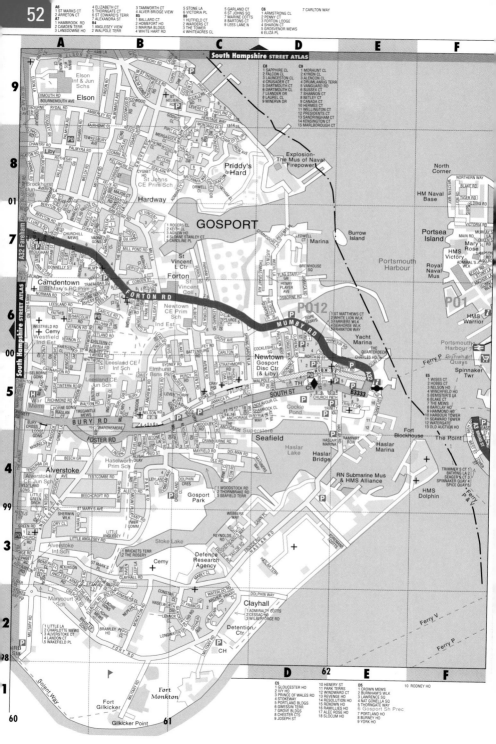

52

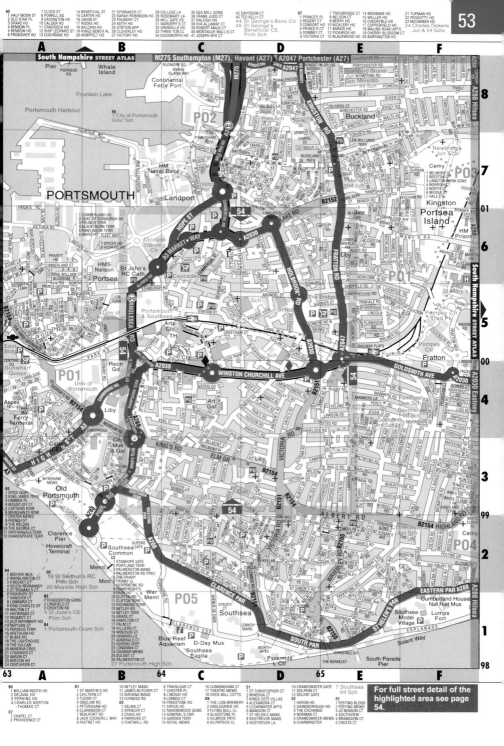

South Hampshire STREET ATLAS

For full street detail of the highlighted area see page 54.

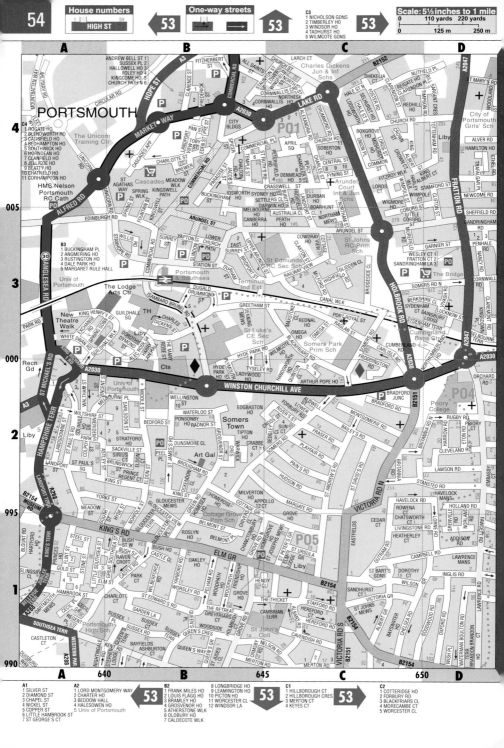

Index

Place name May be abbreviated on the map

Location number Present when a number indicates the place's position in a crowded area of mapping

Locality, town or village Shown when more than one place has the same name

Postcode district District for the indexed place

Page and grid square Page number and grid reference for the standard mapping

Church Rd 6 Beckenham BR2..........**53** C6

Cities, towns and villages are listed in CAPITAL LETTERS **Public and commercial buildings** are highlighted in magenta
Places of interest are highlighted in blue with a star★

Abbreviations used in the index

Acad	**Academy**	Comm	**Common**	Gd	**Ground**	L	**Leisure**	Prom	**Promenade**
App	**Approach**	Cott	**Cottage**	Gdn	**Garden**	La	**Lane**	Rd	**Road**
Arc	**Arcade**	Cres	**Crescent**	Gn	**Green**	Liby	**Library**	Recn	**Recreation**
Ave	**Avenue**	Cswy	**Causeway**	Gr	**Grove**	Mdw	**Meadow**	Ret	**Retail**
Bglw	**Bungalow**	Ct	**Court**	H	**Hall**	Meml	**Memorial**	Sh	**Shopping**
Bldg	**Building**	Ctr	**Centre**	Ho	**House**	Mkt	**Market**	Sq	**Square**
Bsns, Bus	**Business**	Ctry	**Country**	Hospl	**Hospital**	Mus	**Museum**	St	**Street**
Bvd	**Boulevard**	Cty	**County**	HQ	**Headquarters**	Orch	**Orchard**	Sta	**Station**
Cath	**Cathedral**	Dr	**Drive**	Hts	**Heights**	Pal	**Palace**	Terr	**Terrace**
Cir	**Circus**	Dro	**Drove**	Ind	**Industrial**	Par	**Parade**	TH	**Town Hall**
Cl	**Close**	Ed	**Education**	Inst	**Institute**	Pas	**Passage**	Univ	**University**
Cnr	**Corner**	Emb	**Embankment**	Int	**International**	Pk	**Park**	Wk, Wlk	**Walk**
Coll	**College**	Est	**Estate**	Intc	**Interchange**	Pl	**Place**	Wr	**Water**
Com	**Community**	Ex	**Exhibition**	Junc	**Junction**	Prec	**Precinct**	Yd	**Yard**

Index of towns, villages, streets, hospitals, industrial estates, railway stations, schools, shopping centres, universities and places of interest

A

Abbey Ct 6 SO15..........50 F7
Abbeyfield Ho 8 SO18...51 E8
Abbey La PO33 ....12 E5
Abbots Brook SO41 .....48 F2
Abbots Cl PO33..........11 D6
A'Becket Ct 8 PO1......53 A4
Abingdon Cl PO12 ....52 B5
Abingdon Rd PO33.......12 C5
Above Bar St SO14......50 F5
Acacia Cl PO30 ....20 B7
Acacia Rd SO19..........51 F5
Acorn Cl SO40 ....50 A1
Acorn Gdns PO32........3 D2
Acorns The PO33..........10 D4
Acorn Workshops SO14...51 B7
Adames Rd PO1..........53 E6
Addison Rd PO4 ....54 B5
Adelaide Ct
  Lymington SO41..........48 F4
  Ryde PO33..........12 B4
Adelaide Gr PO32..........3 C3
Adelaide Pl PO33 ....12 B4
Adelaide Rd SO17.......51 C8
ADEGESTONE 23 E1
Adgestone Vineyard★
  PO36 ....23 F2
Admiral's Cnr 13 PO5 ...53 D7
Admirals Ct
  2 Portsmouth PO5 .....53 C2
  Portsmouth PO5..........53 C2
Admiral's Wharf PO31...3 B5
Admiral's Wlk PO1......52 F7
Admiralty Cl PO12 ....52 C8
Admiralty Cotts PO12 ...52 C2
Admiralty Ho SO14......51 A2
Admiralty Rd PO1..........53 A5
Admiral Way PO31..........2 F3
Afton Barns PO40..........27 E8
Afton Marsh Nature
  Reserve★ PO40..........27 C8
Afton Park Gdns★ PO40...27 D7
Afton Rd PO40..........27 D7
Agincourt Rd PO2 ......53 D7
Agnew Ho PO12 ....52 B7
Ailsa La SO19..........51 D4
Aisan Way PO38..........45 D7
Albany Ct PO12..........52 B6
Albany Park Ct SO17...50 F8
Albany Rd
  East Cowes PO32 ....3 C5

Albany Rd continued
  Newport PO30 ....20 C8
  Portsmouth PO5..........54 C1
  Southampton SO15 .....50 C6
Albany The 22 SO14......51 A3
Albany View PO30..........8 F1
Albemarle Ave PO12 ...52 B9
Albert Gr PO5 ....54 C1
Albert Mews PO30......20 F8
Albert Rd
  Gurnard PO31..........2 D3
  Portsmouth PO4, PO5 ...53 E2
  Sandown PO36 ....36 A3
  Shanklin PO37 ....43 B7
Albert Road N SO14....51 B3
Albert Road S SO14....51 B3
Albert St
  Cowes PO31..........3 A4
  Gosport PO12..........52 C6
  Newport PO30 ....20 D6
  Ryde PO33..........12 C5
  Ventnor PO38 ....47 B6
Albion Pl 3 SO14......50 F4
Albion Rd PO36..........36 A3
Albion Towers SO14....51 B4
Alcantara Cres SO14...51 B3
Alderbury La PO30......20 C6
Alderbury Rd PO30......20 C6
Aldermore Cl PO33......12 C3
Aldermore Terr PO40...15 A3
Aldrich Rd PO1..........53 A6
Aldwell St PO5..........54 C2
Alec Rose Ho 11 PO12 ...52 C5
Alec Rose La PO1......54 B3
Alecto Rd PO12..........52 C6
Alec Wintle Ho PO2...53 D8
Alencon Cl 3 PO12 ...52 C9
Alexander Cotts PO41...15 A6
Alexander Ct
  Southampton SO15 ....50 D6
  Southampton, Woolston
  SO19..........51 E2
Alexandra Ct 4 PO4....53 E1
Alexandra Gdns PO38...47 A4
Alexandra La PO30......20 D6
Alexandra Mews
  Lymington SO41..........48 D5
  Southampton SO15 .....50 E7
Alexandra Rd
  Cowes PO31..........3 A3
  Lymington SO41..........48 C5
  Portsmouth PO1..........54 C4
  Ryde PO33..........12 E4

Alexandra Rd continued
  Shanklin PO37..........43 C7
  Southampton SO15 .....50 E6
Alexandra Road E PO41...16 C8
Alexandra St 7 PO12 ...52 A7
Alfred Rd
  Portsmouth PO1..........54 A4
  Sandown PO36 ....35 D4
Alfred St
  East Cowes PO32 ....3 C3
  Ryde PO33..........12 C4
Alhambra Rd PO4..........53 E1
Allen's Rd PO4 ....53 E2
Alliance Ho PO1..........53 E6
Allotment Rd PO38......51 B3
Allotment Rd PO38......45 C4
All Saints CE Prim Sch
  PO40..........14 F1
All Saints Ho 7 SO14...51 A3
All Saints Rd SO41......48 F2
All Saints' Rd PO1......53 D7
All Saints' St PO1......54 B4
Alma Ho SO14..........51 A8
Alma Pl 5 PO41..........15 D6
Alma Rd
  Southampton SO14 .....51 A8
  Ventnor PO38 ....47 A5
Alma St PO12..........52 C6
Almond Ct 10 SO15......50 C6
Almond Rd SO15..........50 C6
Almshouses 6 PO33......12 C5
Alpine Rd PO40 ....47 A6
Alresford Lodge PO37...35 D1
Alresford Rd PO33......35 D1
Altofts Gdns PO38......47 A6
Alton Ho SO18..........51 E8
Alum Bay New Rd PO39...26 F6
Alum Bay Old Rd PO39...26 F6
Alvara Rd PO12..........52 A4
Alver Bridge View 4
  PO12..........52 B4
Alver Quay PO12..........52 B4
Alver Rd
  Gosport PO12..........52 B4
  Portsmouth PO1..........53 E6
ALVERSTOKE..........52 A4
Alverstoke CE Jun Sch
  PO12..........52 A4
Alverstoke St PO12......52 A3
Alverstoke Inf Sch PO12...52 A3
ALVERSTONE..........35 B8
Alverstone Cross PO32...10 C5
Alverstone Ct PO36......34 E4

ALVERSTONE GARDEN
  VILLAGE..........35 B7
Alverstone Rd
  Alverstone Garden Village
  PO36..........35 B7
  Winford PO36 ....34 F5
  Wootton PO33 ....10 A6
Alverstone Shute PO36...35 B7
Alverstone Mead Nature
  Reserve★ PO36..........35 B7
Alvington Cl PO30 ......20 A5
Alvington Manor View
  PO30..........19 F6
Alvington Rd PO30......20 A5
Alyne Ho SO15..........50 F8
Aman Ct PO39..........14 C1
Amazon World Zoo Park★
  PO36..........34 C5
Amberley Ho PO37......43 B7
Amberley Rd PO12......52 A9
Ambleside Rd SO41......48 F3
Ambrose Cnr SO41......48 D6
Amberst Pl PO33 ......12 E4
Amoy St SO15..........50 F6
Ampress La SO41..........48 D6
Ampress Pk SO41..........48 D6
Ampthill Rd
  Ryde PO33..........12 E5
  Southampton SO15......50 F8
Ancasta Rd SO14..........51 B7
Anchorage Ho PO38......47 A5
Anchorage The PO12......52 C5
Anchorage Way
  East Cowes PO32 ....3 C2
  Lymington SO41..........48 D3
Anchor Gate Rd PO1......53 A6
Anchor La PO1..........53 A6
Anchor Mews SO14......48 E4
Anderri Way PO37......35 C2
Anderson's Rd SO14......51 B3
Andes Cl SO14..........51 C3
Andover Rd
  Portsmouth PO4 ....53 F2
  Southampton SO15 .....50 D6
Andrew Bell St PO1......54 B4
Andrew's Lodge SO41...48 D5
Angel Ct SO41..........48 F6
Anglesea PO1..........53 B5
Anglesea Rd PO1..........54 A4
Anglesea St 1 PO33......12 C5
Anglesea Terr SO14......51 B3

Anglesey Arms Rd PO12..52 A3
Anglesey Rd PO12 ......52 A3
Anglesey View 1 PO12...52 B4
Angmering Ho 2 PO1 ...54 B3
Ann's Hill Rd PO12......52 A6
Ansells PO34..........13 D2
Anson Ct PO12..........53 A4
Anson Ho SO14..........51 B3
Appleford Rd PO38......40 C5
APPLEY..........12 F5
Appley Farm PO33......12 E4
Appley La PO33..........12 F5
Appley Rd PO33..........12 F4
Appley Rise PO33 ......12 F5
Appley Twr★ PO33......12 F5
Apollo Ct PO5..........54 B2
Appuldurcombe Ho★
  PO38..........42 A4
Appuldurcombe Rd PO38..42 A5
Appuldurcombe Terr
  PO38..........42 C4
April Sq PO1..........54 C4
April St PO33..........54 C4
Ariel Rd PO1..........54 C4
Arlott Ct SO15..........50 E7
Armadale Ho 20 SO14...51 D6
Arminers Cl PO12......52 B2
Armory La PO1..........53 A4
Armoury The SO40......50 A1
Armstrong Cl 1 PO12...52 C4

Arnaud Cl PO2 . . . . 53 D7
Arnhem Rd PO40 . . . . 14 E2
Arnhem Villas PO40 . . . . 14 E2
Arnold Rd
  Cowes PO31 . . . . 3 A3
  Ryde PO33 . . . . 11 E5
ARRETON 21 E2
Arreton Barns Craft Village ★
  PO30 . . . . 21 E2
Arreton Cross PO30 . . . . 21 E2
Arreton Ct 2 PO12 . . . . 52 A6
Arreton St George's CE Prim
  Sch PO30 . . . . 21 F2
Arrow Cl SO19 . . . . 51 D1
Arthur Cott PO2 . . . . 3 E2
Arthur Moody Dr PO30 . . . . . 19 F6
Arthur Pope Ho PO5 . . . . 54 C2
Arthur Rd SO15 . . . . 50 D6
Arthur's Hill PO37 . . . . 35 D1
Arthur St
  Portsmouth PO2 . . . . 53 E7
  Ryde PO33 . . . . 12 B5
Arundel Cl PO33 . . . . 12 E4
Arundel Ct Inf Sch PO1 . . . . . 54 C4
Arundel Ct Jun Sch PO1 . . . . 54 C4
Arundel Ho
  Southampton, Banister's Pk
  SO15 . . . . 50 F8
  18 Southampton, Northam
  SO14 . . . . 51 C6
Arundel Rd PO33 . . . . 12 E4
Arundel St PO1 . . . . 54 C3
Ascupart Ho 6 SO17 . . . . 51 B8
Ascupart St SO14 . . . . 51 C5
Ashborne Ct PO36 . . . . 35 F5
Ashburnham Cl SO19 . . . . 51 D5
Ashburton Ct SO14 . . . . 54 B1
Ashburton Rd PO5 . . . . 53 C2
Ashby Pl PO5 . . . . 53 C2
Ash Cl
  Gosport PO12 . . . . 52 B5
  Newport PO30 . . . . 19 F7
Ashdene 17 SO15 . . . . 50 B8
ASHEY 23 B7
Ashey Cl PO33 . . . . 12 B3
Ashey Pk PO33 . . . . 23 D8
Ashey View PO36 . . . . 35 C3
Ash Gr
  Cowes PO31 . . . . 3 A2
  Shanklin PO37 . . . . 43 C4
Ashknowle La PO38 . . . . 45 D5
Ashlake Copse La PO33 . . . . 11 A5
Ashlake Copse Rd PO33 . . . . 11 A6
Ashlake Farm La PO33 . . . . . 11 A5
Ashley Ct PO12 . . . . 52 A6
Ashley Way SO14 . . . . 30 A2
Ash Rd PO30 . . . . 19 F7
Ashridge Cl SO15 . . . . 50 F8
Ashton Ho SO19 . . . . 51 F1
Ashton Terr 1 SO41 . . . . 3 B4
Ashtree Way PO34 . . . . 13 D2
Aspen Cl PO30 . . . . 20 C7
Aspen Gdns PO33 . . . . 12 F7
Aspex (Gall)★ PO1 . . . . 53 A4
Aspin House Further
  Education Unit SO15 . . . . 50 D6
Astley St PO5 . . . . 54 A2
Aston Rd SO4 . . . . 53 F3
Astra Wlk PO12 . . . . 52 D5
Asturias Way SO14 . . . . 51 C3
Asylum Rd SO15 . . . . 51 A6
Athelstan Rd SO19 . . . . 51 E6
Athelston Ct SO14 . . . . 54 B1
ATHERFIELD GREEN 39 C3
Atherfield Rd PO38 . . . . 39 C8
Atherley Cross Rd PO37 . . . . 43 C8
Atherley Ct
  Shanklin PO37 . . . . 43 C8
  Southampton SO15 . . . . 50 E8
Atherley Rd
  Shanklin PO37 . . . . 43 C8
  Southampton SO15 . . . . 50 D6
Atherstone Wlk 5 PO5 . . . . 54 B2
Atkinson Cl PO12 . . . . 52 A3
Atkinson Dr PO30 . . . . 20 F8
Atlantic Cl SO14 . . . . 51 B2
Atrium The 16 SO17 . . . . 51 A8
Attrill's La PO33, PO34 . . . . . 24 E8
Auckland Road E PO5 . . . . . . 53 C2
Auckland Road W PO5 . . . . . 53 C2
Audley Ct 5 PO40 . . . . 14 E1
Augusta Rd PO33 . . . . 12 B6
Augustine Rd SO14 . . . . 51 B6
Augustus Ho SO18 . . . . 51 C7
Australia Ct PO1 . . . . 54 C3
Autumn Rd SO40 . . . . 50 A1
Avenue Cl
  Gosport PO12 . . . . 52 A3
  2 Southampton SO17 . . . . . . 50 F8
Avenue De Caen PO5 . . . . . . 53 C1
Avenue Nurseries PO36 . . . 36 A4
Avenue Rd
  Freshwater PO40 . . . . 14 E1
  Gosport PO12 . . . . 52 A3
  Lymington SO41 . . . . 48 E4
  Sandown PO36 . . . . 36 A4
  Shanklin PO37 . . . . 43 C8
  Southampton SO14 . . . . 51 A8
  Ventnor PO38 . . . . 42 B5
Avenue Slipway PO12 . . . . . 52 A3
Avenue The
  Bouldnor PO41 . . . . 16 C8
  East Cowes PO32 . . . . 3 E2

Avenue The continued
  Gosport PO12 . . . . 52 A4
  Gurnard PO31 . . . . 2 D3
  Totland PO39 . . . . 14 E1
Avery La PO12 . . . . 52 A8
Avon Cl SO41 . . . . 48 C3
Avondale Rd
  Newport PO30 . . . . 20 E6
  Portsmouth PO1 . . . . 54 C4
Avon Ho 6 SO14 . . . . 51 C6
Avro Cl SO15 . . . . 50 A7
Aylesbury Rd PO2 . . . . 53 F8
Aylett Cl PO36 . . . . 36 A6
Aylward St PO1 . . . . 53 A5
Aynsley Ct SO15 . . . . 50 D7

B

Back of the Walls 26
  SO14 . . . . 51 A3
Bacon Ct SO19 . . . . 51 F1
Badger La PO30 . . . . 28 F4
Badgers Cl PO38 . . . . 42 C4
Badger Terr PO31 . . . . 3 A5
Bagshot Mews SO19 . . . . 51 F3
Bagwich La PO38 . . . . 33 A1
Bailey Cl PO33 . . . . 12 D5
Bailey's Rd PO5 . . . . 54 C2
Bakers Ct PO33 . . . . 11 F5
Baker St PO1 . . . . 53 D7
Balchin Ho 18 PO1 . . . . 53 A5
Ballard Cl 1 PO12 . . . . 52 B5
Balliol Rd PO2 . . . . 53 E8
Balmoral Ct
  4 Southampton, Millbrook
  SO15 . . . . 50 A6
  3 Southampton SO17 . . . . . 51 A8
Banas Cl PO38 . . . . 47 B7
Banbury Cl PO38 . . . . 12 E4
Bangor Rd SO15 . . . . 50 B6
Banister Ct 6 SO15 . . . . 50 F7
Banister Gdns SO15 . . . . 50 F7
Banister Grange 3 SO15 . . . 50 F7
Banister Inf Sch SO15 . . . . . . 50 F7
Banister Mews SO15 . . . . 50 F7
Banister Rd SO15 . . . . 50 F7
BANISTER'S PARK 50 F7
Bank Cotts PO30 . . . . 17 E7
Bank Gdns 8 PO33 . . . . 12 C5
Bankhill Dr SO41 . . . . 48 D4
Bank Pl PO33 . . . . 12 C5
Bankside
  Lymington SO41 . . . . 48 D6
  Shalfleet PO30 . . . . 17 E7
Bankview SO41 . . . . 48 D6
Banner La PO30 . . . . 28 C8
Bannock Rd PO38 . . . . 45 D6
Barclay Ho 8 PO12 . . . . 52 E6
Barfield PO33 . . . . 12 C5
Barfields SO41 . . . . 48 E4
Barfields Ct 2 SO41 . . . . 48 E4
Bargate Mon Mus★ SO14 . . 50 F4
Bargate Sh Ctr 8 SO14 . . . . 51 A4
Bargate St SO14 . . . . 50 F4
Barge La PO33 . . . . 10 F5
Barham Ct PO12 . . . . 52 B7
Baring Dr PO31 . . . . 3 A5
Baring Rd PO31 . . . . 2 E5
Barkis Ho 1 PO1 . . . . 53 D7
Barksdale Ct 7 SO15 . . . . 50 F7
Barn Cl PO38 . . . . 46 B4
Barnes Rd PO1 . . . . 53 E6
Barnfield Cl SO19 . . . . 51 E1
Barnfield Ct SO19 . . . . 51 F1
Barnfield Flats SO19 . . . . 51 F1
Barnfield Rd
  Bembridge PO35 . . . . 25 E4
  Southampton SO19 . . . . 51 F1
Barnfield Way SO19 . . . . 51 F1
Barns The PO30 . . . . 20 B5
Baronsmere PO12 . . . . 52 A5
Barrack Shute PO38 . . . . 45 B3
Barrington Ho 20 PO1 . . . . . 53 D7
Barrington Row PO30 . . . . . . 18 A2
Bars Hill PO31 . . . . 3 A5
Bartlett Ho 2 SO17 . . . . 51 B8
Bartletts Cl PO36 . . . . 24 F7
BARTON 20 F7
Barton Cl PO2 . . . . 9 F8
Barton Prim Sch PO30 . . . . . 20 F7
Barton Rd
  East Cowes PO32 . . . . 3 F2
  Newport PO30 . . . . 20 E7
Bartons Cnr
  Ryde PO33 . . . . 11 E4
  Shalfleet PO30 . . . . 17 F6
Bartons Ct 8 PO12 . . . . 52 B6
Bartonwood Rd PO32 . . . . . . 4 A1
Basepoint Ent Ctr SO14 . . . 51 B3
Basing Ho SO15 . . . . 50 C7
Basin St PO2 . . . . 53 F8
Basketts La 2 PO41 . . . . 15 D6
BATHINGBOURNE 34 B4
Bathingbourne La PO36 . . . 34 B4
Bathing La PO1 . . . . 52 F5
Bath Rd
  Cowes PO31 . . . . 3 B5
  Lymington SO41 . . . . 49 A3
  Portsmouth PO4 . . . . 53 F3
  Ventnor PO38 . . . . 46 F5
Bath Sq PO1 . . . . 52 F5
Bath St SO14 . . . . 51 C5
Battenburg Rd PO12 . . . . 52 C6
Battery Rd PO31 . . . . 2 E5
Battery Row PO1 . . . . 53 A3
Batts Rd PO33 . . . . 23 B7
Bay Ct PO38 . . . . 47 B6

Bayfields PO5 . . . . 54 B1
Baynton Ho SO41 . . . . 48 D7
Bay Rd PO40 . . . . 27 D7
Bays Ct SO41 . . . . 48 C4
Bays Rd SO41 . . . . 48 C3
Bayswater Ho PO5 . . . . 54 C1
Baythorn Cl PO2 . . . . 53 D7
Bay View Ct PO36 . . . . 35 D2
Bay View Rd PO31 . . . . 2 D3
Beachfield Rd
  Bembridge PO35 . . . . 25 F3
  Sandown PO36 . . . . 35 F5
  Wroxall PO38 . . . . 42 B4
Beach House La PO35 . . . . . . 25 F5
Beach Rd
  Bembridge PO35 . . . . 25 C6
  Shanklin PO37 . . . . 35 C4
  Southampton SO19 . . . . 51 E1
Beachside Bowls PO39 . . . . 14 D2
Beacon Alley PO38 . . . . 41 B7
Beaconsfield Rd PO38 . . . . . 47 B6
Beaper Shute PO33, PO36 . . 24 B6
Beatrice Ave
  Portsmouth PO4 . . . . 9 E8
  Shanklin PO37 . . . . 43 D8
Beatrice Cl PO33 . . . . 11 F5
Beatrice Cotts PO41 . . . . 15 A6
Beatrice Rd
  Portsmouth PO4 . . . . 53 E7
  Southampton SO17 . . . . 50 C7
  Ventnor PO38 . . . . 47 D6
Beatty Ho 9 PO1 . . . . 54 C4
Beaufort Rd 7 PO5 . . . . 53 D1
Beaulieu Ho 2 SO15 . . . . 50 F7
Beaumont Ct PO12 . . . . 52 A9
Beckfield Cross PO38 . . . . . . 40 A7
Beckford Rd PO11 . . . . 53 A5
Beck St PO1 . . . . 53 B5
Bedbury La PO40 . . . . 27 B7
Beddow Hall 1 PO5 . . . . 54 A2
Bedford Ave SO19 . . . . 51 E2
Bedford Pl SO15 . . . . 50 F6
BEDFORD PLACE 50 F6
Bedford Row PO30 . . . . 20 C6
Bedford St
  Gosport PO12 . . . . 52 A7
  Portsmouth PO5 . . . . 54 B2
Bedhampton Ho 4 PO1 . . . . 54 C4
Bedhampton Rd PO2 . . . . 53 F8
Bedworth Pl 3 PO33 . . . . 12 C5
Beecham Rd PO1 . . . . 54 C4
Beech Ave SO18 . . . . 51 E7
Beechcroft Ho PO3 . . . . 10 D5
Beechcroft Rd PO12 . . . . 52 B4
Beech Ct
  Shanklin PO37 . . . . 43 C6
  Southampton SO19 . . . . 51 F3
Beeches The PO36 . . . . 35 D3
Beechfield Ct SO15 . . . . 50 B8
Beech Gr
  Gosport PO12 . . . . 52 A4
  Ryde PO33 . . . . 12 A3
Beech Rd
  Newport PO30 . . . . 20 E7
  Southampton SO15 . . . . 50 B6
Beech Tree Dr PO37 . . . . 35 C1
Beechwood Gdns SO18 . . . . 51 F8
Beechwood Ho SO17 . . . . . . 51 C8
Beechwood Jun Sch SO18 51 F7
Beehive Wlk 1 PO1 . . . . 53 A4
Beeston Ct PO1 . . . . 53 F7
Behrendt Cl PO12 . . . . 52 A7
Belgrave Ct PO38 . . . . 46 F5
Belgrave Rd PO38 . . . . 47 A5
Belgrave View PO38 . . . . 46 F6
Bellamy Ct SO17 . . . . 51 D8
Bellcroft Dr PO30 . . . . 20 F7
BELLEVUE 51 C5
Bellevue Rd
  Cowes PO31 . . . . 3 A3
  Ryde PO33 . . . . 12 D6
  Southampton SO15 . . . . 51 A6
Bellevue Terr
  Portsmouth PO5 . . . . 54 A1
  Southampton SO14 . . . . 51 A6
Bellmeade La PO30 . . . . 20 F8
Bell St SO14 . . . . 51 A3
Belmont La PO22 . . . . 9 F3
Belmont Pl PO5 . . . . 54 B1
Belmont St PO5 . . . . 54 B1
Belmore Cl PO1 . . . . 53 E7
Belmore Ct SO41 . . . . 48 D3
Belmore Ho 1 SO41 . . . . 48 E3
Belmore La SO41 . . . . 48 E3
Belmore Rd SO41 . . . . 48 E4
Belvedere St PO33 . . . . 12 C5
BELVIDERE 51 C5
Belvidere Ho 12 SO14 . . . . . 51 C6
Belvidere Rd SO14 . . . . 51 C6
Belvidere Terr SO14 . . . . 51 C5
BEMBRIDGE 25 C4
Bembridge Airport PO35 . . 25 D4
Bembridge CE Prim Sch
  PO35 . . . . 25 D4
Bembridge Cres PO4 . . . . 53 E1
Bembridge Her Str★
  PO35 . . . . 25 C5
Bembridge House Cl
  PO35 . . . . 25 C4
Bembridge Trail PO30 . . . . . . 21 A2
Bembridge Windmill★
  PO35 . . . . 25 B3
Bemister's La 5 PO12 . . . . . . 52 E5
Benbow Ct PO13 . . . . 52 A8
Benbow Ho 4 PO1 . . . . 54 C4
Benbow Pl 5 PO1 . . . . 54 C4
Beneficial St 8 PO1 . . . . 53 A4
Benett St PO33 . . . . 12 D5
Benjamen Mews PO36 . . . . . 35 F5

Benson Rd SO15 . . . . 50 B8
Bentham Rd PO12 . . . . 52 B4
Bentley Way SO41 . . . . 48 D6
Bentley Way SO41 . . . . 48 D7
Benton Cl PO32 . . . . 3 D3
Beresford Rd SO41 . . . . 48 C4
Berkeley Cl SO15 . . . . 50 E7
Berkeley Rd SO15 . . . . 50 E7
Berkeley The PO5 . . . . 53 E1
Bernard Mews 3 PO31 . . . . . 3 B4
Bernard Rd PO31 . . . . 3 B4
Bernard St SO14 . . . . 51 A3
Bernard Way PO30 . . . . 20 D8
Berry Cl PO30 . . . . 20 F6
Berry Hill PO36 . . . . 35 C4
Berryfields PO35 . . . . 25 C4
Berrylands PO35 . . . . 25 C4
Berrymead PO38 . . . . 42 C4
Berry Shute PO30 . . . . 32 A1
Beryton Cl PO12 . . . . 52 A7
Beryton Rd PO12 . . . . 52 A7
Bettesworth Rd
  Portsmouth PO1 . . . . 53 E7
  Ryde PO33 . . . . 12 B3
Betty Haunt La PO30 . . . . 19 C6
Bevan Cl SO19 . . . . 51 E1
Bevis Rd PO12 . . . . 52 B6
Bevois Gdns SO14 . . . . 51 A7
Bevois Hill SO14 . . . . 51 B8
Bevois Mans 2 SO14 . . . . 51 B8
Bevois Mews 4 SO14 . . . . . . 51 A8
BEVOIS MOUNT 51 A7
BEVOIS TOWN 51 A7
Bevois Town Prim Sch
  SO14 . . . . 51 A7
BEVOIS VALLEY 51 B7
Bevois Valley Rd SO14 . . . . . 51 B7
Biddlesgate Ct 5 SO14 . . . . 50 F3
BIERLEY 41 A1
Bignor Pl 15 PO30 . . . . 20 C6
Billington Pl SO41 . . . . 48 D2
Bill Sargent Cres PO1 . . . . . 54 D4
Bindon Ct 12 SO14 . . . . 51 A8
Binfield Cnr PO30 . . . . 9 F4
Bingham Dr SO41 . . . . 48 E3
BINSTEAD 11 F5
Binstead Hill PO33 . . . . 11 E5
Binstead Lodge Rd PO33 . . 11 F4
Binstead Prim Sch PO33 . . 11 F4
Binstead Rd PO33 . . . . 12 A5
Binstead Rd PO33 . . . . 12 A5
Birch Cl
  East Cowes PO32 . . . . 3 D3
  Freshwater PO40 . . . . 14 E2
Birch Ct SO41 . . . . 48 B2
Birch Gdns
  Newport PO30 . . . . 20 C7
  Portsmouth PO1 . . . . 11 F5
Birchmore La PO30 . . . . 32 F8
Birchwood Ct 7 SO18 . . . . . 51 E8
Birdham Ct PO33 . . . . 11 E4
Birkenshaw 5 PO39 . . . . 14 D1
Bishop Lovett CE Mid Sch
  PO33 . . . . 12 E4
Bishops Cl PO30 . . . . 35 E6
Bishops Cres SO19 . . . . 51 E5
Bishops Rd SO19 . . . . 51 E5
Bishops Way PO30 . . . . 9 C1
Bishop St PO1 . . . . 53 A5
Bitterln Ct PO12 . . . . 52 B8
BITTERNE 51 F8
Bitterne CE Inf Sch SO19 . . 51 F6
Bitterne CE Jun Sch SO19 51 F6
BITTERNE MANOR 51 D7
Bitterne Manor Ho SO18 . . 51 C7
Bitterne Manor Prim Sch
  SO18 . . . . 51 D7
Bitterne Road W SO18 . . . . 51 E7
Bitterne Sta SO18 . . . . 51 D7
Bitterne Way
  Lymington SO41 . . . . 48 D2
  Southampton SO19 . . . . 51 F6
Bittern Pl PO30 . . . . 9 E4
Blackberry La PO31 . . . . 3 A4
Blackberry Terr SO14 . . . . . . 51 B7
Blackbridge Rd PO40 . . . . . . 27 C7
Blackfriars Cl 3 PO5 . . . . 54 C2
Blackfriars Rd PO5 . . . . 54 C2
BLACKGANG 44 D4
Blackgang Chine★ PO38 . . 44 D4
Blackgang Sawmill & St
  Catherine's Quay Mus★
  PO38 . . . . 44 D4
Blacklands Rd PO30, PO33 . 21 D8
Blackpan Cl PO36 . . . . 35 C3
Blacksmiths La PO41 . . . . 16 D6
Blackthorn Cl
  Lymington SO41 . . . . 48 B2
  Newport PO30 . . . . 20 C7
  Ryde PO33 . . . . 12 D4
  Southampton SO19 . . . . 51 F5
Blackthorn Rd SO19 . . . . 51 F5
Blackthorn Terr PO1 . . . . 53 A6
Blackwater PO30 . . . . 20 E3
Blackwater Hollow PO30,
  PO38 . . . . 32 F7
Blackwater Junc PO30 . . . . . 20 E3
Blackwood Ho 13 PO1 . . . . . 53 D7
Blake Cl 6 PO12 . . . . 52 E5
Blake Ho 1 PO1 . . . . 54 C4
Blake Rd
  Gosport PO12 . . . . 52 C6
  Portsmouth PO1 . . . . 52 F8

Blechynden Terr SO15 . . . . . 50 E5
Blendworth Ho 2 PO1 . . . . . 54 C4
Blenheim Gdns PO12 . . . . . . 52 B9
Blighmont Ave SO15 . . . . 50 B6
Blighmont Cres SO15 . . . . . . 50 B6
Bloomfield Cotts PO33 . . . . 24 F7
Bloomsbury Pk PO30 . . . . . . 9 B1
Bloomsbury Wlk SO19 . . . . 51 E2
Blossom Sq PO1 . . . . 53 A6
Blue Anchor La PO30 . . . . . . 53 B3
Blue Anchor La 10 SO14 . . . 50 F3
Blue Reef Aquarium★
  PO5 . . . . 53 C1
Bluett Ave PO34 . . . . 13 D4
Blythe Shute PO38 . . . . 44 D5
Blythe Way PO37 . . . . 43 A8
Blyth Mews 4 SO15 . . . . 50 E5
Boardwalk Way SO40 . . . . . . 50 A3
Boarhunt Cl PO2 . . . . 54 C3
Boldens Rd PO12 . . . . 52 B6
Boldre La SO41 . . . . 48 D8
Bolton Dr PO12 . . . . 52 A6
Boltons The PO33 . . . . 10 F5
BONCHURCH 47 D6
Bonchurch Pottery★
  PO38 . . . . 47 D6
Bonchurch Shute PO38 . . . . 47 D7
Bonchurch Village Rd
  PO38 . . . . 47 C7
Bond St SO14 . . . . 51 C7
Bonfire Cnr PO1 . . . . 53 A6
Bosham Rd PO2 . . . . 53 F8
BOULDNOR 15 F6
Bouldnor Mead PO41 . . . . . 15 F6
Boulton Rd PO5 . . . . 54 D1
Boundary Dr PO2 . . . . 4 B3
Bound Rd PO40 . . . . 14 F2
Bournemouth Ave PO12 . . 52 A9
Bourne Rd SO15 . . . . 50 D5
BOWCOMBE 19 E2
Bowcombe Bsns Pk PO30 19 E2
Bowcombe Rd PO30 . . . . 19 E3
Bowdens Mead Cl PO30 . . . 20 C7
Bower Cl SO19 . . . . 51 F1
Bower The PO36 . . . . 34 F5
Bowler Ave PO1 . . . . 53 F6
Bowler Ct PO1 . . . . 53 F6
Bowling Green La 13
  PO30 . . . . 20 D6
Boxgrove Ho PO1 . . . . 54 C4
Bracken Dell PO2 . . . . 43 C4
Brackens Way SO41 . . . . 48 F2
Bracklesham Cl SO19 . . . . . . 51 F3
Bradford Junc PO5 . . . . 54 C2
Bradford Rd PO5 . . . . 54 C2
BRADING 24 A3
Brading CE Prim Sch
  PO36 . . . . 24 A3
Brading Marshes RSPB
  Reserve★ PO35 . . . . 24 D3
Brading Rd PO33 . . . . 12 E2
Brading Roman Villa★
  PO36 . . . . 23 F1
Brading Sta PO36 . . . . 24 B2
Braeside Cl SO19 . . . . 51 E5
Braeside Cres SO19 . . . . 51 E5
Braeside Rd SO19 . . . . 51 E5
Bramber Rd PO12 . . . . 52 A4
Bramble Rd PO4 . . . . 53 E4
Brambles La PO31 . . . . 2 E7
Bramble Wlk SO41 . . . . 48 C4
Bramdean Mews SO19 . . . . 51 E6
Bramley Cl SO41 . . . . 48 E2
Bramley Gdns PO12 . . . . 52 B2
Bramley Ho
  Gosport PO12 . . . . 52 B2
  3 Portsmouth PO5 . . . . 53 C2
Bramleys PO30 . . . . 20 A6
Bramsdon Ct 5 PO4 . . . . 53 F2
Bramshott Rd PO4 . . . . 53 F2
Bramston Rd SO15 . . . . 50 C8
Brandon Ct PO5 . . . . 54 D1
Brandon La PO31 . . . . 3 A4
Brandon Rd PO5 . . . . 54 D1
Brandon Rd PO5 . . . . 54 D1
Brannon Way PO33 . . . . 10 E4
BRANSTONE 34 D3
Branstone Cross PO36 . . . . . 34 D3
Braxton Mdw PO41 . . . . 15 A5
Brecon Ho 22 PO1 . . . . 53 A4
Brewer St PO1 . . . . 52 F8
Brewhouse Sq PO12 . . . . 52 D7
Briary Ct PO31 . . . . 2 E5
Brickets Terr PO12 . . . . 52 B3
Brickfield La
  Freshwater PO39 . . . . 27 A8
  Lymington SO41 . . . . 48 F5
Brickfields Horse Country★
  PO33 . . . . 11 E3
Brickfields Way PO36 . . . . . . 36 A4
Briddlesford Rd PO33 . . . . . . 21 F6
Bridge Ho SO15 . . . . 50 C5
Bridge Rd
  Cowes PO31 . . . . 3 B4
  East Cowes PO32 . . . . 3 F4
  Lymington SO41 . . . . 48 F5
  Southampton SO19 . . . . 51 D3
  6 Yarmouth PO41 . . . . 15 C6
Bridge Sh Ctr The PO1 . . . . 54 D3
Bridgeside Cl PO33 . . . . 54 C3
Bridge Sq PO12 . . . . 54 C3
Bridge Terr 8 SO14 . . . . 51 B3
Bridgeway PO33 . . . . 10 E5
Bridgeway The SO19 . . . . . . 51 E3

Column 1

Bridgwater Ct S015 . . . . .50 D5
Bridlington Ave S015 . . . . . . .50 D8
Bridport Ct S015 . . . . .50 C5
Bridport St P01 . . . . .54 B3
BRIGHSTONE 30 C2
Brighstone CE Prim Sch
  P030 . . . . .30 B2
Brighstone Forest Wlk*
  P030 . . . . .30 A6
Brighstone Mus* P030 . . . . . .30 A6
Brighton Rd S015 . . . . .51 A5
Brigstoke Terr 4 P033 . . . . .12 C6
Brinkcliffe Gdns P036 . . . . . .35 E3
Brinton's Rd S014 . . . . .51 B5
Brinton's Terr S014 . . . . .51 A6
Brisbane Ho 4 P01 . . . . .53 F7
Bristol Rd P04 . . . . .53 F2
Britain St P01 . . . . .53 A5
Britannia Ct S014 . . . . .51 C5
Britannia Rd P01 . . . . .48 F4
Britannia Rd
  Portsmouth P05 . . . . .54 C2
  Southampton S014 . . . . . . .51 B5
Britannia Road N P05 . . . . . . .54 D2
Britannia Way
  East Cowes P032 . . . . .3 C2
  Gosport P012 . . . . .52 B7
Britannic Ho 5 S014 . . . . . . .51 C5
Briton St S014 . . . . .51 A3
Brittany Cl S040 . . . . .50 A1
Broadbeach Ct P036 . . . . . . .35 E4
Broadfields Ave P031 . . . . . . .2 F2
Broad Gn 2 S014 . . . . .51 A4
Broad La
  Brighstone P030 . . . . .30 B1
  Lymington S041 . . . . .48 F2
  Southampton S014 . . . . . . .50 F3
  Thorley P041 . . . . .16 D3
Broadlea Prim Sch P036 . . . .35 C4
Broadly Cl S041 . . . . .48 B2
Broadmead Cl 2 S041 . . . . . .48 F2
Broadsmith Ave P032 . . . . . . .3 D2
Broad St P01 . . . . .52 F4
Broadstone Cres P036 . . . . . .24 B3
Broadway P036 . . . . .35 F5
Broadway Cres P033 . . . . . . .12 A5
Broadway The P039 . . . . .14 D1
Broadwood La P030 . . . . .19 F7
Brockhurst Jun Sch P012 . . .52 D8
Brocks Copse Rd P033 . . . . . .10 D6
Brockwood Dr P07 . . . . .43 B8
Brodrick Ave P012 . . . . .52 A4
Brompton Rd P04 . . . . .53 F3
Bronte Way S019 . . . . .51 E6
BROOK 29 A4
Brook Cl
  Ryde P033 . . . . .12 D3
  Sandown P036 . . . . .35 F7
Brook Ct S015 . . . . .50 D5
Brookedge P030 . . . . .30 A3
Brooke Rd P030 . . . . .20 C6
Brook Farm Cl P030 . . . . .29 A4
Brookfield Cotts P036 . . . . . .23 F2
Brookfield Gdns P033 . . . . . .11 F5
Brookfield Rd P01 . . . . .53 E6
Brook Furlong P035 . . . . .25 D8
Brook Hill Ho P030 . . . . .29 B6
Brook Ho P033 . . . . .11 F5
Brook La P030 . . . . .32 C6
Brookland Cl S041 . . . . .48 C3
Brooklands Rd P031 . . . . .2 F3
Brooklyn Gdns P04 . . . . .27 C7
Brookmead P037 . . . . .43 C8
Brook Rd
  Lymington S041 . . . . .48 F2
  Shalcombe P041 . . . . .29 B8
  Shanklin P037 . . . . .43 C8
Brookside Cl P040 . . . . .14 F1
Brookside Cres P038 . . . . . . .42 A4
Brookside Rd P040 . . . . .14 F1
Broomfield La S041 . . . . .48 E4
Broomhill Cl S041 . . . . .48 B2
Broomlands Cl P033 . . . . .24 A7
Brougham La P012 . . . . .52 A7
Brougham Rd P05 . . . . .54 B2
Brougham St P012 . . . . .52 A7
Broughton Ho 12 S018 . . . . . .51 E8
Brownings Cl S041 . . . . .48 A4
Brownlow Cl P01 . . . . .53 D7
Brownlow Rd P04 . . . . .53 F2
Bruce Rd P04 . . . . .53 F2
Brunswick Ct 6 P031 . . . . . . .3 B4
Brunswick Ho 11 S015 . . . . . .51 A6
Brunswick Pl
  Lymington S041 . . . . .48 E4
  Southampton S015 . . . . . . .51 A6
Brunswick Rd P031 . . . . .3 B4
Brunswick Sq S014 . . . . .51 A3
Brunswick St P05 . . . . .54 B2
Bryanston Rd S019 . . . . .51 E5
Buckbury Cl P030 . . . . .21 A7
Buckbury Hts P030 . . . . .21 B7
Buckbury La P030 . . . . .21 B7
Buckingham Cl P033 . . . . .12 B6
Buckingham Cres P030 . . . . . .21 A7
Buckingham Ct 2 S017 . . . . .51 A8
Buckingham Gn P01 . . . . .53 D7
Buckingham Pl 1 P01 . . . . . . .54 B3
Buckingham Rd P033 . . . . . . .12 B6
Buckingham St P01 . . . . .54 B4
BUCKLAND
  Lymington 48 D5
  Portsmouth 53 E8
Buckland Ct S041 . . . . .48 E5

Column 2

Buckland Dene S041 . . . . . . .48 D5
Buckland Gdns
  Lymington S041 . . . . .48 D6
  Ryde P033 . . . . .12 A6
Buckland Grange P033 . . . . . .12 A6
Buckland Path P02 . . . . .53 D7
Bucklands Ct 3 . . . . .3 C4
Buckland St P02 . . . . .53 E7
Buckland View S041 . . . . .48 E5
Bucklers Ct S041 . . . . .48 D3
Bucklers Dr P033 . . . . .12 B4
Bucklers Mews S041 . . . . . . .48 D3
Bucklers Rd P012 . . . . .52 C9
Bucklers View P031 . . . . .2 D3
Bugle St S014 . . . . .50 F3
Bullar Rd S018 . . . . .51 E8
Bullar St S014 . . . . .51 A4
Bullen Cross P033 . . . . .13 B3
Bullen Rd P033 . . . . .12 F2
BULLEN VILLAGE 12 F2
Bull Ring P030 . . . . .24 B3
Bullys Hill P036 . . . . .24 A2
Bunkers La P038 . . . . .32 F5
Buona Vista Rd P038 . . . . . . .47 B5
Buona Vista Terr P038 . . . . . .47 B5
Burgoyne Rd P05 . . . . .53 D1
Buriton Ct S019 . . . . .51 E3
Buriton St P01 . . . . .54 C4
Burleigh Rd P01 . . . . .53 D7
Burley Ho 2 S014 . . . . .50 B8
Burlington Mans 1 S015 . . . .50 C7
Burlington Rd S015 . . . . .50 E6
Burnaby Rd P01 . . . . .53 B4
Burney Ho 2 S014 . . . . .50 B8
Burnham's Wlk 2 P012 . . . . .52 D5
Burnt House La
  Alverstone P036 . . . . .35 B7
  Downend P030 . . . . .21 C4
  Sandown P036 . . . . .35 D3
Burrard Gr S041 . . . . .48 F2
Burton Rd S015 . . . . .50 E6
Bury Cl P012 . . . . .52 B5
Bury Cres P012 . . . . .52 B5
Bury Cross P012 . . . . .52 A5
Bury Rd P012 . . . . .52 A5
Bush St E P05 . . . . .54 B1
Bush St E P05 . . . . .54 B1
Bush St W P05 . . . . .54 B1
Butcher St P01 . . . . .53 A5
Butler Gdns P037 . . . . .43 C7
Butterfly World* P033 . . . . . .10 B2
Butt's Rd P033 . . . . .12 A3
Byams La S040 . . . . .50 C2
Byerley Rd P01 . . . . .53 C7
Byron Ct S015 . . . . .51 D6
Byron Rd P02 . . . . .53 F8

Column 3 — C

Cable St 2 S014 . . . . .51 C5
Cadets Wlk P032 . . . . .3 D2
Cadington Ho 9 P01 . . . . .53 A5
Cadland Ct S014 . . . . .51 C2
Caernarvon Lodge P037 . . . .35 C1
Caesars Rd P030 . . . . .20 C7
Cairo Terr P02 . . . . .53 D7
CALBOURNE 18 B1
Calbourne Rd P030 . . . . .19 D4
Calbourne Water Mill*
  P030 . . . . .17 E2
Caldecote Wlk 7 P05 . . . . . . .54 B2
Calder Ho 10 P01 . . . . .53 A5
Calder Rd S019 . . . . .51 E3
Callaway Ho 2 P01 . . . . .53 A5
Calshot Ct S014 . . . . .51 C2
Calthorpe Rd P033 . . . . .13 A4
Camber Pl 3 S014 . . . . .53 A3
Cambrian Terr P01 . . . . .53 A3
Cambridge Ct 17 S014 . . . . . .51 A8
Cambridge Junc P01 . . . . . . .53 A4
Cambridge Rd
  East Cowes P032 . . . . .3 C5
  Portsmouth P01 . . . . .53 B4
  Southampton S014 . . . . . . .51 A8
Camden Ct P033 . . . . .12 D6
Camden Ct S014 . . . . .51 A4
Camden Rd P031 . . . . .2 F2
Camden Terr 2 P012 . . . . . . .52 A7
CAMDENTOWN 52 A6
Cameron Cl
  Freshwater P040 . . . . .27 B8
  Newport P030 . . . . .9 A1
Camley Ct S019 . . . . .51 E1
Campbell Rd P05 . . . . .54 D1
Campbell Rd S014 . . . . .51 C6
Campbell Rd P03 . . . . .9 F8
CAMP HILL 8 E1
Campion Way S041 . . . . .48 E5
Camp Rd P040 . . . . .27 B8
Canada Ct 9 P02 . . . . .54 A1
Canada Rd S019 . . . . .51 E2
Canalside The P01 . . . . .53 A4
Canal Wlk
  Portsmouth P01 . . . . .54 C3
  Southampton S014 . . . . . . .51 A3
Canberra Ho P01 . . . . .53 B3
Candlemas Pl 13 S017 . . . . . .51 A8
Cannon Ho S041 . . . . .48 E4
Cannon St
  Lymington S041 . . . . .48 E4
  Southampton S015 . . . . . . .50 C8
Canteen Rd P038 . . . . .34 D1
Canterbury Rd P04 . . . . .53 F3
Canute Rd S014 . . . . .51 A3
Canute Ho 13 S014 . . . . .51 A3
Canute Rd S014 . . . . .51 A3
Captains Row 5 P012 . . . . . . .51 A3
Captains Row 5 P012 . . . . . . .53 A3
Captain's Row S041 . . . . .48 F4

Column 4

CARISBROOKE 20 B5
Carisbrooke Castle* 20 B4
Carisbrooke Castle Mus*
  P030 . . . . .20 B4
Carisbrooke CE Prim Sch
  P030 . . . . .20 C6
Carisbrooke Dr S019 . . . . . . .51 F6
Carisbrooke High Sch
  P030 . . . . .20 C6
Carisbrooke Rd P030 . . . . . . .20 C6
Carita Ho P030 . . . . .20 C6
Carlisle Ct 3 S016 . . . . .50 B8
Carlisle Rd
  Portsmouth P05 . . . . .54 C3
  Southampton S016 . . . . . . .50 B8
Carlton Commerce Ctr The
  P01 . . . . .53 B7
Carlton Cres S015 . . . . .50 F6
Carlton Ct 6 S015 . . . . .50 F6
Carlton Ho 4 S041 . . . . .48 E4
Carlton Pl S015 . . . . .50 F6
Carlton Rd
  Gosport P012 . . . . .52 C6
  Ryde P033 . . . . .12 D3
  Southampton S015 . . . . . . .50 F7
Carlton Way 7 P012 . . . . .52 C6
Carlyle Rd P012 . . . . .52 B6
Carnarvon Rd
  Gosport P012 . . . . .52 A5
  Portsmouth P02 . . . . .53 F8
Caroline Ct S015 . . . . .50 F7
Caroline Pl P012 . . . . .52 B7
Carolyn Ct S019 . . . . .51 E2
Carpathia Dr 13 S014 . . . . . .51 B3
Carpenter Cl
  Lymington S041 . . . . .48 D5
  Sandown S014 . . . . .35 D3
CARPENTERS 24 E6
Carpenters La P030 . . . . .28 F4
Carpenters Quay P030 . . . . . .24 D6
Carpenters Rd P033, P036 . . .24 D6
Carronades The 3 S014 . . . .51 A5
Carter Ave P037 . . . . .43 B8
Carter Ho 16 P01 . . . . .53 A5
Carters Rd P033 . . . . .12 B1
Carter St P030 . . . . .35 F6
Carval Ct P031 . . . . .3 B5
Cascades App P01 . . . . .54 B4
Cascades Sh Ctr P01 . . . . . . .54 B4
Castle Cl
  Portsmouth P05 . . . . .54 B1
  Ventnor P038 . . . . .46 E5
Castle Crag P030 . . . . .20 A5
Castle Ct
  Southampton, Millbrook
    S015 . . . . .50 A6
  Ventnor P038 . . . . .46 D5
Castlehaven La P038 . . . . . . .45 A2
Castle Hill
  Carisbrooke P030 . . . . .20 A4
  Cowes P031 . . . . .3 A6
Castle La
  Carisbrooke P030 . . . . .20 B4
  1 Southampton S014 . . . . .50 F3
  Wroxall P038 . . . . .42 C5
Castle Mews S014 . . . . .51 A4
Castle Rd
  Cowes P031 . . . . .3 A5
  Newport P030 . . . . .20 C5
  Portsmouth P05 . . . . .54 B1
  Ventnor P038 . . . . .46 E5
  Wroxall P038 . . . . .42 C5
Castle Sq 3 S014 . . . . .50 F3
Castle St
  Carisbrooke P030 . . . . .20 B4
  East Cowes P032 . . . . .3 C6
  Newport P030 . . . . .20 C5
  Portsmouth P05 . . . . .54 B1
  1 Southampton S014 . . . . .51 A4
Castleton Ct P05 . . . . .54 A1
Castle View P05 . . . . .54 A1
Castle Way S014 . . . . .50 F3
Catherine Terr P030 . . . . .24 B3
Catisfield Ho 3 P01 . . . . .53 A5
Causeway Ct S018 . . . . .51 E8
Causeway The P040 . . . . .27 E8
Cavalier Quay P030 . . . . .3 C3
Cavendish Mews 3 S015 . . . .50 F8
Cavendish Pl P030 . . . . .20 C6
Cavendish Rd P05 . . . . .54 C3
Caws Ave P04 . . . . .13 D2
Cecil Gr P05 . . . . .54 A1
Cecil Pl P05 . . . . .54 A1
Cecil Rd S019 . . . . .51 F3
Cedar Ave S015 . . . . .50 D8
Cedar Cl P07 . . . . .35 C2
Cedar Gdns S014 . . . . .51 A8
Cedar Hill P030 . . . . .20 B5
Cedar Rd S014 . . . . .51 A8
Cedar Wood Dr P034 . . . . . . .13 D2
Cedar Ho S014 . . . . .51 A8
Cement Terr 2 S014 . . . . . . .50 F3
Cemetery Rd
  Ryde P033 . . . . .11 E5
  Sandown P036 . . . . .35 D2
  Southampton S014 . . . . . . .51 B4
Centaur St P02 . . . . .53 D8
Central Bridge S014 . . . . .51 A3
Central Cres S040 . . . . .50 A3
Central Rd S014 . . . . .51 A3
Central Sq P01 . . . . .53 A3
Central St P01 . . . . .54 C4

Column 5

Central Station Bridge
  S015 . . . . .50 E5
Central Trading Est S014 . .51 C4
Central Way P036 . . . . .35 E6
Centurion Ct 24 P01 . . . . . . .53 A4
Centurion Ho S018 . . . . .51 C7
Centurion Ind Pk S018 . . . . . .51 C7
Cessac Ho P012 . . . . .52 A4
Chadderton Gdns 1 P01 . . . .53 B3
Chafen Rd S018 . . . . .51 D7
Chain La P030 . . . . .20 D7
CHALE 44 C7
Chale CE Prim Sch P038 . . . .44 C6
Chale Gn P038 . . . . .40 A4
CHALE GREEN 40 B4
Chale La P038 . . . . .44 C7
Challenger Dr P012 . . . . .52 C8
Challis Ct 10 S014 . . . . .51 A3
Chalton Ho P01 . . . . .54 B4
Chambers Dr P036 . . . . .34 F5
Chanctonbury Ho P05 . . . . . . .54 B1
Chandler Cl P030 . . . . .20 C5
Chandlers Ct 2 S014 . . . . . . .51 A3
Chandlers The P031 . . . . .2 F3
Chandos Ho 3 S041 . . . . . . .48 E4
Chandos St S014 . . . . .51 A4
Channel Way S014 . . . . .51 C3
Channon Ct 11 S015 . . . . . . .50 E7
Chantry Rd
  Gosport P012 . . . . .52 A8
  Southampton S014 . . . . . . .51 B3
CHAPEL 51 B4
Chapel Cl P030 . . . . .20 A6
Chapel Ct 1 P01 . . . . .53 C7
Chapel La P030 . . . . .33 C7
Chapel Rd
  Ryde P033 . . . . .11 E5
  Southampton S014 . . . . . . .51 B4
Chapel St
  Gosport P012 . . . . .52 B9
  Newport P030 . . . . .20 C6
  Portsmouth, Buckland P02 . .53 D8
  3 Portsmouth P05 . . . . .54 A1
  Southampton S014 . . . . . . .51 B4
Charlecote Ho 11 S014 . . . . .51 C6
Charles Dickens' Birthplace
  Mus* P01 . . . . .53 A4
Charles Dickens Jun & Inf
  Schs P01 . . . . .53 D7
Charles Dickens St P01 . . . . .54 B3
Charles Ho P012 . . . . .52 E6
Charles Knott Gdns S015 . . .50 F8
Charles Miller Ct 8 S015 . . .50 F8
Charles Norton-Thomas Ct
  4 P01 . . . . .53 B5
Charles Rd P031 . . . . .2 F4
Charles St
  Portsmouth P01 . . . . .54 C4
  Southampton S014 . . . . . . .51 A4
Charles Wyatt Ho P05 . . . . . .54 C3
Charliejoy Gdns 1 S014 . . . .51 C6
Charlott Ct P05 . . . . .54 B4
Charlotte Ct S019 . . . . .51 F2
Charlotte Pl S014 . . . . .51 A6
Charlotte Mews P012 . . . . . . .52 A3
Charlotte Pl S014 . . . . .51 A6
Charlton House Sch S018 . .51 E8
Charlton Rd S015 . . . . .50 D7
Charminster 8 P05 . . . . .53 E2
Charnwood Cl P030 . . . . .24 A3
Charnwood Cotts P036 . . . . .24 A3
Charter Ho 2 P01 . . . . .53 A5
Chase The P036 . . . . .34 F4
Chatfield Ave P02 . . . . .53 A8
Chatfield Ho 10 P01 . . . . .54 C4
Chatfield Lodge P030 . . . . . . .20 C5
Chatham Dr P01 . . . . .53 B3
Chatham Ct P012 . . . . .52 A3
Chatham Dr P01 . . . . .53 B3
Chatsworth Ave P037 . . . . . . .43 A7
Chatsworth Rd S019 . . . . . . .51 E3
Chatsworth Mews P036 . . . . .36 A4
Chawton Farm Barns P031 . .30 A7
Cheddar Cl S019 . . . . .51 E3
Cheeryble Ho 18 P01 . . . . . . .53 D7
Chelsea Rd P05 . . . . .54 C1
Chelsfield Ave P036 . . . . .35 D2
Chequers Cl S041 . . . . .48 E5
Chequers Inn Rd P038 . . . . . .33 A3
Cheriton Ct 8 S015 . . . . .50 C6
Cherry Blossom Ct 14 . . . . . .53 D7
Cherry Ct 16 S014 . . . . .51 A8
Cherry Side P036 . . . . .35 D3
Cherrytree Rd P04 . . . . .13 D2
Cherry Wlk S015 . . . . .50 C6
Cherrywood View P030 . . . . . .22 A1
Chesham Terr P016 . . . . .36 A4
Chessel Ave S019 . . . . .51 E6
Chessel Cres S019 . . . . .51 E6
CHESSELL 29 B8
Chessell Cl P033 . . . . .52 C5
Chessell Pottery* P041 . . . . .29 B8
Chester Pl P033 . . . . .53 D1
Chestnut Ave P04 . . . . .53 F3
Chestnut Cl
  Newport P030 . . . . .20 E5
  Ryde P033 . . . . .11 E4
  Ventnor P038 . . . . .46 E7
Chestnut Ct 1 P030 . . . . .20 E6
Chestnut Gr P033 . . . . .12 F4
Chestnut Mews P037 . . . . . . .43 C6
Chetwynd Rd P04 . . . . .53 E3

Column 6

Cheverton Shute P030 . . . . . .31 B5
Chewter Cl P04 . . . . .53 E1
Chichester Cl P036 . . . . .35 F6
Chichester Rd P02 . . . . .53 E8
Chichester Wlk P030 . . . . . . .20 F7
CHILLERTON 32 C5
Chillerton & Rookley Prim
  Sch P030 . . . . .32 C5
Chiltern Ct
  Gosport P012 . . . . .52 B6
  2 Portsmouth P05 . . . . .53 D1
CHILTON GREEN 29 E2
Chilton La P030 . . . . .29 F2
Chilworth Gr P012 . . . . .52 A6
Chine Ave
  Shanklin P037 . . . . .43 C7
  Southampton S019 . . . . . . .51 E6
Chine Cl P040 . . . . .14 D2
Chine La P030 . . . . .38 H7
Chivers Ct P05 . . . . .54 B1
Chiverton Wlk P030 . . . . .21 A7
Christine Ct 8 S018 . . . . .51 E8
Christ the King Coll P030 . .20 B5
Church Cl P033 . . . . .10 E5
Church End S015 . . . . .50 C8
Church Hill
  Godshill P038 . . . . .41 D8
  Totland P039 . . . . .26 G8
Church Hollow P038 . . . . .41 D8
Churchill Cl
  Cowes P031 . . . . .2 F4
  Sandown P036 . . . . .35 D3
Churchill Mews P012 . . . . . . .52 A7
Churchill Rd P031 . . . . .2 F4
Church La
  Brading P036 . . . . .24 C6
  Cowes P031 . . . . .9 A6
  Cowes P031 . . . . .9 A8
  Lymington S041 . . . . .48 E3
  Ryde P033 . . . . .12 C6
  Shalfleet P030 . . . . .18 D1
  12 Southampton S014 . . . .50 F3
Church Lane Cotts 14
  P033 . . . . .12 C6
Church Litten P030 . . . . .20 E6
Church Mead 9 S041 . . . . . . .48 E2
Church Mews 1 P033 . . . . . . .12 C6
Church Path
  East Cowes P032 . . . . .3 C4
  Gosport P012 . . . . .52 D5
Church Path N P01 . . . . .54 B4
Church Pl
  Freshwater P040 . . . . .44 C6
  Freshwater P040 . . . . .15 B1
Church Rd
  Bembridge P035 . . . . .25 C5
  Cowes P031 . . . . .3 A5
  Gosport P012 . . . . .52 A3
  Gurnard P031 . . . . .2 D3
  Havenstreet P033 . . . . .11 C7
  Portsmouth P01 . . . . .54 C4
  Ryde P033 . . . . .11 E6
  Shanklin P037 . . . . .43 B6
  Southampton S019 . . . . . . .51 D2
  Wootton P033 . . . . .10 E5
Church St
  Niton P038 . . . . .45 B4
  Portsmouth P01 . . . . .54 C4
  Seaview P034 . . . . .13 D3
  Ventnor P038 . . . . .47 B6
Church View S019 . . . . .51 D2
Cinnamon St 3 S015 . . . . . . .50 E6
Circle The P05 . . . . .53 D2
Circular Rd
  Portsmouth P01 . . . . .53 C7
  Ryde P033 . . . . .12 E3
  Seaview P034 . . . . .13 D4
City Bldgs P01 . . . . .54 B4
City Commerce Ctr 6
  S014 . . . . .51 B3
City Ct 3 S014 . . . . .51 A3
City Ind Pk S015 . . . . .50 A3
City of Portsmouth Girls' Sch
  P04 . . . . .53 E6
Civic Centre Rd S014 . . . . . . .50 F5
Clanfield Ho 7 P01 . . . . .54 C4
Claremont Cres S015 . . . . . . .50 A7
Claremont P7 P031 . . . . .3 B5
Claremont Rd
  Portsmouth P04 . . . . .54 D3
  Ventnor P038 . . . . .47 B6
Clarence Espl P05 . . . . .53 C1
Clarence Gdns P031 . . . . .35 D1
Clarence Ho 6 S014 . . . . . . .51 C6
Clarence Par P05 . . . . .53 C2
Clarence Rd
  East Cowes P032 . . . . .3 C3
  Gosport P012 . . . . .52 D6
  Newport P030 . . . . .20 C6
  Shanklin P037 . . . . .35 C1
  Ventnor P038 . . . . .47 B6
  Wroxall P038 . . . . .42 C5
Clarence St P01 . . . . .54 B4
Clarendon Cl P036 . . . . .24 B1
Clarendon Ct 6 P05 . . . . .53 D1
Clarendon Ct P031 . . . . .3 B5
Clarendon Pl
  Newport P030 . . . . .20 C5
  Portsmouth P01 . . . . .54 C4
Clarendon Rd
  Portsmouth, Southsea
    P05 . . . . .53 D2
  Shanklin P037 . . . . .43 C8

Clarendon Rd continued
Southampton SO16 . . . .**50** A8
Clarendon St
Newport PO30 . . . .**20** C6
Portsmouth PO1 . . . .**54** C4
Clarkes Rd PO1 . . . .**53** F6
Classic Boat Mus★
Cowes PO31 . . . .**3** C4
Newport PO30 . . . .**9** B2
CLATTERFORD **20** A4
Clatterford Rd PO30 . . . .**20** A5
Clatterford Shute PO30 . . . . .**20** A4
Clausentum Ho SO18 . . . .**51** C7
Clausentum Rd SO14 . . . .**51** B7
Clausen Way SO41 . . . .**48** C1
Claxton St PO1 . . . .**54** C3
CLAYHALL **52** D2
Clayhall Rd PO12 . . . .**52** B3
Clay La PO41 . . . .**17** E3
Clayton Rd PO40 . . . .**14** E1
Clearwater Apartments 🖪
PO4 . . . .**53** E1
Cleaver Ho PO33 . . . .**11** C1
Cleaver's Cl PO33 . . . .**11** E4
Cleveland Rd
Gosport PO12 . . . .**52** B4
Portsmouth PO5 . . . .**54** D2
Clevelands Rd PO30 . . . .**42** C5
Cleveland Terr PO38 . . . .**42** B5
Cleverley Ho PO1 . . . .**53** A5
Cliff Cl PO36 . . . .**24** B3
Cliff Ct PO36 . . . .**35** E4
Cliff End PO40 . . . .**14** E4
Cliff Farm App PO37 . . . .**42** F7
Cliff Gdns PO36 . . . .**35** E3
Cliff Ho
Sandown PO36 . . . .**35** E4
Ventnor PO38 . . . .**47** D7
Cliff La PO30 . . . .**38** C8
Clifford Dibben Mews 🖪
SO14 . . . .**51** A8
Clifford St
Newport PO30 . . . .**20** C6
Southampton SO14 . . . .**51** B5
Cliff Rd
Cowes PO31 . . . .**2** F5
Sandown PO36 . . . .**35** E4
Southampton SO15 . . . .**50** D5
Totland PO39 . . . .**26** G8
Cliff The SO19 . . . .**51** A3
Cliff Way PO36 . . . .**35** E3
Clifton Ct 🖪 SO15 . . . .**50** A8
Clifton Gdns 🖪 SO15 . . . .**50** A8
Clifton Lodge SO15 . . . .**50** A8
Clifton Rd
Southampton PO05 . . . .**53** C2
Southampton SO15 . . . .**50** A8
Clifton St PO1 . . . .**54** D4
Clifton Terr
🖽 Portsmouth PO5 . . . .**53** C2
🖪 Totland PO40 . . . .**14** E1
Clinton Rd SO41 . . . .**48** E5
Clissold Rd PO30 . . . .**9** A2
Clive Rd PO1 . . . .**53** E6
Clock St 🖪 PO1 . . . .**53** A5
Cloisters The
Lymington SO41 . . . .**48** E3
Sandown PO36 . . . .**35** F6
Close The PO34 . . . .**13** E2
Clovelly Rd SO14 . . . .**51** B6
Clydebank Rd PO2 . . . .**53** D8
Clyde Ho
🖪 Southampton SO14 . . . .**51** C5
Ventnor PO38 . . . .**47** B6
Coach House La PO33 . . . .**12** A4
Coach House Mews PO33 . . . .**43** C8
Coach La PO30 . . . .**24** A3
Coastal Visitors Ctr★
PO38 . . . .**47** A5
Coastguard Cotts
Bembridge PO36 . . . .**37** A6
Brighstone PO30 . . . .**38** C8
Brook PO30 . . . .**28** F4
Little Atherfield PO38 . . . .**39** A3
Lymington SO41 . . . .**49** A2
🖬 Yarmouth PO41 . . . .**15** C6
Coastguard La
Brook PO30 . . . .**28** F4
Freshwater Bay PO40 . . . .**27** D6
Cobbett Ct 🖪 SO18 . . . .**51** E1
Cobbett Rd SO18 . . . .**51** E8
Cobden Ave SO18 . . . .**51** E8
Cobden Cres SO18 . . . .**51** F8
Cobden Ct SO18 . . . .**51** E8
Cobden Dell 🖪 SO18 . . . .**51** E8
Cobden Marine Ct SO17 . . .**51** D8
Cobden St PO12 . . . .**52** B6
Coburg Ct PO32 . . . .**3** D2
Coburg Ho 🖪 SO14 . . . .**51** C6
Coburg St
Portsmouth PO1 . . . .**54** C3
Southampton SO14 . . . .**51** C6
Cochrane Ho 🖪 PO1 . . . .**53** A5
COCKEREL **34** D7
Cockerell Rise PO32 . . . .**3** D2
Cockleshell Sq PO12 . . . .**52** D6
Cockleton La PO31 . . . .**2** E2
Colborne Cl SO41 . . . .**48** E5
Coleman's Animal Farm★
PO30 . . . .**7** E1
Coleman's La PO30 . . . .**7** E1
Coleman St SO14 . . . .**51** B4
Colenutt's Rd PO33 . . . .**12** A3
Coles Cl PO40 . . . .**14** D2
Coleson Rd SO18 . . . .**51** E8

Collards Cl PO40 . . . .**14** F1
College Cl PO36 . . . .**36** A4
College Keep SO14 . . . .**51** B3
College La 🖽 PO1 . . . .**53** A5
College Pl 🖪 SO15 . . . .**51** A6
College Rd
Newport PO30 . . . .**20** E5
Portsmouth PO1 . . . .**53** A5
Southampton SO19 . . . .**51** E2
College St
Portsmouth PO1 . . . .**53** A5
Southampton SO14 . . . .**51** A3
College Way PO32 . . . .**3** D2
Collier Cl SO17 . . . .**51** C8
Collingwood Ct PO33 . . . .**12** E5
Collingwood Rd
Newport PO30 . . . .**20** D6
Portsmouth PO5 . . . .**53** D2
Shanklin PO37 . . . .**43** D8
Colmar Way PO30 . . . .**14** D1
Colonnades The PO37 . . . .**43** B6
Colonnade The SO19 . . . .**51** D3
Colpoy St PO5 . . . .**54** A2
Columbine Rd PO32 . . . .**3** C4
Columbus Ho PO37 . . . .**35** D1
Cozens Cl SO19 . . . .**51** E1
Colwell Chine PO40 . . . .**14** D2
Colwell Chine Rd PO40 . . . . . .**14** E2
Colwell Cl PO40 . . . .**14** E2
Colwell Common Rd
PO39 . . . .**14** D1
Colwell La PO40 . . . .**14** E1
Colwell Rd
Freshwater PO39 . . . .**14** E2
Norton Green PO40 . . . .**15** A3
Combley La PO30 . . . .**21** F5
Comforts Farm PO31 . . . .**8** D7
Commercial Pl PO1 . . . .**54** B4
Commercial Rd
Portsmouth PO1 . . . .**54** B4
Southampton SO15 . . . .**50** E5
Commodore Ct 🖪 SO14 . . . . .**51** B3
Commodore Pl PO12 . . . .**52** D7
Commodores Ct PO34 . . . .**13** C4
Common St PO1 . . . .**54** C4
Compton Ho 🖪 SO16 . . . .**50** E8
Compton Wlk 🖪 SO14 . . . .**51** A5
Condor Cl SO19 . . . .**51** D3
Conference Pl 🖪 SO41 . . . . . .**48** F2
Conifer Cres SO41 . . . .**48** B3
Coniston Ave PO33 . . . .**11** E4
Coniston Dr PO33 . . . .**12** B6
Coniston Ph PO33 . . . .**35** D1
Connaught Rd PO32 . . . .**3** B4
Consort Ho 🖪 PO1 . . . .**53** D7
Consort Rd PO1 . . . .**3** B4
Constable Ct PO12 . . . .**52** C2
Consulate Ho 🖪 SO14 . . . .**51** B3
Conway La PO39 . . . .**14** D2
Cook Ave PO30 . . . .**20** D6
Cook St SO14 . . . .**51** A4
Cookworthy Rd PO30 . . . .**9** A2
Coombe La PO30 . . . .**30** B4
Coombe Pk PO38 . . . .**42** B4
Coombe Rd PO12 . . . .**52** B8
Cooper Rd PO30 . . . .**20** F8
Coopers Cl PO40 . . . .**14** E1
Coopers Ct 🖪 SO14 . . . .**51** A3
Coopers La PO41 . . . .**16** F5
Cooper's La SO19 . . . .**51** D3
Copperfield Ho 🖽 PO1 . . . . . .**53** D7
Copper St 🖪 PO5 . . . .**54** A1
Coppice End PO33 . . . .**12** E7
Coppins Cl PO30 . . . .**20** E7
Copse Butt PO33 . . . .**25** E4
Copse End PO36 . . . .**35** F7
Copsefield Dr PO33 . . . .**12** B6
Copse La
Blackwater PO30 . . . .**20** D2
Freshwater PO40 . . . .**15** A2
Copse Rd PO37 . . . .**43** B8
Corbett Rd PO33 . . . .**12** A3
Corbin Cl SO41 . . . .**48** B2
Corbin Rd SO41 . . . .**48** B2
Corhampton Rd PO11 . . . .**54** C4
Cornel Rd SO19 . . . .**51** F5
Cornwallis Cres PO1 . . . .**54** C4
Cornwallis Ho PO1 . . . .**54** C4
Cornwall Rd
Portsmouth PO1 . . . .**53** E5
Ventnor PO38 . . . .**46** F6
Cornwall St PO33 . . . .**12** D6
Coronado Rd PO12 . . . .**52** B8
Coronation Ave PO31 . . . .**9** A7
Coronation Cotts
Freshwater PO40 . . . .**27** C8
🖽 Yarmouth PO41 . . . .**15** D6
Coronation Gdns PO37 . . . . . .**35** C1
Coronation Rd PO31 . . . .**3** A4
Corve Hill PO30 . . . .**31** B1
Cossack Gn 🖪 SO14 . . . .**51** A4
Cothey Way PO33 . . . .**12** F2
Cotswold Ct PO33 . . . .**12** E5
Cottage Gr
Gosport PO12 . . . .**52** B6
Portsmouth PO5 . . . .**54** A2
Cottage Grove Prim Sch
PO5 . . . .**54** B1
Cottage Ho 🖽 PO30 . . . .**20** D6
Cottage Mews 🖪 PO30 . . . . . .**20** D6
Cottage View PO1 . . . .**54** C3
Cotteridge Ho 🖪 PO5 . . . .**54** C2
Cotton Cl PO31 . . . .**3** A3
Coulmere Rd PO12 . . . .**52** A7
County View PO37 . . . .**35** D2
Court Cl SO41 . . . .**48** D2
Courtenay Pl SO41 . . . .**48** E3
Courtlands 🖪 SO41 . . . .**48** E4

Court Rd
Freshwater PO40 . . . .**27** A8
Southampton SO15 . . . .**50** F7
Court Royal Mews SO15 . . . . .**50** F8
Court The SO41 . . . .**48** D2
Courtyard The
East Cowes PO32 . . . .**3** C3
Newport PO30 . . . .**9** B2
Cousins Gr PO4 . . . .**53** F2
Coventry Rd SO15 . . . .**50** F6
Cowdray Ho PO1 . . . .**54** C3
COWES **3** B5
Cowes Cty Prim Sch PO31 . . . .**3** A4
Cowes High Sch PO31 . . . .**2** F5
Cowes Maritime Mus★
PO31 . . . .**3** B4
Cowes Rd PO30 . . . .**9** A5
Cow La PO31 . . . .**2** E4
COWLEAZE **47** B6
Cowleaze Hill PO37 . . . .**43** B6
Cowley Rd SO41 . . . .**48** C4
Cowper Rd PO1 . . . .**53** E7
Cox's Cnr PO30 . . . .**20** C1
Cox's Green PO36 . . . .**35** E6
Cox's La SO19 . . . .**51** D3
Cozens Cl SO19 . . . .**51** E1
Crabbe Ct PO5 . . . .**54** B2
Cracknore Hard SO40 . . . .**50** A1
Cracknore Hard La SO40 . . . . .**50** A1
Cracknore Ind Pk SO40 . . . . . .**50** C2
Cracknore Rd SO15 . . . .**50** D5
Craddock Ho 🖽 PO1 . . . .**53** A5
Craig Ho 🖪 PO5 . . . .**53** C2
Craigmore Ct PO37 . . . .**35** D1
Cranbourne Rd PO12 . . . .**52** C4
Cranbury Ave SO14 . . . .**51** B6
Cranbury Ct SO19 . . . .**51** F3
Cranbury Pl SO14 . . . .**51** A6
Cranbury Rd SO19 . . . .**51** F3
Cranbury Terr 🖪 SO14 . . . . . .**51** A6
Cranbury The 🖪 SO14 . . . .**51** A6
Cranbury Twrs 🖪 SO14 . . . . . .**51** A6
Craneswater Ave PO4 . . . .**53** E2
Craneswater Gate 🔟 PO4 . . . .**53** E1
Craneswater Jun Sch PO4 . . .**53** F2
Craneswater Mews 🖪
PO4 . . . .**53** E2
Craneswater Park PO1 . . . .**53** E6
Cranleigh Ave PO1 . . . .**53** E6
Cranleigh Gdns PO31 . . . .**8** F8
Cranleigh Ho SO17 . . . .**51** A8
Cranleigh Rd PO1 . . . .**53** E6
CRANMORE **17** B8
Cranmore Ave PO41 . . . .**5** D1
CRANMORE PARK **16** F8
Cranstoun Cl PO30 . . . .**26** G8
Crasswell St PO1 . . . .**54** C4
Craven St 🖪 SO14 . . . .**51** A5
Cray Ho PO12 . . . .**52** D5
Creek Gdns PO33 . . . .**10** F6
Creek Rd PO12 . . . .**52** D5
Crescent Ct PO37 . . . .**43** D8
Crescent Rd
Gosport PO12 . . . .**52** A2
Sandown PO36 . . . .**36** A3
Shanklin PO37 . . . .**43** D8
Cressy Rd PO2 . . . .**53** D7
Cresta Ct 🖪 PO4 . . . .**53** F2
CRIDMORE **32** D2
Crocker Rd PO38 . . . .**45** B6
Crocker St PO30 . . . .**20** D7
Cromwell Rd SO15 . . . .**50** F7
Crossfield Ave PO1 . . . .**2** F4
CROSSHOUSE **51** C3
Cross House Ctr SO14 . . . .**51** C3
Crosshouse Rd SO14 . . . .**51** C3
Cross La PO30 . . . .**20** F8
Crossland Cl PO12 . . . .**52** C4
Crossley Ct 🖪 SO15 . . . .**50** C6
Crossley Pl 🖪 SO15 . . . .**50** C6
Cross Rd
Sandown PO36 . . . .**35** D3
Shanklin PO37 . . . .**43** C8
Southampton SO19 . . . .**51** E7
Cross St
Brading PO36 . . . .**24** B3
Cowes PO31 . . . .**3** B5
Newport PO30 . . . .**20** D6
Portsmouth PO5 . . . .**54** C2
Portsmouth, Portsea PO1 . . . . .**53** A6
Ryde, Oakfield PO33 . . . .**12** C4
Ryde PO33 . . . .**11** C6
Sandown PO36 . . . .**36** A4
Shanklin PO37 . . . .**43** C7
Crossway PO35 . . . .**25** E4
Crossways Rd
Camp Hill PO30 . . . .**8** F1
East Cowes PO32 . . . .**3** E2
Crossways The PO12 . . . .**52** B7
Crouchers Cross PO30 . . . .**33** D8
Crown Ct
Cowes PO31 . . . .**3** B5
Newport PO30 . . . .**20** D6
Crown Mews 🖪 PO12 . . . .**52** D5
Crown St
Portsmouth PO1 . . . .**54** C4
🖪 Ryde PO33 . . . .**12** C6
Southampton SO15 . . . .**50** E6
Croxton Rd PO1 . . . .**53** B3
Crozier Rd PO41 . . . .**15** A6
Crundles The PO40 . . . .**15** A1
Crusader Ct 🖪 PO12 . . . .**52** C8
Cuckoo La 🔟 SO14 . . . .**51** A3
Culver Par PO36 . . . .**36** B4
Culver Rd PO4 . . . .**43** D8
Culver Way PO36 . . . .**36** B5
Cumberland Bsns Ctr
Cumberland **54** C3

Cumberland Ho PO1 . . . .**53** A6
Cumberland House Natural
History Mus**★** PO4 . . . .**53** F1
Cumberland Pl SO15 . . . .**50** F5
Cumberland Rd PO5 . . . .**54** D3
Cumberland St
Portsmouth PO1 . . . .**53** A6
Southampton SO14 . . . .**51** B4
Cunard Ave SO15 . . . .**50** C8
Cunard Rd SO14 . . . .**51** A2
Cunningham Ct 🔞 PO5 . . . . . .**53** D2
Cupressus Ave PO30 . . . .**34** E5
Curve Rd PO36 . . . .**35** F7
Curzon Howe Rd PO1 . . . .**53** A5
Curzon Pl SO41 . . . .**48** D2
Cuthbert Rd PO1 . . . .**53** F6
Cut The PO31 . . . .**3** B5
Cygnet Ho PO12 . . . .**52** B8
Cynthia Gr PO30 . . . .**20** F8
Cypress Ave SO19 . . . .**51** F5
Cypress Rd PO30 . . . .**34** E5
Cyprus Rd PO2 . . . .**53** E8

D

Dagmar Mews 🔁 PO5 . . . .**53** C2
Dairy La PO30 . . . .**20** E5
Daish's La PO33 . . . .**24** F6
Daish Way PO30 . . . .**9** B1
Daisy La PO12 . . . .**52** B5
Dale Park Ho 🖪 PO1 . . . .**54** B3
Dalmally Gdns SO18 . . . .**51** F8
Dame Anthonys Cl PO33 . . . . .**11** F4
Daneshill Flats PO32 . . . .**3** E2
Daniell's Cl SO41 . . . .**48** E3
Daniell's Wlk SO41 . . . .**48** E3
Daniel St PO33 . . . .**12** D5
Dapple Pl SO40 . . . .**50** D1
Darlington Rd PO4 . . . .**53** F2
Darnan Ho 🖪 SO14 . . . .**51** A7
Dart Ho SO18 . . . .**51** F8
Dartmouth Cl 🖪 PO12 . . . .**52** C8
Dartmouth Ct 🖪 PO12 . . . .**52** C8
Dartmouth Mews PO5 . . . .**54** A1
Darts La PO35 . . . .**25** D5
Darwin Ho PO1 . . . .**54** A4
Darwin Rd SO15 . . . .**50** E7
Daulston Rd PO1 . . . .**53** F7
Davidson Ct 🔂 PO30 . . . .**20** F8
Davies Ct PO37 . . . .**35** C2
Dawlish Ave SO15 . . . .**50** C6
D–Day Mus★ PO5 . . . .**53** D1
Deacons La PO33 . . . .**23** C7
Dean Cl 🖪 SO18 . . . .**51** E8
Deans Cl PO36 . . . .**35** D3
Deans Ct PO33 . . . .**12** D6
Dean St PO1 . . . .**53** A5
Debourne Cl PO12 . . . .**52** A6
Debourne Manor Dr PO31 . . . . .**2** E4
Deepdene
Shanklin PO37 . . . .**43** B7
Southampton SO18 . . . .**51** E8
Deeping Cl SO19 . . . .**51** F1
Defender Rd SO19 . . . .**51** D3
Defender Wlk SO19 . . . .**51** D3
Delamere Rd PO4 . . . .**53** F3
Delaval Ho 🖪 PO1 . . . .**53** A5
Dell Sq PO30 . . . .**14** F1
Dell The
Cowes PO31 . . . .**9** A8
Southampton SO15 . . . .**50** E6
Delphi Ct PO37 . . . .**43** D8
Delphi Rd PO17 . . . .**43** D8
De Mowbray Way SO41 . . . . . .**48** D2
Deneside Copse SO41 . . . .**48** B1
Denmark Rd PO31 . . . .**3** A4
Denmead Ho PO1 . . . .**54** C4
Denness Path PO36 . . . .**35** D4
Denness Rd PO36 . . . .**35** E4
Dennett Rd PO35 . . . .**25** C5
Denning Mews PO5 . . . .**53** C3
Dennison Ct 🔞 SO15 . . . .**50** B8
Denny Gdns PO37 . . . .**43** B8
Denton Gdns PO32 . . . .**3** D4
Denzil Ave SO14 . . . .**51** B6
Derby Rd SO14 . . . .**51** C7
Derwent Dr PO33 . . . .**12** F4
Desmond Price Cl PO36 . . . . . .**35** D4
Devonia Gdns PO36 . . . .**36** A6
Devon Mews 🖪 SO15 . . . .**50** E5
Devonshire Inf Sch PO4 . . . . .**53** F3
Devonshire Mans 🔟 SO15 . . .**50** F6
Devonshire Rd SO15 . . . .**50** F6
Devonshire Sq PO4 . . . .**53** F4
Devonshire Terr PO38 . . . .**47** B5
Dhekelia Cl PO1 . . . .**54** C4
Diamond St 🖪 PO5 . . . .**54** A1
Diana Cl PO39 . . . .**14** D1
Dickens Cl PO2 . . . .**53** D7
Dickinson Rd PO4 . . . .**53** F5
Diggings The PO33 . . . .**24** F7
Digital Pl PO12 . . . .**52** C3
Dimbola Lodge Photographic
Mus**★** PO40 . . . .**27** C6
Dimond Rd SO18 . . . .**51** E7
Dinosaur Farm Mus★
PO30 . . . .**38** G6
Dinosaur Isle★ PO36 . . . .**36** B4
Disa Ho SO15 . . . .**50** F6
Ditchbury SO41 . . . .**48** D6
Dock Mill Cotts PO5 . . . .**53** D2
Dock Rd PO12 . . . .**52** D4
Doctors La PO30 . . . .**39** A8
Doctor's La PO36 . . . .**24** A3
Dodnor Creek Nature
Reserve**★** PO30 . . . .**9** B4
Dodnor La PO30 . . . .**9** A1

Dodnor Mews PO30 . . . .**9** B2
Dodnor Pk PO30 . . . .**9** B1
Dodpits La PO30, PO41 . . . . . .**17** C2
Dolcroft Rd PO38 . . . .**32** F5
Dolman Rd PO12 . . . .**52** C4
Dolphin Cres PO12 . . . .**52** C4
Dolphin Ct
🔟 Portsmouth PO5 . . . .**53** E1
🔟 Totland PO40 . . . .**14** E1
Dolphin Way PO12 . . . .**52** D2
Dombey Ct 🖪 PO12 . . . .**53** D7
Donnelly St PO12 . . . .**52** A7
Donnington Dr PO37 . . . .**35** B1
Dorchester Ct SO15 . . . .**50** F8
Dorothy Ct PO5 . . . .**54** C1
Dorothy Dymond St PO1 . . . .**54** B3
Dorrick Ct 🔟 SO15 . . . .**50** F7
Dorrien Rd PO12 . . . .**52** B8
Dorrita Cl PO4 . . . .**53** F2
Dorset St SO14 . . . .**51** A6
Dorval Ho 🖪 SO15 . . . .**50** E7
Dorval Manor 🔳 SO15 . . . .**50** E7
Douglas Rd PO2 . . . .**53** F7
Dove Cl PO33 . . . .**24** F6
Dovecotes PO30 . . . .**33** D6
Dover Park Cty Prim Sch
PO33 . . . .**12** D5
Dover Rd PO32 . . . .**3** C3
Dover St
Ryde PO33 . . . .**12** D6
Southampton SO14 . . . .**51** A7
Downcourt La PO38 . . . .**44** F7
DOWNEND **21** E4
Downend Rd PO30 . . . .**21** E3
Down La
Carisbrooke PO30 . . . .**20** A5
Ventnor PO38 . . . .**46** F6
Downlands Cres PO38 . . . .**46** F6
Downland View PO37 . . . .**35** C2
Down Lane Cotts PO38 . . . . . .**46** F6
Downside PO30 . . . .**46** F6
Downside Ave PO4 . . . .**45** B4
Downside Mid Sch 🖬
PO30 . . . .**9** A1
Downs View PO40 . . . .**27** B8
Downs View La PO30 . . . .**24** A3
Downsview Gdns PO33 . . . . . .**10** E4
Downsview Rd PO35 . . . .**25** D4
Downs View Rd
Newport PO30 . . . .**20** F6
St Helens PO33 . . . .**24** F6
Doyle Cl SO19 . . . .**51** F1
Drabbles La PO36 . . . .**35** E5
Dracaena Gdns PO37 . . . .**35** C2
Drake Cl SO40 . . . .**50** A2
Drake Ho 🖪 PO1 . . . .**53** A5
Drake Rd PO30 . . . .**20** A3
Drakes Ct SO40 . . . .**50** A3
Drill Hall Rd PO30 . . . .**20** D5
Drive The PO35 . . . .**25** C5
Droffatts Ho SO15 . . . .**50** D7
Drumlanrig Terr 🔳 PO12 . . . . .**52** C9
Drummond Ct SO15 . . . .**51** E3
Drummond Dr SO41 . . . .**51** C8
Drummond Rd PO1 . . . .**54** C4
Dubbers PO38 . . . .**33** C1
Ducie Ave PO35 . . . .**25** C6
Duckworth Ho 🔢 PO1 . . . .**54** B3
Dudley Rd PO33 . . . .**47** B5
Dugald Drummond St
PO1 . . . .**54** B3
Duisburg Way PO5 . . . .**53** B2
Duke Cres PO1 . . . .**53** D7
Duke of Edinburgh Ho
PO1 . . . .**53** A6
Dukes Rd
Gosport PO12 . . . .**52** A7
Southampton SO14 . . . .**51** B7
Duke St SO14 . . . .**51** B3
Dumbarton Cl PO2 . . . .**53** D8
Duncan Cl SO19 . . . .**51** E1
Duncan Rd PO4 . . . .**53** F2
Duncroft Gdns PO37 . . . .**35** C1
Dundonald Cl SO19 . . . .**51** D1
Dungewood La PO30,
PO38 . . . .**39** B6
Dunkeld Rd PO12 . . . .**52** B8
DUNSBURY **28** F5
Durban Cl PO05 . . . .**54** B2
Durban Ct 🖪 SO15 . . . .**50** E7
Durban Ho PO1 . . . .**54** C4
Durban Rd PO1 . . . .**53** F7
Durham St
Gosport PO12 . . . .**52** A7
Portsmouth PO1 . . . .**54** B3
Durley Rd PO12 . . . .**52** A7
Durnford Rd SO14 . . . .**51** B6
Duver Rd
Seaview PO34 . . . .**13** C4
St Helens PO33 . . . .**25** C6
Dyer Rd SO15 . . . .**50** D5
Dymott Cl SO15 . . . .**50** D5

E

Earley Ct SO41 . . . .**48** F4
Earlsdon St PO5 . . . .**54** C2
Earls Rd SO14 . . . .**51** A7
East Ashey La PO33 . . . .**23** D5
East Bldg PO1 . . . .**53** A5
Eastbourne Ave SO15 . . . .**50** D8
East Cl PO41 . . . .**5** C5
Eastcliff Ct PO37 . . . .**43** D8
Eastcliff Prom PO37 . . . .**43** D7
Eastcliff Rd PO37 . . . .**43** C7
EAST COWES **3** E4

East Cowes Heritage Ctr*
PO32 . . . . 3 C3
East Cowes Prim Sch PO32 3 D3
East Cowes Rd PO32 . . . . . .10 E5
East Ct PO1 . . . . .53 E7
Eastern Par PO4 . . . . .53 F2
Eastern Rd SO41 . . . . .48 A3
Eastern Villas Rd PO4 . . . . .53 D1
Eastfield Rd SO17 . . . . .51 C8
Eastfields PO5 . . . . .54 C1
Eastgate St SO14 . . . . .51 A3
East Gn PO34 . . . . .13 C2
East Hill SO41 . . . . .48 E4
East Hill Rd PO33 . . . . .12 C5
East La PO30 . . . . .33 C6
East Mead PO37 . . . . .43 A7
Eastmore Ct PO41 . . . . .15 F6
East Mount Rd PO37 . . . . . .43 D8
Easton La PO40 . . . . .27 C7
East Park Terr SO14 . . . . . . .51 A5
East Rd SO40 . . . . .50 B2
East St
  Newport PO30 . . . . .20 E7
  Portsmouth PO1 . . . . .53 A4
  Ryde PO33 . . . . .12 D6
  Southampton SO14 . . . . . .51 A4
  Ventnor PO38 . . . . .47 B6
East Street Sh Ctr **9**
  SO14 . . . . .51 A4
East Surrey St PO1 . . . . .54 B3
East View PO30 . . . . .20 D6
East Yar Rd PO36 . . . . .36 A5
Easy View La PO38 . . . . .40 A4
Eddington Rd PO34 . . . . . . .24 F8
Eden Grange **8** SO14 . . . . .51 A7
Eden Pl PO31 . . . . .26 G8
Eden Rd PO39 . . . . .26 G8
Eden St PO1 . . . . .54 B4
Edgbaston Ho PO5 . . . . .54 B2
Edinburgh Ct PO31 . . . . .3 A4
Edinburgh C **2** SO15 . . . . . .50 A6
Edinburgh Rd
  Freshwater PO40 . . . . .15 A1
  Portsmouth PO1 . . . . .54 A3
Edith Haisman Cl SO15 . . . .50 C5
Edmund Rd PO4 . . . . .53 F3
Edward Rd SO15 . . . . .50 C7
Edward Sl SO41 . . . . .48 B3
Edward St PO33 . . . . .12 C5
Edwin Jones Gn SO15 . . . . .50 C8
Efford Cl SO41 . . . . .48 B2
Efford Farm Cotts SO41 . . .48 A1
Efford Way SO41 . . . . .48 B2
Egerton Rd PO35 . . . . .25 E4
Egypt Copse PO31 . . . . .2 F5
Egypt Espl PO31 . . . . .2 E6
Egypt Hill PO31 . . . . .2 F5
Elder Cl SO40 . . . . .50 A1
Eldon Ct PO5 . . . . .54 B2
Eldon Ho **9** SO14 . . . . .51 A3
Eldon St PO5 . . . . .54 B2
Elenors Gr PO33 . . . . .11 C5
Elfin Ct **10** SO17 . . . . .51 B8
Elgar Cl PO12 . . . . .52 A3
Elgar Ct SO41 . . . . .48 F4
Elgin Rd SO15 . . . . .50 D5
Elizabeth Ct
  Bembridge PO35 . . . . .25 C5
  4 Gosport PO12 . . . . . . .52 A7
Elizabeth Gdns
  Havenstreet PO33 . . . . . . .11 C1
  Portsmouth PO4 . . . . .53 F2
Eliza Pl **6** PO12 . . . . .52 B6
Ellachie Gdns PO12 . . . . .52 B2
Ellachie Mews PO12 . . . . . . .52 B2
Ellachie Rd PO12 . . . . .52 B2
Ellery Gn SO41 . . . . .48 E5
Elliston Rd PO39 . . . . .14 F3
Elm Ave SO41 . . . . .48 C1
Elmbank Gdns SO16 . . . . . .35 E5
Elm Cl
  Freshwater PO40 . . . . .14 E1
  Nettlestone PO34 . . . . .13 C2
  Ryde PO33 . . . . .12 D4
Elm Ct
  Ryde PO33 . . . . .12 E4
  Southampton, Sholing SO19 12 E3
ELMFIELD 12 E3
Elmfield North Block
  SO15 . . . . .50 D5
Elmfield West Block
  SO15 . . . . .50 D5
Elm Gr
  Cowes PO31 . . . . .3 A3
  Gosport PO12 . . . . .52 B6
  Newport PO30 . . . . .20 D5
  Portsmouth PO5 . . . . .54 B1
Elmhurst Bsns Pk PO12 . . . .52 E5
Elmhurst Rd PO12 . . . . .52 C5
Elm La PO30 . . . . .18 B4
Elm Lodge PO12 . . . . .54 C1
Elms Ct PO35 . . . . .25 E5
Elm St
  Portsmouth PO5 . . . . .54 A1
  Southampton SO14 . . . . . .51 B4
Elmsworth La PO30 . . . . .7 D3
Elm Terr SO41 . . . . .48 E5
Elphinstone Rd PO5 . . . . . . .53 C2
ELSON 52 A9
Elson Inf Sch PO12 . . . . .52 A9
Elson Jun Sch PO12 . . . . . . .52 A9
Elson Rd PO12 . . . . .52 A8
Elstree Rd SO19 . . . . .51 E5
Emanuel St PO12 . . . . .53 D7
Embankment Rd PO33,
  PO35 . . . . .25 B5
Embassy Ct PO4 . . . . .54 C2

Embassy Way PO36 . . . . . . .35 B4
Emmadale Ct **7** SO14 . . . .51 A6
Emmett Hill PO38 . . . . .40 A6
Emperor Way SO18 . . . . .51 C7
Empress Pk SO14 . . . . .51 B7
Empress Rd SO14 . . . . .51 B7
Empshott Rd PO4 . . . . .53 F4
Emsworth Rd
  Lymington SO41 . . . . .48 E4
  Southampton SO15 . . . . . .50 B7
Endeavour Cl
  Gosport PO12 . . . . .52 D5
  Southampton SO15 . . . . . .50 B7
Endeavour Ct **8** SO14 . . . .51 B3
Endle St SO14 . . . . .51 B3
Enfield Gr SO19 . . . . .51 E3
Englefield Rd SO18 . . . . .51 D7
English Rd SO15 . . . . .50 B7
Ensign Cl PO31 . . . . .3 A3
Enterprise Cl PO33 . . . . .12 D3
Enterprise Way **1** 3 A2
Eremue Ct **1** PO41 . . . . . . .15 C6
Ernest Rd PO1 . . . . .53 E7
Esplanade
  Cowes PO31 . . . . .3 A6
  East Cowes PO32 . . . . .3 D5
  Nettlestone PO34 . . . . .13 E2
  Ryde PO33 . . . . .12 D6
  Sandown PO36 . . . . .36 A3
  Seaview PO34 . . . . .13 D4
  Shanklin PO37 . . . . .43 D7
  Ventnor PO38 . . . . .47 A5
Esplanade Rd
  Sandown PO36 . . . . .36 A3
  Ventnor PO38 . . . . .47 A5
Esplanade The PO12 . . . . . . .52 E5
Esslemont Rd PO4 . . . . .53 F3
Estella Rd PO2 . . . . .53 D8
Ethel Rd PO1 . . . . .53 E7
Eton Rd PO5 . . . . .54 D2
European Ct PO30 . . . . .35 F5
European Way SO14 . . . . . . .51 B3
Eva Allaway Ct **38** PO1 . . .53 A5
Evans St SO14 . . . . .51 A4
Evelyn Cres SO15 . . . . .50 D8
Everard Cl PO31 . . . . .3 A4
Everard Cl PO12 . . . . .27 C7
Everton La PO37 . . . . .43 C7
Ewart Rd PO1 . . . . .53 E8
Ewer Comm PO12 . . . . .52 B3
Exchange Rd PO1 . . . . .54 A3
Exchange The **3** PO4 . . . . .53 E2
Exeter Rd PO4 . . . . .53 F2
Exmoor Cl SO14 . . . . .51 B6
Exmouth Rd
  Gosport PO12 . . . . .52 A9
  Portsmouth PO5 . . . . .53 D2
Exmouth St SO14 . . . . .51 B6
Explosion–The Mus of Naval
  Firepower* PO12 . . . . .52 D8

F

Fairfield Cl SO41 . . . . .48 E3
Fairfield Gdns PO36 . . . . . . .35 E5
Fairfield Pk **6** PO36 . . . . . .35 E5
Fairfield Way PO39 . . . . .14 E1
Fairhaven Cl PO35 . . . . .25 E4
Fairhome Cl PO12 . . . . .52 B8
Fairlead Rd SO31 . . . . .2 F3
Fairlea Rd SO41 . . . . .48 E5
FAIRLEE 9 D1
Fairlee Rd PO30 . . . . .9 D1
Fairmead PO36 . . . . .35 D4
Fairmount Dr PO30 . . . . .20 F8
Fairthorne Gdns PO12 . . . . .52 A5
Fairview Cres PO36 . . . . .35 D5
Fairway Cvn Site PO36 . . . . .35 F6
Fairway The PO36 . . . . .35 E5
Fairy Rd PO34 . . . . .13 A4
Fakenham Farm* PO33 . . . . .25 A7
Falcon Cl **2** PO12 . . . . .52 B7
Falcon Cross Rd PO37 . . . . .43 C8
Falkland Rd SO15 . . . . .50 A8
Fanshawe St SO14 . . . . .51 A6
Farlington Rd PO2 . . . . .53 E8
Farm La PO30 . . . . .3 D2
Farnleys Mead SO41 . . . . . . .48 E2
Farriers Ct **4** PO12 . . . . . . .53 D2
Farriers La PO30 . . . . .31 B2
Farriers Wlk PO12 . . . . .52 D6
Farringford Farm Rd
  PO40 . . . . .27 B7
Farthingale Terr **11** PO1 . .53 A3
Farthing Cl PO12 . . . . .52 A6
Farthing La PO1 . . . . .53 A3
Farthings Way PO39 . . . . . . .14 D1
Fastnet Ho **8** PO5 . . . . . . .53 D1
Faulkner La PO36 . . . . .36 A5
Fawcett Rd PO4 . . . . .53 E3
Fawley Rd PO5 . . . . .50 A6
Felix Rd PO12 . . . . .52 B8
Fellows Rd PO31 . . . . .3 A4
Fennel Gdns SO41 . . . . .48 E5
Ferncliff Apartments
  PO36 . . . . .35 F4
Ferncliff Rd PO36 . . . . .35 E4
Fern Cl SO18 . . . . .51 E7
Ferndene Way SO18 . . . . . . .51 F8
Fernhill PO30 . . . . .10 D4
Fernhill Ct PO36 . . . . .34 F4
Fernhill Pk PO30 . . . . .10 D4
Fernhurst Jun Sch PO4 . . . . .53 F4
Fernhurst Rd PO4 . . . . .53 F4
Fernicose Rd PO34 . . . . .13 E2
Fern Rd SO19 . . . . .51 E5
Fernside Way PO33 . . . . .10 E4

Fernwood Cres SO18 . . . . . .51 F8
Ferrol Rd PO12 . . . . .52 C7
Ferrypoint SO41 . . . . .49 A4
Ferry Rd PO32 . . . . .3 C4
Festing Bldgs **1** PO4 . . . . .53 F2
Festing Mews **2** PO4 . . . . .53 F2
Festing Rd PO4 . . . . .53 F2
Fey Rd PO12 . . . . .52 C6
Field Ct PO30 . . . . .20 C6
Fieldfare Rd PO30 . . . . .20 A6
Field La PO33 . . . . .24 F7
Fieldmore Rd PO12 . . . . .52 B8
Field Pl PO30 . . . . .20 C6
Field View PO33 . . . . .12 B3
Fieldway Cres PO31 . . . . .8 F8
Field Wlk SO41 . . . . .48 C1
Fifth St PO1 . . . . .53 F6
Fighting Cocks Cross
  PO36 . . . . .34 C5
Filton Rd SO41 . . . . .48 D4
Finches The PO30 . . . . .20 A6
Findon Rd PO12 . . . . .52 B9
Fine La PO30 . . . . .31 B2
Firbank Lodge PO37 . . . . . . .43 C8
Firestone Copse Rd PO33 . . .11 B3
Firestone Glade PO33 . . . . . .11 A4
Firgrove Ct SO15 . . . . .50 C7
Firgrove Rd SO15 . . . . .50 C7
Firs Cl PO31 . . . . .2 F4
Fir Tree Cl PO37 . . . . .35 D2
Fisgard Rd PO12 . . . . .52 B8
FISHBOURNE 11 B6
Fishbourne La PO33 . . . . . . .11 A6
Fishermans Wlk PO35 . . . . . .25 F5
Fishers PO33 . . . . .66 B4
Fitzherbert St PO1 . . . . .54 B4
FITZHUGH 50 E6
Fitzhugh Ho **8** SO15 . . . . .50 E6
Fitzhugh Pl SO15 . . . . .50 F7
Fitzhugh St **3** SO15 . . . . . .50 F5
Fitzroy St PO36 . . . . .35 E4
Fitzroy Wlk PO1 . . . . .54 C4
Five Houses La PO30 . . . . . . .18 B4
Five Post La PO12 . . . . .52 B7
Flagstaff Gn PO12 . . . . .52 D7
Flathouse Rd PO1 . . . . .53 C7
Fleet Cl PO33 . . . . .11 F4
Fleet Way
  Portsmouth PO1 . . . . .53 B6
  Portsmouth PO1 . . . . .54 A4
  Shalfleet PO30 . . . . .17 D7
Fleming Cl PO33 . . . . .11 E4
Fleming St SO19 . . . . .51 D2
Flint St PO5 . . . . .54 A1
Flitcroft Gdns PO36 . . . . . . .35 D3
Floating Bridge Rd SO14 . . .51 C3
Florence Ct **2** SO18 . . . . . .51 E8
Florence Rd
  Portsmouth PO5 . . . . .53 D1
  Shanklin PO37 . . . . .43 C7
  Southampton SO19 . . . . . .51 D2
Flushards SO41 . . . . .49 A5
Flying Bull Cl **3** PO2 . . . . .53 D8
Flying Bull La PO2 . . . . .53 D8
Flying Bull Prim Sch PO2 . . .53 D8
Foley Ho PO1 . . . . .54 B4
Folly La PO32 . . . . .9 F7
Fontwell Rd **5** PO5 . . . . . .53 D3
Footways PO33 . . . . .10 D5
Forbury Rd **2** PO5 . . . . . . .53 D2
Ford Mews **3** PO30 . . . . . .20 D7
Foreland Farm La PO35 . . . .25 F4
Foreland Rd PO35 . . . . .25 E5
Forelands Field Rd PO35 . . . .25 E5
Forelands Middle Sch
  PO35 . . . . .25 D4
Foremans Cotts PO12 . . . . . .52 E3
Forest Cl PO30 . . . . .8 F1
Forest Ct
  Lymington SO41 . . . . .48 B2
  Winford PO36 . . . . .34 E4
Forest Dell PO36 . . . . .34 E5
Forest End PO30 . . . . .8 F1
Forest Gate Gdns SO41 . . . .48 C1
Forest Hills PO30 . . . . .19 F6
Forest Rd
  Newport PO30 . . . . .19 E8
  Winford PO36 . . . . .34 E5
FOREST SIDE 20 A8
Forest View **4** SO14 . . . . .50 F4
Forest Way PO34 . . . . .13 C2
Forster Rd SO14 . . . . .51 B7
Forsythia Pl SO19 . . . . .51 F5
Forth Ho **11** SO14 . . . . . . .51 C6
Fort Mews PO36 . . . . .36 A4
FORTON 52 C7
Forton Lodge **3** PO12 . . . .52 C6
Forton Rd
  Gosport PO12 . . . . .52 B6
  Portsmouth PO1 . . . . .53 C6
Fort Rd
  Gosport PO12 . . . . .52 B2
  Southampton SO19 . . . . . .51 E3
Fort Spinney PO36 . . . . .36 C5
Fort Victoria Cotts PO41 . . . .14 F6
Fort Victoria Country Pk*
  . . . . .14 F6
Fort Warden Rd PO39 . . . . . .14 D2
Forward Dr SO41 . . . . .48 C2
Foster Rd
  Gosport PO12 . . . . .52 B6
  Portsmouth PO1 . . . . .54 C4
Foundry Ct **22** PO1 . . . . . .53 A5
Foundry La SO15 . . . . .50 B7
Foundry Lane Prim Sch
  SO15 . . . . .50 B7

Fountain Ct PO31 . . . . .3 B5
Fountain Quay PO31 . . . . .3 B5
Fountain Rd PO1 . . . . .53 B7
Fountain St PO1 . . . . .54 B3
Fourposts Hill **3** SO15 . . .50 E5
Fourth St PO1 . . . . .53 F6
Foxes Cl PO36 . . . . .35 F6
Foxes Rd PO30 . . . . .20 C8
Foxhills PO38 . . . . .46 D5
Foxlea **3** SO15 . . . . .50 E7
Foxlea Gdns PO12 . . . . .52 B8
Fox Pl PO30 . . . . .20 A5
Fox Pond La PO41 . . . . .48 D1
Foyes Ct SO15 . . . . .50 D8
Frampton Way PO35 . . . . . . .25 D5
Francis Ave PO4 . . . . .53 F3
Francis Bright Cotts PO38 . .33 A4
Frank Judd Ct **28** PO1 . . .53 A5
Frank Miles Ho **1** PO5 . . .54 B2
Frankton Way PO12 . . . . . . .52 C6
Frank Williams Ct PO12 . . . .20 F7
Fraser Cl PO31 . . . . .3 A5
Fraser Rd PO4 . . . . .54 C2
Fraser St PO1 . . . . .53 F7
FRATTON 53 F5
Fratton Rd PO1 . . . . .54 D3
Fratton Rd PO1 . . . . .54 D4
Fratton Sta PO1 . . . . .53 E5
Fratton Way PO4 . . . . .53 F5
Frederick St
  Portsmouth PO1 . . . . .54 B4
  Southampton SO14 . . . . . .51 B6
FREEMANTLE 50 C6
Freemantle Bsns Ctr
  SO19 . . . . .51 F6
Freemantle CE Controlled Inf
  Sch SO15 . . . . .50 C6
Freemantle Cl SO19 . . . . . . .51 F5
Freemantle Common Rd
  SO19 . . . . .51 F6
Freemantle Rd PO12 . . . . . . .52 B8
Freestone Rd **10** PO5 . . . .53 D2
French St
  8 Portsmouth PO1 . . . . .53 A3
  Southampton SO14 . . . . . .50 F3
Frensham Ct PO4 . . . . .53 F4
Frensham Rd PO4 . . . . .53 F4
Freshfield Rd SO15 . . . . .50 B7
Freshfield Sq SO15 . . . . .50 B7
FRESHWATER 14 E1
FRESHWATER BAY 27 C6
Friary Cl
  Gosport PO12 . . . . .52 C2
  8 Portsmouth PO5 . . . .53 C2
Friary The **5** PO5 . . . . .53 C2
Friendship Ho PO5 . . . . .54 B1
Frigate Rd PO1 . . . . .53 B8
Frobisher Ct SO40 . . . . .50 A3
Frobisher Ho PO1 . . . . .53 A5
Frobisher Ho **6** PO1 . . . . .53 A5
Froddington Rd PO5 . . . . . . .54 C2
Froglands La PO30 . . . . .20 A3
Frome Cl SO40 . . . . .50 A1
Fromond Cl SO41 . . . . .48 E5
Froude Ave PO12 . . . . .52 A8
Froude Rd PO12 . . . . .52 A8
Froxfield Ho PO1 . . . . .54 C4
Fullerton Rd SO41 . . . . .48 C4
Funtington Rd PO2 . . . . .53 F8
Furness Rd **13** PO5 . . . . . .53 D1
Furzlings PO30 . . . . .20 A4
Furze Hill Rd SO41 . . . . .43 B7
FURZYHURST 8 E7
Fyning St PO1 . . . . .54 C4

G

Gage Cl SO40 . . . . .50 A2
Gaggerhill La PO30 . . . . .30 A3
Gainsborough Ct SO41 . . . . .48 D2
Gainsborough Ho **2** PO4 . .53 E2
Gainsford Rd SO19 . . . . .51 E5
Gain's Rd PO4 . . . . .53 E2
Galley La PO30 . . . . .30 A2
Gamble Cl SO19 . . . . .51 F4
Gamble Rd PO12 . . . . .52 D8
Garden La PO5 . . . . .54 B1
Garden Terr **14** PO5 . . . . . .53 D2
Garden Way PO30 . . . . .20 F6
Gardiner Cl SO40 . . . . .50 A2
Garfield Rd
  Portsmouth PO5 . . . . .53 D8
  Ryde PO33 . . . . .12 C6
  Shanklin PO37 . . . . .43 B7
Garland Ct **5** PO12 . . . . . . .52 B6
Garlic Farm The* PO36 . . . . .32 C2
Garnier St PO1 . . . . .54 D3
Garnier Rd **6** PO33 . . . . . .12 C6
Garnock Rd SO19 . . . . .51 D2
Garrow Dr SO41 . . . . .48 E5
Garton Rd SO19 . . . . .51 E3
Gassiot Cl PO33 . . . . .12 E4
Gas Works La PO41 . . . . .15 B5
GATCOMBE 32 C7
Gatcombe Rd PO33 . . . . .12 C6
Gatehouse Rd PO33 . . . . . . .23 B8
Gatehouse The **11** SO18 . .51 E8
Gate La PO40 . . . . .27 C6
Gawn Pl PO12 . . . . .52 B3
Gaynor Ho PO37 . . . . .43 C8
Genoa Cl SO41 . . . . .48 C1
George Byng Way PO12 . . . .53 C8
George Ct PO5 . . . . .54 B1
George Rd PO12 . . . . .53 D2
George Ct The **10** PO1 . . . .53 A5
George St
  Gosport PO12 . . . . .52 C6
  Portsmouth PO1, PO2 . . . .53 F7
  Ryde PO33 . . . . .12 C6

George St continued
  Sandown PO36 . . . . .35 F5
Gibbs Rd SO14 . . . . .50 F5
Gilbert Cl SO41 . . . . .48 D2
Giles Cl PO12 . . . . .52 A7
Gilkicker Rd PO12 . . . . .52 C2
Gill's Cliff Rd PO38 . . . . .46 E5
Glade The
  Nettlestone PO34 . . . . .13 C2
  Sandown PO36 . . . . .35 E4
Gladiola Rd PO38 . . . . .42 C5
Gladstone Pl **4** PO12 . . . . .52 A8
Gladstone Rd PO12 . . . . .52 A8
Glamis Gdns PO32 . . . . .3 D3
Glebe Gdns PO33 . . . . .10 E5
Glebe Rd SO14 . . . . .51 B3
Glen App PO38 . . . . .45 B3
Glencoe Rd PO1 . . . . .54 B1
Glendale Cl PO33 . . . . .10 D4
Glenfield Ave SO18 . . . . .51 F7
Glenfield Cres SO18 . . . . . . .51 F7
Glenfield Ct PO30 . . . . .20 B5
Glenfield Inf Sch SO18 . . . . .51 F7
Glenfield Way SO18 . . . . .51 F7
Glenheadon Dr PO39 . . . . . .26 G7
Glenmore Ct SO17 . . . . .51 A8
Glen Rd SO19 . . . . .51 D2
Glen The
  Cowes PO31 . . . . .3 A4
  Niton PO38 . . . . .45 B3
  8 Yarmouth PO41 . . . . .15 D6
Glidden Cl PO1 . . . . .54 C2
Glossop Cl PO32 . . . . .3 D3
Gloster The PO31 . . . . .3 A5
Gloucester Ho **1** PO12 . . . .52 C5
Gloucester Mews PO5 . . . . . .54 B2
Gloucester Pl PO5 . . . . .54 B1
Gloucester Rd
  Portsmouth PO1 . . . . .53 A6
  Ventnor PO38 . . . . .46 E6
Gloucester Sq **28** SO14 . . .51 A3
Gloucester Terr PO5 . . . . . . .54 B1
Gloucester View PO5 . . . . . .54 B2
Glynn Cl PO34 . . . . .13 D1
Gobles Cl PO33 . . . . .12 D5
GODSHILL 41 D7
Godshill Model Village*
  PO38 . . . . .41 D8
Godshill Prim Sch PO38 . . . .41 D8
Godwit Cl PO12 . . . . .52 B9
Goldcrest Cl PO30 . . . . .20 A6
Golden Gr SO14 . . . . .51 B5
Golden Groves PO33 . . . . . . .11 F4
Golden Hill Country Pk*
  PO40 . . . . .14 F2
Golden Ridge PO40 . . . . .14 F1
Golden Ridge PO40 . . . . .14 F1
Goldings Way PO40 . . . . .14 E2
Gold Mead Cl **3** SO41 . . . .48 E2
Goldsmith Ave PO4 . . . . .53 F4
Goldsmith Inf Sch PO4 . . . . .53 F4
Goldsmiths Ct **17** SO14 . . .51 A3
Goldt St PO5 . . . . .54 A1
Golf Links Rd PO36 . . . . .35 E6
Goodwood Cl PO12 . . . . .52 B9
Goodwood Rd
  Gosport PO12 . . . . .52 B9
  Portsmouth PO5 . . . . .54 D1
Gordon Ave SO14 . . . . .51 A8
Gordon Cl
  Ryde PO33 . . . . .11 E5
  Sandown PO36 . . . . .35 F6
Gordon Ct **7** PO33 . . . . . . .12 C5
Gordon Lodge PO32 . . . . .3 D2
Gordon Rd
  Cowes PO31 . . . . .3 B4
  Gosport PO12 . . . . .52 A5
  Lymington SO41 . . . . .48 C3
  Newport PO30 . . . . .20 F8
  Portsmouth PO1 . . . . .53 B3
  Ryde PO33 . . . . .12 C5
Gort Rd PO32 . . . . .3 D2
GOSPORT 52 C7
Gosport Discovery Ctr*
  PO12 . . . . .52 D5
Gosport Sh Prec **6** PO12 . .52 D5
Gosport St SO41 . . . . .48 F4
Gosport War Meml Hospl
  PO12 . . . . .52 A5
Gotten La PO38 . . . . .40 B3
Grace Ct **15** PO5 . . . . .53 C2
Graeme Rd PO41 . . . . .15 A6
Grafton Cl PO12 . . . . .52 C8
Grafton Gdns SO41 . . . . .48 C1
Grafton La PO12 . . . . .35 F5
Grafton St
  Portsmouth PO2 . . . . .53 D7
  Southampton SO15 . . . . . .35 F5
Graham Ho **4** SO14 . . . . . .51 C6
Graham Rd
  Gosport PO12 . . . . .52 A8
  Portsmouth PO5 . . . . .54 D1
  Southampton SO14 . . . . . .51 B6
Graham St SO14 . . . . .51 C6
Granada Rd PO4 . . . . .53 E1
Granary Cl PO33 . . . . .11 F5
Grand Par PO1 . . . . .53 A3
Grange Ave PO33 . . . . .12 A4
Grange Cl
  Shanklin PO37 . . . . .43 C7
  Ventnor PO38 . . . . .47 C6
Grange Dr PO30 . . . . .20 D8
Grange Gdns PO35 . . . . .25 C4
Grange Rd
  East Cowes PO32 . . . . .3 D3

Grange Rd continued
Sandown PO36 . . . . **35** E4
Shanklin PO37 . . . . **43** C7
Grangeside PO38 . . . . **47** D6
Grange The
Bembridge PO35 . . . . **25** C4
Newport PO30 . . . . **20** D8
Grantham Ct PO31 . . . . **3** A6
Grantham Rd SO19 . . . . **51** F6
Granville Ct SO15 . . . . **50** E7
Granville Rd
Cowes PO31 . . . . **3** A4
Totland PO39 . . . . **14** C1
Granville Rise ⒊ PO39 . . **14** D1
Granville Road Bridge ⒋
PO31 . . . . **3** A4
Granville St SO14 . . . . **51** B8
Grasmere Ave PO33 . . . . . . **12** F4
Gravel Pit Rd PO33 . . . . **10** D4
Grays Ct PO1 . . . . **53** A4
Grayshott Rd PO4 . . . . **53** F4
Grayswood Cl PO36 . . . . . . **35** F6
Great Appleford Barns
PO38 . . . . **40** E5
Great Preston Rd PO33 . . . **12** D3
Great Southsea St PO5 . . **54** B1
GREAT THORNESS **7** E6
Green Cnr PO34 . . . . **13** C2
Greenfield Cl PO33 . . . . **12** E4
Greenfields Rd PO30 . . . . . **20** F8
Greenfinch Cl PO30 . . . . . . **20** A6
Greengate Ind Est PO31 . . . **3** B4
Greengates PO37 . . . . **35** C1
Greenham Dr PO34 . . . . **13** D2
Greenidge Ct ⒏ SO15 . . **50** F8
Green La
Cowes PO31 . . . . **9** A8
Freshwater PO40 . . . . **27** B6
Gosport, Alverstoke PO12 . . **52** A5
Gosport, Elson PO12 . . . . . . **52** C9
Ryde PO33 . . . . **23** D6
Shanklin PO37 . . . . **35** C2
Green Land Cl PO30 . . . . . . **32** B4
Greenlands PO30 . . . . **32** B4
Greenlands Rd PO32 . . . . . . **3** D2
Greenlydd PO38 . . . . **45** B3
Green Mount Prim Sch
PO33 . . . . **12** C5
Green Rd
Gosport PO12 . . . . **52** A3
Portsmouth PO5 . . . . **54** B2
Green St
Newport PO30 . . . . **20** F7
Ryde PO33 . . . . **12** C5
Green The
Cowes PO31 . . . . **2** F5
Shanklin PO37 . . . . **43** C4
Shorwell PO30 . . . . **31** B3
Greenway PO33 . . . . **11** E4
Greenway Cl
Lymington SO41 . . . . **48** C3
Ryde PO33 . . . . **11** E4
Greenway Rd PO12 . . . . **52** B7
Greenways
Cowes PO31 . . . . **8** F8
Newport PO30 . . . . **21** A7
Totland PO39 . . . . **26** G8
Greenways The ⒉4 SO13 . . **8** F8
Greenway The PO38 . . . . . . **45** B4
Greenwich The ⒉4 SO14 . . **51** A3
Greenwood La PO36 . . . . . . **35** F8
Greenwood Wlk PO30 . . . . **20** F6
Greetham St PO5 . . . . **54** B3
Gregory Ave PO33 . . . . **13** B3
Gregory Cl PO33 . . . . **13** B3
Grenville Cl PO32 . . . . **3** D2
Grenville Dr PO33 . . . . **12** A3
Grenville Ho ⒔2 PO1 . . . . . . **53** A5
Grenville Rd PO4 . . . . **54** D1
Greville Rd SO15 . . . . **50** D7
Greycliff PO38 . . . . **47** D7
Greyfriars Ct PO5 . . . . **54** B1
Greystone La PO33 . . . . **24** F7
Greystones La PO40 . . . . . . **27** D6
Griffin Ct SO17 . . . . **51** C8
Griffin Ho PO31 . . . . **3** A5
Grosvenor Ho
⒋ Portsmouth PO5 . . . . . . **54** B2
⒓ Portsmouth SO15 . . . . **50** F6
Grosvenor Mews
⒌ Gosport PO12 . . . . **52** C6
Lymington SO41 . . . . **48** D5
Grosvenor Sq SO15 . . . . . . **50** F6
Grosvenor St PO5 . . . . **54** B2
Grove Ave PO12 . . . . **52** C6
Grove Bldgs ⒎ PO12 . . . . **52** C5
Grove Ct PO30 . . . . **20** F6
Grove Cotts PO30 . . . . **17** E2
Grove Ho PO5 . . . . **54** B1
Grove Pastures SO41 . . . . **48** E3
Grove Pl PO30 . . . . **48** E3
Grove Rd
Cowes PO31 . . . . **3** A3
Gosport PO12 . . . . **52** B8
Lymington SO41 . . . . **48** F3
Ryde PO33 . . . . **12** A3
Sandown PO36 . . . . **35** F6
Southampton SO15 . . . . . . **50** G2
Ventnor PO38 . . . . **47** A6
Wroxall PO38 . . . . **42** C4
Grove Road N PO5 . . . . **54** B1
Grove Road S PO5 . . . . **54** B1
Groves Cl PO40 . . . . **14** E2
Grove St SO14 . . . . **51** B4

Grove The
Bembridge PO35 . . . . **25** C6
Cowes PO31 . . . . **3** A5
Ventnor PO38 . . . . **47** A6
Guadeloupe Rd PO36 . . . . **35** F5
Guardhouse Rd PO1 . . . . . **53** B7
Guildford Park Camp
PO33 . . . . **24** F7
Guildford Rd
Portsmouth PO1 . . . . **53** E6
St Helens PO33 . . . . **25** A7
Guildford St ⒈ SO14 . . . . **51** C5
Guildhall Sq PO1 . . . . **53** A5
Guildhall Wlk PO1 . . . . **54** A3
Guild Ho ⒙ SO14 . . . . **51** A3
Gully Rd PO34 . . . . **13** D2
Gunville Cres PO30 . . . . . . **20** A6
Gunville Rd PO30 . . . . **20** A6
Gunville W PO30 . . . . **19** F6
Gunwharf Quays PO1 . . . . **52** F6
Gunwharf Quays (Sh Ctr)
PO1 . . . . **53** A4
Gunwharf Rd PO1 . . . . **53** A4
Guppy Cl PO31 . . . . **2** E4
GURNARD **2** E4
Gurnard Cty Prim Sch
PO31 . . . . **2** D3
Gurnard Hts PO31 . . . . **2** D4
Gurney Rd SO15 . . . . **50** C8
Gustar Gr PO32 . . . . **3** D1
Gusters Shute PO30 . . . . . **18** B2
Guyers Rd PO40 . . . . **27** C7
Gwen-Rhian Ct ⒋ SO15 . . **50** F7
Gwessin Terr ⒍ SO15 . . . **52** C5
Gwydyr Cl PO33 . . . . **12** A5

H

Hadrians Way PO36 . . . . . . **24** A1
Haglane Copse SO41 . . . . **48** C2
Haig Cl PO30 . . . . **35** D3
Halberry Ho PO30 . . . . **20** F8
Halberry La PO30 . . . . **20** F8
HALE COMMON **34** B5
Hale Ct PO1 . . . . **53** E7
Halesowen Ho ⒋ PO5 . . . **54** A2
Hale Street N PO1 . . . . **54** C4
Hale Street S PO1 . . . . **54** C4
Half Moon St ⒈ PO1 . . . . . **53** A5
Halford Cl PO36 . . . . **35** F7
Halfpenny La PO1 . . . . **53** A3
Halletts Shute PO41 . . . . . **15** A5
Halliday Cl PO12 . . . . **52** B6
Hall of Aviation (Mus)★
SO14 . . . . **51** B3
Hallowell Ho PO1 . . . . **54** B4
Hambrook Rd ⒈ PO12 . . . **52** A7
Hambrook St PO5 . . . . **54** A1
Hambrougn La PO39 . . . . . **26** D3
Hambrougn Rd PO38 . . . . **47** A5
Hamilton Ct ⒒ PO5 . . . . . **53** C2
Hamilton Ho PO1 . . . . **54** D4
Hamilton Mews SO41 . . . . **48** F4
Hamilton Pl SO41 . . . . **48** D3
Hamilton Rd
Portsmouth PO5 . . . . **53** D2
Ryde PO33 . . . . **11** F4
Hamlet Ct PO31 . . . . **3** A6
Hammond Cl PO41 . . . . **15** A5
Hammond Ho ⒐ PO12 . . . **52** A7
Hampshire Cres ⒊ PO30 . . **9** A1
Hampshire St PO1 . . . . **53** E7
Hampshire Terr PO1 . . . . . **54** A2
HAMSTEAD **5** F3
Hamstead Dr PO41 . . . . **6** A2
Hamstead Rd PO41 . . . . . . **17** B8
Hamtun St SO14 . . . . **50** F3
Hamwic Ho ⒊ SO14 . . . . . **51** A6
Handel Rd SO15 . . . . **50** F5
Handel Terr SO15 . . . . **50** E6
Handford Pl ⒉ SO15 . . . . **50** F6
Handsworth Ho PO5 . . . . . **54** C2
Hanley Rd SO15 . . . . **50** D8
Hannah Ho PO30 . . . . **20** D8
Hanover Bldgs SO14 . . . . . **51** A4
Hanover Ct ⒎ PO1 . . . . . . **53** A4
Hanover Ho ⒎ SO14 . . . . **51** A4
Hanover St PO1 . . . . **53** A5
Hanway Rd PO1, PO2 . . . . **53** E7
Harborough Rd SO15 . . . . **50** F6
Harbors Lake La PO36 . . . **34** D6
Harbour Cl SO40 . . . . **50** C2
Harbour Par SO15 . . . . **50** F4
Harbour Rd PO1 . . . . **52** E6
Harbour St PO12 . . . . **52** E6
Harbour Twr ⒒ PO12 . . . . **52** E5
Harbour Way PO31 . . . . **2** F3
Harcourt Rd
Gosport PO12 . . . . **52** A6
Portsmouth PO1 . . . . **53** E7
Southampton SO18 . . . . . **51** E8
Harding Rd PO12 . . . . **12** D4
Harding Shute PO33 . . . . . **23** F6
Hard The PO1 . . . . **53** A5
HARDWAY **52** B8
Hardy Cl SO15 . . . . **50** B6
Harford Cl SO41 . . . . **48** C1
Harley Wlk PO1 . . . . **54** C4
Harness La PO31 . . . . **2** C1
Harold Rd
Portsmouth PO4 . . . . **53** E3
Southampton SO15 . . . . . **50** C7
Harrison's Cut SO14 . . . . . **51** A4
Harris Rd PO30 . . . . **9** A2
Harrow Rd PO5 . . . . **54** D2
Harry Cheek Gdns PO31 . . . **8** B1
Harry Law Hall PO1 . . . . . . **54** B3

Hart Ct SO19 . . . . **51** F3
Hartford Ho PO1 . . . . **54** A1
Hartington Rd SO14 . . . . . **51** B6
Hartley Ct ⒌ SO17 . . . . . . **51** A8
Harts La PO38 . . . . **32** F3
Harvester Way SO41 . . . . **48** D6
Harvey Cl PO32 . . . . **3** D1
Harvey Rd PO30 . . . . **20** F8
Haselworth Dr PO12 . . . . . **52** B2
Haselworth Prim Sch
PO12 . . . . **52** B4
Haskell Rd PO30 . . . . **9** A2
Haslar Marina PO12 . . . . . **52** E4
Haslar Rd
Gosport, Clayhall PO12 . . . **52** D3
Gosport, Newtown PO12 . . **52** E5
Haslar Terr PO12 . . . . **52** D3
Haslegrave Ho ⒉ PO2 . . . **53** D8
Haslemere Rd PO4 . . . . . . **54** D1
Hatherley Mans ⒋ SO15 . . **50** C7
Hatherton Rd PO37 . . . . . . **43** C7
Havant St PO1 . . . . **53** A5
Havelock ⒉ PO40 . . . . **14** E1
Havelock Mans PO5 . . . . . **54** D2
Havelock Rd
Portsmouth PO5 . . . . **54** C2
Southampton SO14 . . . . . **50** F5
Haven Crest PO36 . . . . **24** B2
HAVENSTREET **11** C1
Havenstreet Main Rd
PO33 . . . . **11** C1
Havenstreet Sta★ PO33 . . **22** D8
Haven The
Gosport PO12 . . . . **52** B3
Southampton SO19 . . . . . **51** E4
Havisham Rd PO2 . . . . **53** C7
Hawke St PO1 . . . . **53** A5
Hawkeswood Rd SO18 . . . **51** C7
Hawk Ho ⒔ PO33 . . . . **12** C6
Hawkins PO31 . . . . **2** E5
Hawkins Cl PO36 . . . . **24** A3
Hawthorn Cl
Newport PO30 . . . . **20** C7
Ryde PO33 . . . . **11** F5
Hawthorns The SO40 . . . . **50** A1
Hawthorns Urban Wildlife
Ctr★ SO15 . . . . **50** F8
Haydens Ct SO41 . . . . **48** F4
HAYLANDS **12** A3
Haylands Cty Prim Sch
PO33 . . . . **12** A4
Hayling Cl PO12 . . . . **52** C9
Hayward Ave PO33 . . . . . . **12** E3
Haywards Ct ⒒ PO1 . . . . . **53** A4
Hazel Cl PO33 . . . . **46** E7
Hazel Ct PO4 . . . . **53** F4
Hazeleigh Ave SO19 . . . . . **51** E2
Hazel Green Village PO33 . **10** F6
Hazelmount Paddock
PO33 . . . . **11** E6
Hazel Rd
Lymington SO41 . . . . **48** A4
Southampton SO19 . . . . . **51** D3
Hazelwood Cl PO33 . . . . . . **12** B4
Hazely Combe PO30 . . . . . **34** A8
Hazlemere Ave PO33 . . . . **11** E4
Hearn St PO30 . . . . **20** D7
Hearts of Oak Mews
SO41 . . . . **48** D4
Heasley La PO30 . . . . **34** B8
Heath Cl PO30 . . . . **20** E6
Heatherley Ct PO5 . . . . **54** C1
Heatherwood Park Rd
PO39 . . . . **26** G8
Heathfield Cl
Bembridge PO35 . . . . **25** C4
Freshwater PO40 . . . . **14** F2
Newport PO30 . . . . **21** A7
Heathfield Ho PO37 . . . . . . **43** C7
Heathfield Mdws PO40 . . . **14** E2
Heathfield Rd
Bembridge PO35 . . . . **25** C4
Freshwater PO40 . . . . **14** F2
Heath Gdns PO36 . . . . **35** D3
Heath Rd PO36 . . . . **35** D3
Heath Villas PO40 . . . . **14** E2
Heaton Rd PO12 . . . . **52** A8
Hedley Ct PO37 . . . . **43** A7
Hefford Rd PO32 . . . . **3** D4
Heidelberg Rd PO4 . . . . . . **53** F4
Heights Leisure Ctr PO30 . **35** E4
Helena Rd PO4 . . . . **53** F3
Hendy Cl PO5 . . . . **54** B1
Hendy Rd PO32 . . . . **3** D4
Henery St ⒑ PO12 . . . . . . **52** C5
Henley Rd PO4 . . . . **53** F3
Henry Player Ave PO12 . . **52** D7
Henry Rd SO15 . . . . **50** C7
Henry St SO15 . . . . **50** F6
Henstead Ct ⒐ SO15 . . . . **50** F6
Henstead Rd SO15 . . . . . . **50** F6
Henty Rd SO16 . . . . **50** B8
Herbert Rd PO4 . . . . **53** E2
Herbert St PO1 . . . . **53** C7
Herbert Walker Ave SO15 . **50** C4
Hercules St PO2 . . . . **53** D8
Hereford Ct PO5 . . . . **54** C1
Hereford Rd PO5 . . . . **54** C1
Heritage Way, Priddy's Hard
PO12 . . . . **52** C9
Hermes Ct ⒑ PO12 . . . . . . **52** C5
Heron Ho ⒈ PO5 . . . . **53** E2
Heron Rd PO38 . . . . **33** A4
Hersey Rise PO34 . . . . **13** D2
Hertford Pl PO1 . . . . **53** D7
Hesketh Rd ⒋ SO15 . . . . . **50** C6
Heversdwood PO33 . . . . . . **12** E4
Hewitt Cl PO33 . . . . **12** A8

Hewitt Cres PO30 . . . . **9** A2
Hewitt's Rd SO15 . . . . **50** D5
Heysham Rd SO15 . . . . . . **50** B7
Heyshott Rd PO4 . . . . **53** F4
Heytesbury Cl PO41 . . . . . **15** D5
Heytesbury Rd
Newport PO30 . . . . **20** D8
Yarmouth PO41 . . . . **15** D5
Heyward Rd PO4 . . . . **53** E4
Highbury Ct PO35 . . . . **25** E4
Highbury St ⒍ PO1 . . . . . . **53** A4
Highcliff Ave SO14 . . . . . . **51** A8
Highcliffe Lodge PO36 . . . **35** D2
Highdown La PO39 . . . . . . **26** G6
Highfield SO41 . . . . **48** D3
Highfield Ave SO41 . . . . . . **48** C3
Highfield Ct PO33 . . . . **12** E4
Highfield Rd
Cowes PO31 . . . . **2** F2
Lymington SO41 . . . . **48** C3
Newport PO30 . . . . **20** E7
Portsmouth PO1 . . . . **54** C3
Shanklin PO37 . . . . **43** B7
Highlands Ho SO19 . . . . . . **51** D3
Highland Terr PO4 . . . . **53** F3
High Park Rd PO33 . . . . . . **12** E3
High Point SO18 . . . . **51** F8
High Rd PO30 . . . . **9** F1
High Salterns PO34 . . . . . . **13** D3
High St
Bembridge PO35 . . . . **25** C4
Brading PO36 . . . . **24** B3
Carisbrooke PO30 . . . . **20** B5
Cowes PO31 . . . . **3** A5
Freshwater PO40 . . . . **14** F1
Godshill PO38 . . . . **41** D8
Gosport PO12 . . . . **52** D5
Lymington SO41 . . . . **48** E4
Newchurch PO36 . . . . **34** E7
Newport PO30 . . . . **20** D7
Niton PO38 . . . . **45** B4
Portsmouth PO1 . . . . **53** A3
Rhyde, Oakfield PO33 . . . . **12** D4
Ryde PO33 . . . . **12** C5
Sandown PO36 . . . . **35** F5
Seaview PO34 . . . . **13** D4
Shanklin PO37 . . . . **43** C7
⒐ Southampton SO14 . . . **51** A3
Ventnor PO38 . . . . **47** B6
Whitwell PO38 . . . . **45** E7
Wootton PO33 . . . . **10** E5
Wroxall PO38 . . . . **42** C4
Yarmouth PO41 . . . . **15** D6
High View Way SO18 . . . . **51** F8
Highway The PO37 . . . . . . **43** C4
Highwood La PO30, PO28 . **32** E6
Hilbre Rd PO33 . . . . **24** F6
Hilda Cl ⒈ SO14 . . . . **51** C5
Hilda Pl ⒉ SO14 . . . . **51** C5
Hildyards Cres PO2 . . . . . . **53** D2
Hillborough Cres ⒉ PO5 . . **54** C1
Hillborough Ct ⒈ PO5 . . . **54** C1
Hillcrest Rd PO38 . . . . **32** F4
Hillcroft SO14 . . . . **48** E4
Hilldetch SO41 . . . . **48** D6
Hill Farm Rd SO15 . . . . . . **50** E6
Hillgrove Cvan Site PO33 . **24** F7
Hill Ho PO30 . . . . **26** H8
Hillis Cnr PO31 . . . . **8** C7
HILLISGATE **8** D5
Hillis Gate Rd PO30, PO31 . **8** C6
Hill La PO40 . . . . **14** F3
Hill Place La PO40 . . . . **16** C7
Hilrise Ave PO33 . . . . **11** F4
Hills Ct ⒉ PO33 . . . . **12** D5
Hilton Rd SO19 . . . . **51** D1
HULVERSTONE **29** B5
Hulverstone La PO30 . . . . **29** B4
Hundred La SO41 . . . . **49** A7
Hungerberry Cl PO37 . . . . **43** A7
Hunnycross Way PO30 . . . **20** D7
HUNNY HILL **20** C8
Hunny Hill
Brighstone PO30 . . . . **29** F3
Newport PO30 . . . . **20** D8
Hunnyhill Prim Sch PO30 . **20** C8
Hunter Rd PO4 . . . . **53** F3
Huntly Way SO18 . . . . **51** F8
Hunts Rd PO38 . . . . **46** A3
Hurstake Rd PO30 . . . . **20** F8
Hurst Castle★ SO41 . . . . . **54** B6
Hurst Hill PO39 . . . . **26** G7
Hurst Point View PO39 . . . **14** D1
Hurst View PO39 . . . . **26** G8
Hutchinson Dr PO33 . . . . . **13** B3
Hutfield Cl ⒈ PO12 . . . . . . **52** B6
Huxford PO30 . . . . **34** A8
Hyde Park Rd PO5 . . . . **54** B3
Hyde Park Rd PO5 . . . . **54** B3
Hyde Rd PO17 . . . . **43** B8
Hyde St PO5 . . . . **54** B2
Hynes Ct ⒈ SO17 . . . . **51** B8

I

Idsworth Ho PO1 . . . . **54** B4
Imperial Appartments ⒏
SO14 . . . . **51** B3
Imperial Ave SO15 . . . . . . **50** B7
Imperial Pk SO15 . . . . **50** B7
Imperial Rd SO14 . . . . **51** B7
Imperial Way SO15 . . . . . . **50** C5
Ingledene Cl PO12 . . . . **52** B5
Inglewood Pk PO38 . . . . . . **46** C4
Inglis Rd PO5 . . . . **54** C2
Ingram Ct SO17 . . . . **51** C8
Inkerman Rd SO19 . . . . . . **51** D8
Institute Hill PO38 . . . . **45** B4

nverness Rd
Gosport PO12.........52 A7
Portsmouth PO1.........53 E7
requois Ct SO14.........51 B7
ronside 7 SO14.........50 F3
rwin Hts PO12.........52 A9
sambard Brunel Jun Sch
PO2.........53 E8
sambard Brunel Rd PO1..54 B3
semhurst Ct PO35.........25 D4
sland Planetarium *
PO41.........14 F6
sland Point SO41.........48 F4
sland View Chalets PO39..14 C2
sle of Wight Airport
PO36.........35 B5
sle of Wight Bus *
PO30.........44 A3
sle of Wight Coll PO30 ..20 D8
sle of Wight Donkey
Sanctuary* PO38.........42 B7
sle of Wight Lavender*
PO33.........21 C6
sle of Wight Military Mus*
PO31.........9 A4
sle of Wight Natural History
Ctr* PO38.........41 D8
sle of Wight Owl & Falconry
Ctr* PO38.........42 A4
sle of Wight Pearl*
PO30.........29 E1
sle of Wight Shipwreck Ctr
& Maritime Mus* PO30..21 E2
sle of Wight Steam
Railway* PO33.........22 E8
sle of Wight Studio Glass*
.........26 A3
sle of Wight Zoo* PO36..36 B4
TCHEN.........51 F4
vy Cl PO38.........45 B4
vy Ho 2 PO12.........52 C5
vy La PO12.........53 A6
vy Rd SO17.........51 C8

J

Jack Cockerill Way 8
PO5.........53 D1
Jackmans Cl SO19.........51 D3
Jacob's St PO1.........54 B4
Jago Rd PO1.........52 F7
Jamaica Pl PO12.........52 C5
Jamaica Rd PO12.........52 D6
James Ave PO36.........35 D3
James Butcher Ct 11 PO5.53 D1
James Mews PO36.........35 D3
Jameson Gdns PO39.......14 E1
Jameson Rd SO19.........51 F3
James St SO14.........51 A4
Janaway Gdns SO17.......51 D8
Janson Rd SO15.........50 D8
Jarndyce Wlk PO2.........53 D7
Jasmine Ct
  Lymington SO41.........48 C4
  1 Southampton PO5.....50 F8
Jasmine's Wlk PO33 ....10 E4
Jeal's La PO30.........35 F7
Jellicoe Ho 8 PO1.........54 C4
Jellicoe Rd PO33.........12 A5
Jennifer Way PO32.........3 D3
Jennings Cl PO40.........27 C7
Jenny Streets La PO35...25 C2
Jensen Ct SO15.........50 F7
Jersey Rd PO2.........53 E8
Jervis Dr PO12.........52 B7
Jessie Rd
  Gosport PO12.........52 A5
  Portsmouth PO4.........54 F1
Jessie Terr 23 SO14.......51 A3
Jireh Pl 3 PO1.........53 F2
Jo Benson Ct 3 PO4.....53 F2
Jocelyn Ct PO36.........36 A5
John Nash Ave PO32.......3 D3
Johnson Rd PO30.........20 E7
Johnson St 4 SO14.......51 A4
John's Rd SO19.........51 D3
John St
  Newport PO30.........20 E7
  Ryde PO33.........12 C5
  Southampton SO14.......51 A3
Jonas Nichols Sq SO14...51 B4
Jonathan Cl SO41.........48 E5
Jordan Cl PO31.........2 D4
Jordan Ho SO15.........50 C5
Jordans La SO41.........49 B8
Joseph Nye Ct 41 PO1 ..53 A3
Joseph St 9 PO12.........52 C5
Josephs Way PO7.........43 B8
Josian Wlk SO14.........51 B5
Joys La SO41.........49 E8
Jubilee Cl
  Freshwater PO40.........27 C8
  Godshill PO38.........41 C8
Jubilee Pl PO33.........12 D5
Jubilee Rd
  Gosport PO12.........52 B6
  Portsmouth PO4.........53 F3
Jubilee Terr PO5.........54 A1
Juniper Cl
  Carisbrooke PO30.........20 B7
  Lymington SO41.........48 B3
Juniper Ct 5 SO18.........51 E7
Juniper Rd SO18.........51 F7
Jupiter Ct PO33.........53 A4
Jurds Lake Way SO19.....51 E1
Justin Cl PO12.........52 D7

K

Kealy Rd PO12.........52 A7
Keats Mews PO37.........43 C7
Keats Retreat PO37.......43 C7
Keelan Ct PO5.........53 D2
Keel Gdns 6 SO41.........48 E4
Keith Cl PO12.........52 D7
Keith Ho 6 PO12.........53 A5
Kellett Rd SO15.........50 E8
Kelly Cl 1 SO18.........51 E8
Kelsey Cl PO32.........3 E3
Kelston Cl SO15.........50 A7
Kemming Rd PO30.........44 A5
Kemmin La PO38.........45 F7
Kempfelt Ho 20 PO1.......53 A5
Kemps Quay Ind Pk SO18.51 C7
Kendal Rd PO30.........26 H8
Kenilworth Ho 15 SO14...51 C6
Kenilworth Rd
  Portsmouth PO5.........53 D1
  Southampton SO15.......50 F6
Kennedy Cl PO33.........10 E4
KENNERLEY HEATH.........33 B4
Kennet Cl PO12.........52 B2
Kensington Ct 14 PO12...52 C7
Kensington Rd PO12.......52 C4
Kent Ave PO32.........3 D3
Kent Ho 4 SO14.........51 C5
Kentish Rd SO15.........50 C7
Kent Rd
  Portsmouth PO5.........54 B1
  Ventnor PO38.........47 B6
Kent St
  Portsmouth PO1.........53 A5
  Ryde PO33.........12 C4
  Southampton SO14.......51 C6
Kerrigan Ct SO17.........51 A7
Kerry Cl SO41.........48 C3
Kerry Fields PO34.........13 D1
Kestrel Cl PO30.........52 D3
Kestrel Way PO30.........20 A6
Keswick Rd SO19.........51 D2
Kettering Terr PO33.......53 C8
Keyes Ct 4 PO5.........54 C4
Key Haven Ct 1 PO39.....14 D1
Kidson Ct PO2.........53 D8
Kilbride Path 6 PO12.......53 D8
Kilmiston Cl PO1.........53 E7
Kilpatrick Cl 6 PO2.........53 D8
Kimberley Ct SO19.........51 E2
Kinchington Rd PO30.......20 B6
King Albert Ct PO1.........54 C4
King Albert St PO1.........54 C4
King Arthur Ct PO33.......12 B5
Kingates La PO30.........45 C6
King Charles 1st Ct PO38.47 A6
King Charles St 9 PO1....53 A4
Kingcome Ho PO1.........54 B4
King Edward Ave SO16....50 B8
King Edwards Cl PO37....43 A6
King Edward VI Sch SO15.50 E8
Kingfisher Cl PO30.........20 A6
King George V Cl PO33...12 B4
King Henry 1 St PO1.......54 A3
King James Cl PO31.......2 F4
King James Terr 2 PO5..54 A3
King Richard 1 Rd PO1....54 A3
Kings Bay PO38.........47 C6
Kings Bench Alley 19 PO1.53 A5
Kingsbury Rd PO1.........51 B7
Kings Cl
  Bembridge PO35.........25 C6
  Lymington SO41.........48 D4
Kingsclere Cl SO19.......51 F1
Kings Cote Villas 3 PO5.3 B4
Kings Cres SO41.........48 D2
Kingsdown Pl PO1.........54 D3
Kingsfield SO41.........49 A2
King's Ho 6 SO14.........51 A8
Kings Huts SO41.........48 A3
Kingsland Cl 4 SO14.....51 A4
Kingsland Ho 4 SO14....51 A4
Kingsland Mkt SO14.......51 A4
KINGSLAND PLACE.........51 A5
Kingsland Sq 5 SO14.....51 A4
Kingslea 2 PO30.........3 B3
Kingslea Pk PO32.........3 D1
Kingsley Rd SO15.........50 B7
Kings Manor Rd PO40.....15 B2
Kingsmere 1 PO31.........3 A4
Kings Park Rd PO5.........53 D2
Kings Park Rd SO15.......51 A6
Kings Rd
  East Cowes PO32.........3 C3
  Gosport PO12.........52 B6
  Lymington SO41.........48 D4
King's Rd
  Bembridge PO35.........25 C6
  Portsmouth PO5.........54 B1
  Ryde PO33.........12 C4
King's Saltern Rd SO41...49 A2
King St
  Gosport PO12.........52 D6
  Portsmouth PO4.........54 B2
  Southampton SO14.......51 A3
King's Terr PO1, PO5.....54 A1
KINGSTON
  40 A7
  Portsmouth.........53 F7
Kingston Cres PO2.........53 D8
Kingston Cross PO2.......53 D8
Kingston Rd PO41.........48 D2
Kingston Rd
  East Cowes PO32.........3 C2
  Portsmouth PO1, PO2....53 E8
  Southampton SO15.......50 D6

Kingsway
  Cowes PO31.........3 A4
  Southampton SO14.......51 A5
Kingswell Path PO1.......54 B4
Kingswell St PO1.........54 B3
Kingswood
  3 Cowes PO31.........3 A4
  Marchwood SO40.........50 A1
King William St PO1.......53 A6
Kinterbury St PO1.........54 A1
Kipling Ct SO19.........51 F1
Kirkstall Rd PO4.........53 E1
Kitbridge Rd PO30.........20 C7
Kite Hill PO33.........11 A5
KNIGHTON.........22 E2
Knighton Rd SO19.........51 F4
Knighton Shute PO36.....22 F3
Knight's Cross PO33.......21 F8
Knights Ct PO38.........47 B6
Kyngs Cl PO30.........24 A3
Kynon Cl 2 PO12.........52 C9

L

Laburnum Cl PO30.........20 E5
Laburnum Ct SO19.........51 D3
Lacey's La PO38.........35 D4
Lacon Cl SO18.........51 E8
Ladywood Ho PO5.........54 B2
Lake Common Rd PO36...35 D4
Lake Green Rd PO36......35 D4
Lake Hill PO36.........35 E4
Lake Ho SO15.........50 C6
Lake Industrial Way PO36.35 B3
Lakelands Dr SO15.........50 C6
Lake Mid Sch PO36.......35 C3
Lake Rd
  Portsmouth PO1.........54 C4
  Southampton SO19.......51 D2
Laker Ho SO15.........50 F7
Lakeside Ct PO4.........53 F2
Lake Sta PO33.........35 D4
Lamnas Cl PO31.........2 E5
Lamorbey Cl PO36.........35 D3
Lamorbey Terr PO36......35 D3
Lamward Mans 1 SO14...51 A7
Lance's Hill SO18.........51 E8
Landguard Manor Rd
  PO37.........35 C1
Landguard Rd
  Shanklin PO37.........43 C8
  Southampton SO15.......50 D6
Landon Ct PO12.........52 A3
LANDPORT.........53 C7
Landport St
  Portsmouth PO1.........54 C4
  Portsmouth, Southsea PO5.54 A2
Landport Terr PO1.........54 A2
Landport View PO1.........54 C4
Landscape La PO30.........21 B7
Landsdowne St PO5.......54 A2
Lane End Cl PO35.........25 C4
Lane End Ct PO35.........25 C4
Lane End Rd PO35.........25 C4
Lanes End PO39.........14 C1
Lane The
  Gosport PO12.........52 A2
  Portsmouth PO4.........53 F2
  Sandown PO36.........36 A4
Langbar SO41.........51 E6
Langford Rd PO1.........54 C4
Langley Ct PO30.........20 E7
Langley Rd
  5 Cowes PO31.........3 B4
  Portsmouth PO5.........53 E8
  Southampton SO15.......50 A6
Langton Farm Gdns PO1..53 A7
Langtry PO33.........3 A3
LANSDOWNE HILL.........50 F4
Lansdowne Hill 4 SO14..50 F4
Lansdowne Ho 3 PO12...52 A7
Lansdowne Rd SO15.......50 F7
Lansdown Gdns PO30.....32 B4
Lanterns The PO5.........25 C5
Lanyards Lea PO33.........3 A3
Lapwing Cl PO12.........52 B8
Larch Ct PO1.........54 C4
Lark Rise
  Carisbrooke PO30.........20 A5
  Shanklin PO37.........35 C1
Lasham Ho 10 SO30.......50 B8
Latham Ct SO15.........50 F7
Latimer Gate 22 SO14...51 A3
Latimer Ho 5 SO15.......50 F6
Latimer St PO33.........25 A6
Latimer St SO14.........51 A3
Launceston Cl 3 PO12...52 C8
Laundry La PO30.........20 C6
Laurel Cl
  6 Gosport PO12.........52 C8
  Southampton SO19.......51 D3
Laurel Est PO31.........3 B3
Laurel Ho 6 PO30.........20 D6
Lavender Cl SO19.........51 F5
Lavender Glade SO41.....51 A2
Lavinia Rd
  Gosport PO12.........52 B5
  Portsmouth PO2.........53 D8
Lawn Ct SO17.........51 A7
Lawn Rd
  Lymington SO41.........48 B3
Lawns The PO30.........9 D2
Lawrence Ct SO19.........51 D1
Lawrence Gr SO19.........51 F2
Lawrence Mans PO5......54 D1

Lawrence Rd PO5.........54 D1
Lawrence Sq 3 PO12.....52 D5
Lawson Rd PO5.........54 D2
Lea Ct PO36.........35 D4
Leamington Ho 9 PO5....54 D2
Leander Dr 7 PO12.........52 C8
Lea Rd PO36.........35 D4
Lear Rd PO12.........52 A8
Ledwell Ct PO12.........52 D7
Leed St PO36.........35 F5
Lee Lands SO41.........48 D1
Leep La PO12.........52 B3
Lee Rd PO12.........52 A7
Lees La PO12.........52 B5
Leesland CE Inf Sch PO12.52 B5
Leesland Ct Jun Sch
  PO12.........52 B5
Leesland Rd PO12.........52 A6
Lees Lane N 9 PO12......52 B5
Leeson Rd PO38.........47 D7
Leigh Pk SO41.........48 C3
Leighton Ave 10 SO15...50 B8
Leighton Mount PO5......43 A7
Leighton Rd SO19.........51 F3
Leighwood Cl PO33.......12 B3
Lemon Rd SO15.........50 B7
Lennox Cl PO12.........52 C2
Lennox Ct PO33.........12 A4
Lennox Mans PO5.........53 D2
Lennox Road N PO5......53 D2
Lennox Road S PO5......53 D2
Lentune Way SO41.........48 D2
Len Williams Terr PO12..53 F7
Leonard Rd PO12.........52 C6
Leopold St PO4.........54 F1
Leroux Cl SO15.........50 F5
Leslie Loader Ho SO19...51 C3
Lessland La PO38, PO36...34 B2
Le Tissier Ct 6 SO15......50 F5
Leventhorpe Ct PO12.....52 C5
Leveret Cl PO12.........52 C9
Lewis Ho 6 SO14.........51 A5
Leyland Cl PO12.........52 A5
Leyton Rd SO14.........51 D5
Lichfield Dr PO12.........52 C8
Lift Rd PO37.........35 C2
Lighthouse The 18 PO1...53 A4
Lilliput Antique Dolls & Toy
  Mus* PO5x.........24 B3
Lime Kiln Shute PO36....34 D5
LIMERSTONE.........30 E2
Limerstone Rd PO30......30 D2
Lime St SO14.........51 A3
Limes The
  Marchwood SO40.........50 A1
  Newport PO30.........20 C7
  Shanklin PO37.........43 C6
Lime Tree Ct PO40.........27 B8
Lime Tree Ho 11 SO41...48 E4
Lincoln Cl PO35.........25 D3
Lincoln Rd PO1.........53 E5
Lincoln Way PO35.........25 D3
Linden Gr PO12.........52 B4
Linden Rd SO19.........20 C5
Linden Terr PO30.........20 C5
Linden Way SO41.........48 C4
Lind Hill 10 PO33.........12 C6
Lindon Ct PO4.........53 F4
Lind Pl PO33.........12 B6
Lindsay Ho 8 PO5.........53 D2
Lindsay Rd SO19.........51 C2
Liners Ind Est SO15.......51 C6
Lingdale Pl 3 SO17.........51 A8
Lingfield Ct 3 PO1.........53 B3
Linington Ct 11 PO30......20 C6
Linklater Path PO1.........53 D7
Link Rd 8 PO32.........3 C4
Linkside PO30.........43 A6
Linnet Ct PO36.........20 A6
Linnet Rise PO30.........35 C3
Linstone Dr PO41.........15 A5
Lion Brewery The 1 PO2..53 D8
Lion Rd PO1.........52 F8
Lion Terr PO1.........53 B5
Lisbon Rd SO15.........50 D6
Lisle Cl SO41.........48 D3
Lisle Ct SO14.........51 A3
LISLE COURT.........49 C3
Lisle Court Rd SO41......49 C3
Lisle La PO4.........53 F4
Little Anglesey PO12.....52 A2
Little Anglesey Rd PO12.52 A3
Little Arthur St PO2......53 E7
Little Coburg St PO5.....54 C3
Little Dene Copse SO41..48 A3
Little George St PO1......53 E7
Little Gn PO12.........52 A7
Little Green Orch PO12...52 A3
Little Hambrook St 6
  PO5.........54 A1
Little La PO12.........52 A3
Little Lance's Hill SO19..51 F4
Little London PO30.........20 E8
Little Preston Rd PO33...12 E1
Little Princelett Cross
  PO36.........34 E2
Little Southsea St PO5...54 A1
Littlestairs Rd PO37......35 D1
Littleton Cl PO8.........54 A6
Littletown La PO33.........10 D2
LITTLE WHITEHOUSE......7 D5
Little Whitehouse Rd PO31.7 D5
Liverpool Rd PO1.........53 E5
Liverpool St SO14.........51 A4
Livesay Gdns PO1.........53 F6

Livingstone Rd
  Portsmouth PO5.........54 C1
  Southampton SO14.......51 A8
Loane Rd SO19.........51 F3
Lockerley Cl SO41.........48 C2
LOCKSGREEN.........7 C2
LOCKSLEY.........27 B7
Locksley Cl PO40.........27 B7
Locksley Cl SO15.........50 F7
Locksley Mews 7 PO41..54 B3
Lodge Arts Ctr The* PO1.54 B3
Lodge Cl PO30.........30 A2
Lodge Gdns PO12.........52 A4
Lodge Rd
  Lymington SO41.........48 B3
  Southampton SO14.......51 A4
Lodgeside PO32.........3 D2
Lodge The PO5.........50 F7
Lodsworth Ho PO1.........53 A4
Lombard Ct 8 PO1.........53 A4
Lombard St PO1.........53 A3
Lomond Cl PO2.........53 D8
Londesborough Pl SO41..48 D2
Londesborough Rd PO4...53 E3
Long Acre Ct SO15.........53 F2
Longbeach PO4.........14 D2
LONGBRIDGE.........34 D8
Longbridge Ho 8 PO5....54 B2
Longbridge Ind Pk SO14..51 C3
Long Cl SO41.........48 A3
Long Curtain Rd PO5.....53 A2
Longford Pl SO41.........48 D1
Long La
  Downend PO30.........21 E4
  Newport PO30.........21 B6
Longlands La PO36.........34 C6
Longlands Shute PO33....24 C2
Long Lane Shute PO30....21 D5
Longman Ct 2 PO5.........53 C2
Longmead Rd PO33.........12 C4
Longmore Ave SO19.......51 D1
Longmore Cres SO19......51 D2
Longs Wlk PO1.........53 D7
Long Water Dr PO12......52 C2
Lonsdale Ave PO30.........9 A2
Lord Montgomery Way 1
  ....54 A2
Lords Ct PO1.........54 C4
Lords St PO1.........54 C4
Lorne Rd PO5.........54 D1
Louis Flagg Ho 2 PO5...54 B2
Louis Rd PO36.........35 D4
Love La
  Bembridge PO35.........25 D6
  Cowes PO31.........3 A3
  Ventnor PO38.........46 E4
Lovett Way PO37.........35 C2
Lowcay Rd PO5.........53 E2
Lower Adgestone Rd
  ....23 F1
Lower Alfred St SO14.....51 B6
Lower Banister St 7
  ....51 A8
Lower Bettesworth Rd
  PO33.........12 B3
Lower Brookfield Rd PO1.53 E6
LOWER BUCKLAND.........48 E5
Lower Buckland Rd SO41.48 D5
Lower Canal Wlk SO14....51 A3
Lower Church Path PO1...53 E5
Lower Church Rd PO31....2 D3
Lower Fields PO38.........45 C4
Lower Forbury Rd PO5....54 C2
Lower Furlongs PO36.....24 D3
Lower Green Rd PO33.....6 B2
LOWER HAMSTEAD.........6 B2
Lower Highland Rd PO33..12 D4
Lower Horn Hill PO31......2 C3
LOWER HYDE.........43 C8
Lower Hyde Est PO37.....43 B8
Lower Mortimer Rd SO19.51 D8
Lower Vicarage Rd SO19.51 D3
Lower William St Ind Est
  SO14.........51 D6
Lower William St SO14....51 D6
Lower Wingfield St PO1...54 C4
Lower Woodside PO33 ....10 E8
Lower York St SO14.......51 C6
LOWTHERVILLE.........46 E6
Lowtherville Rd PO38......46 F7
Luccombe Ct PO37.........43 C6
Luccombe Rd PO37.........43 C5
LUCCOMBE VILLAGE.......43 C6
Lucerne Rd PO37.........43 C8
Lucerne Villa PO37.........43 C8
Lucia Foster Welch Coll
  Student Village 7 SO14.51 B3
Lucknow St PO1.........53 C6
Ludbrook Way PO30......45 F7
Ludlow Inf Sch SO19......51 E4
Ludlow Jun Sch SO19.....51 E4
Ludlow Rd SO19.........51 E4
Lugley St PO30.........20 D7
Lukely Ct PO30.........20 C6
Lukely Gdns PO30.........20 C6
Lumsden Ave SO15.......50 D7
Lumsden Mans 3 SO15...50 D7
Lushington Hill PO33......10 C4
LYMINGTON.........48 C5
Lymington CE Inf Sch
  SO41.........48 D4

Lymington Jun Sch SO41 . .48 D4
Lymington New Forest Hospl
SO41 . . . . .48 D4
Lymington Pier Sta SO41 . .49 A3
Lymington Rehabilitation
Unit SO41 . . . . .48 E4
Lymington Town Sta
SO41 . . . . .48 F4
Lynchens Cl PO35 . . . . .25 C4
Lynch La
  Brighstone PO30 . . . . .30 A5
  Calbourne PO30 . . . . .30 A7
Lyndhurst Rd PO12 . . . . . . .52 A5
Lyndock Cl SO19 . . . . .51 E2
Lyndock Pl SO19 . . . . .51 E2
Lynn Rd PO2 . . . . .53 F8
Lynwood Ct SO41 . . . . .48 D3
Lyon St SO14 . . . . .51 A6
Lysander Ct 21 PO1 . . . . . . .53 A4
Lytellane Rd SO41 . . . . .48 D2

M

Mabey Cl PO12 . . . . .52 C3
Machin Cl PO30 . . . . .20 B6
Macketts La PO30 . . . . .34 B5
Macnaghten Rd SO18 . . . . .51 D8
Macnamara Almshouses
PO31 . . . . .3 B5
Macrocarpa Rd PO38 . . . . . .47 A6
Maddison St 8 SO14 . . . . .50 F4
Madeira Ct PO18 . . . . .47 C6
Madeira La PO40 . . . . .14 D2
Madeira Rd
  Seaview PO34 . . . . .13 D3
  Totland PO39 . . . . .14 C1
  Ventnor PO38 . . . . .47 C6
Madeira Vale PO38 . . . . . . .47 C6
Madrisa Ct SO41 . . . . .48 E4
Mafeking Rd PO4 . . . . .53 F3
Magazine La SO40 . . . . .50 A3
Magdalen Cres PO30 . . . . . . .2 F4
Magnolia Rd SO19 . . . . .51 F5
Magnum Hall PO37 . . . . . . .35 D1
Maida Vale Rd PO37 . . . . . . .35 D1
Maiden La SO41 . . . . .48 F1
Main Rd
  Brighstone PO30 . . . . .30 B2
  Newport PO30 . . . . .7 D3
  Portmore SO41 . . . . .49 B7
  Rookley PO38 . . . . .33 A4
  Wellow PO41 . . . . .17 D4
Maitland Ct SO14 . . . . .48 D3
Maitland St PO1 . . . . .53 D7
Major Ct PO12 . . . . .52 B8
Makings Cl PO40 . . . . .27 C7
Malcolm Dyer Ct 8 PO30 . .20 D6
Malcroft Mews SO40 . . . . . .50 A1
Maldon Rd SO19 . . . . .51 E4
Malins Rd PO2 . . . . .53 D8
Malins Road Apts 18 PO2 . .53 D7
Mallard Point PO31 . . . . .9 B8
Mallfield Terr PO36 . . . . .24 B2
Mall Marlands (Sh Ctr) The
SO14 . . . . .50 F4
Mall The
  Brading PO36 . . . . .24 B2
  Ryde PO33 . . . . .11 E4
  Sandown PO36 . . . . .35 E4
  Totland PO39 . . . . .14 D1
Malmesbury Pl SO15 . . . . . .50 D7
Malmesbury Rd SO15 . . . . . .50 D7
Malta Rd PO2 . . . . .53 E8
Malthouse Ct 2 PO30 . . . . .20 D7
Malthouse Gn PO41 . . . . . . .17 E4
Malthouse Rd PO2 . . . . .53 D8
Malvern Rd PO5 . . . . .53 D1
Manchester Rd PO1 . . . . . . .53 E5
Mandela Way SO15 . . . . . . .50 E5
Manna Rd PO35 . . . . .25 C4
Manners La PO4 . . . . .53 E4
Manners Rd PO4 . . . . .53 E4
Manners View PO30 . . . . .9 B1
Manor Cres
  Newport PO30 . . . . .20 F7
  Rookley PO38 . . . . .32 F4
Manor Ct PO36 . . . . .35 D4
Manor Gn PO30 . . . . .17 E2
Manor Inf Sch PO1 . . . . .53 D6
Manor Park Ho 1 SO18 . . . .51 E1
Manor Quay SO41 . . . . .51 D7
Manor Rd
  Freshwater Bay PO40 . . . . .27 C7
  Portsmouth PO1 . . . . .53 E7
  Sandown PO36 . . . . .35 D4
  Shanklin PO37 . . . . .43 B6
  Wroxall PO38 . . . . .42 D3
Manor Road N SO19 . . . . . .51 E4
Manor Road S SO19 . . . . . . .51 E3
Manor Villas 4 PO39 . . . . . .14 D1
Manor Wharf SO41 . . . . .51 C7
Mansion Ct 4 PO4 . . . . .53 E1
Mansion Rd
  Portsmouth PO4 . . . . .53 E1
  Southampton SO15 . . . . . .50 D6
Maple Ct
  Lymington SO41 . . . . .48 B2
  Southampton, Woolston
  SO19 . . . . .51 E2
Maple Dr PO30 . . . . .20 C7
Maple Rd
  Portsmouth PO5 . . . . .53 D2
  Southampton SO18 . . . . . .51 E7
Maples Dr PO38 . . . . .47 C7

Maples The PO36 . . . . .35 D2
Marchwood Ind Pk SO40 . . .50 A3
Marchwood Rd SO15 . . . . . .50 B6
Maresfield Rd PO32 . . . . .3 C4
Margam Ave SO19 . . . . .51 F5
Margaret Rule Hall 5
PO1 . . . . .54 B3
Margate Rd PO5 . . . . .54 C2
Margery's Ct 51 PO1 . . . . . .53 A5
Marina Ave PO33 . . . . .12 F5
Marina Bldgs 3 PO12 . . . . .52 B5
Marina Cl PO32 . . . . .3 C2
Marine Cotts 2 PO12 . . . . . .52 B6
Marine Cross Rd PO37 . . . . .43 C8
Marine Ct PO38 . . . . .47 A5
Marine Dr PO41 . . . . .16 C8
Marine Par
  Southampton SO14 . . . . . .51 B4
  Ventnor PO38 . . . . .47 A5
Mariners Ct SO41 . . . . .48 F2
Mariners Way
  Cowes PO31 . . . . .3 A2
  Gosport PO12 . . . . .52 D4
Marine View PO32 . . . . .3 C3
Marion Rd PO4 . . . . .53 E2
Maritime Chambers SO14 . .51 B2
Maritime Way SO14 . . . . . . .51 A2
Maritime Wlk SO14 . . . . . . .51 A2
Mark Cl SO15 . . . . .50 A7
Market Hill PO31 . . . . .3 B5
Market Pl 19 SO14 . . . . .51 A3
Market Sq 1 PO41 . . . . .15 C6
Market St
  Ryde PO33 . . . . .12 C6
  Ventnor PO38 . . . . .47 A6
Marketway PO1 . . . . .54 B4
MARK'S CORNER 8 C5
Marlborough Cl PO33 . . . . . .12 E3
Marlborough Ct 15 PO12 . . .52 C9
Marlborough Ho SO15 . . . . .50 F8
Marlborough Pl SO15 . . . . . .48 D5
Marlborough Rd
  Carisbrooke PO30 . . . . .20 B6
  Ryde PO33 . . . . .12 E3
  Southampton SO15, SO30 . .50 B8
  Ventnor PO38 . . . . .47 A6
Marlborough Row PO1 . . . . .53 A6
Marlowe Ct SO19 . . . . .51 F1
Marmion Ave PO5 . . . . .53 D2
Marmion Rd PO5 . . . . .53 D2
Marram Ct SO41 . . . . .48 E5
Marshall Ct 10 SO15 . . . . . .50 F8
Marshall Sq SO15 . . . . .50 F8
Marsh Cl
  Freshwater Bay PO40 . . . . .27 C7
  Sandown PO36 . . . . .36 A4
Marsh Ho 8 SO41 . . . . .51 A3
Marsh La
  Lymington SO41 . . . . .48 E5
  Southampton SO14 . . . . . .51 B3
Marsh Rd
  East Cowes PO32 . . . . .3 C4
  Gurnard PO31 . . . . .2 C3
Martine Ct PO40 . . . . .14 E2
Marvel La PO30 . . . . .20 E2
Marycourt Sch PO12 . . . . . . .52 A2
Maryfield SO14 . . . . .51 B4
Marymead Cl PO33 . . . . .12 B5
Mary Rose* PO1 . . . . .52 F7
Mary Rose Ave PO1 . . . . . . .10 E4
Mary Rose St The PO1 . . . . .54 B3
Matthews Way PO34 . . . . . . .13 D2
Maturin Cl SO41 . . . . .48 D3
Mauretania Ho 18 SO14 . . .51 C6
Maxstoke Cl PO5 . . . . .54 C3
Maxted Cl PO31 . . . . .3 A3
May Ave SO41 . . . . .48 D5
Maybrick Rd PO33 . . . . .12 A5
May Cl PO38 . . . . .33 C1
Maycroft Ct 4 SO15 . . . . . .50 F8
Mayfair Gdns SO15 . . . . .50 F7
Mayfield CE Mid Sch
PO33 . . . . .12 A5
Mayfield Dr PO33 . . . . .21 A7
Mayfield Rd
  East Cowes PO32 . . . . .3 D2
  Gosport PO12 . . . . .52 C4
  Ryde PO33 . . . . .12 A5
Mayflower Ct SO41 . . . . .49 A2
Mayflower Ct
  Cowes PO31 . . . . .3 B4
  7 Southampton, Banister's Park
  SO15 . . . . .50 F7
  10 Southampton SO15 . . . .50 B8
Mayflower Rd SO15 . . . . . . .50 B8
Mayo Cl PO1 . . . . .53 D7
May Rd SO15 . . . . .50 C8
Maythorne Way PO37 . . . . . .43 C4
Maytree Int Sch SO14 . . . . .51 B6
Mayville High Sch 20 PO5 . .53 D2
Meaders Rd PO33 . . . . .12 D4
Meadow Barn Cl PO39 . . . . .26 H8
Meadowbrook PO33 . . . . . . .11 F5
Meadow Cl
  Bembridge PO35 . . . . .25 D5
  Sandown PO36 . . . . .35 D3
  Whitwell PO38 . . . . .45 E7
Meadow Dr PO35 . . . . .25 D5
Meadow End PO35 . . . . .25 D5
Meadow Glade PO40 . . . . . . .27 C8
Meadow Rd PO30 . . . . .20 D5
Meadowlands SO14 . . . . . . .48 C4
Meadowmead Ave SO15 . . .50 A7
Meadow Rd
  East Cowes PO32 . . . . .3 D2
  Lymington SO41 . . . . .48 C2
Meadows Cl PO30 . . . . .30 B2

Meadowside PO30 . . . . .21 A7
Meadow St PO5 . . . . .54 A2
Meadow View Cl PO33 . . . . .12 B3
Meadow Way PO36 . . . . .36 C5
Meadow Wlk SO14 . . . . .54 B4
Mead Rd SO41 . . . . .48 B2
Medeway PO36 . . . . .35 D4
Medham Farm La PO31 . . . . .9 A8
Medina Ave PO30 . . . . .20 E6
Medina Court Ind Est PO31 . .3 B2
Medina High Sch PO30 . . . . . .9 D1
Medina House SO30 . . . . . . .20 F7
Medina L Ctr PO30 . . . . .9 D1
Medina Pk PO32 . . . . .9 E6
Medina Rd PO33 . . . . .3 B4
Medina View PO32 . . . . .3 C2
Medina Village Ind Est
PO31 . . . . .3 B4
Medina Way PO30 . . . . .20 D8
Medley Pl SO15 . . . . .50 A7
Melbourne Ho PO31 . . . . . . .54 B3
Melbourne Pl
  Cowes PO31 . . . . .3 A6
  Portsmouth PO5 . . . . .54 B2
Melbourne St
  Newport PO30 . . . . .20 C6
  Southampton SO14 . . . . . .51 B4
Melbury Cl PO33 . . . . .48 D3
Melcombe Ho PO31 . . . . .2 F6
Melton Hall PO33 . . . . .12 D5
Melville Gdns PO36 . . . . .35 F5
Melville Rd PO12 . . . . .52 B8
Melville St
  Ryde PO33 . . . . .12 D6
  Sandown PO36 . . . . .35 E5
Merchants Row 6 PO1 . . . . .53 A3
Merchants Wlk 16 SO14 . . .50 F3
Meredith Inf Sch PO2 . . . . . .53 E8
Merganser Ct PO12 . . . . .52 B8
Meriden St PO5 . . . . .54 A2
Merlin Lodge SO19 . . . . .51 D3
Mermaid Way SO14 . . . . . . .51 B2
Merridale Rd SO19 . . . . .51 E5
Merrie Gdns PO36 . . . . .35 C3
Merryl La PO38 . . . . .41 C7
MERRY OAK 51 F5
Merryoak La SO19 . . . . .51 F5
Merryoak Rd SO19 . . . . .51 F5
MERSTONE 33 C6
Merstone La PO30, PO38 . . .33 D6
Merton Ct 3 PO5 . . . . .54 C1
Merton Rd PO5 . . . . .54 C1
Methuen St SO14 . . . . .51 A7
Mews La
  Newport, Fairlee PO30 . . . . .9 D1
  Newport, Staplers PO30 . . .21 B8
Mews The
  7 Gosport PO12 . . . . .52 E5
  Newport PO30 . . . . .20 D7
Micawber Ho 22 PO1 . . . . . .53 D7
Midanbury Ct 9 SO18 . . . . .51 E8
Midanbury La SO18 . . . . .51 E8
Middle Barn La PO38 . . . . . .42 E3
Middle Common Rd SO41 . .48 A3
Middle Ct PO1 . . . . .53 E7
Middle Rd SO41 . . . . .48 D3
Middle St
  Portsmouth PO5 . . . . .54 B2
  Southampton SO14 . . . . . .51 A7
MIDDLETON 27 A7
Middleton Terr PO31 . . . . .3 B5
Midhurst Ho PO1 . . . . .54 C4
Mile End Rd PO2 . . . . .53 C7
Milestone Cres PO36 . . . . . .34 E7
Milford Rd
  Lymington SO41 . . . . .48 C1
  Portsmouth PO1 . . . . .54 C3
  Shanklin PO37 . . . . .43 C8
Military Rd
  Brighstone PO30 . . . . .38 F7
  Brook PO30 . . . . .28 D6
  Chale PO38 . . . . .39 C2
  Gosport, Alverstoke PO12 . .52 A2
  Gosport, Clayhall PO12 . . . .52 C2
  Portsmouth, Landport PO1 . .53 B7
Millais Rd SO19 . . . . .51 E3
MILLBANK 51 C5
Millbank Ho 14 SO14 . . . . . .51 C6
Millbank St SO14 . . . . .51 C5
Millbrook Point Rd SO15 . . .50 A6
Millbrook Road E SO15 . . . . .50 D5
Millbrook Road W SO15 . . . .50 A6
Millbrook Sta SO15 . . . . .50 B6
Millennium Way PO36 . . . . . .35 D4
Miller Cl PO37 . . . . .35 C2
Millers' La PO30 . . . . .20 A4
Miller's Pond Gdns SO19 . . .51 F3
Millfield Ave PO2 . . . . .53 E8
Millfield Rd PO30 . . . . .20 B6
Mill Gate Ho 30 PO1 . . . . . .53 A5
Mill Hill Rd PO31 . . . . .3 A3
Mill House Bsns Ctr SO19 . .51 D4
Milligan Ho PO33 . . . . .12 B4
Milligan Rd PO33 . . . . .12 B4
Mill La
  Brighstone PO30 . . . . .30 B1
  Brighstone PO30 . . . . .30 F1
  Gosport PO12 . . . . .52 B7
  Lymington SO41 . . . . .48 F4
  Newport PO30 . . . . .9 E4
  Portsmouth, Landport PO1 . .53 C7
  South Baddesley SO41 . . . .49 F4
Mill Pond Rd PO12 . . . . .52 B7
Mill Rd
  Bembridge PO35 . . . . .25 C4
  Gosport PO12 . . . . .52 A7
  Shalfleet PO30 . . . . .17 E7

Mill Rd continued
  Southampton SO15 . . . . . .50 A7
  St Helens PO33 . . . . .25 A6
  Yarmouth PO41 . . . . .15 D5
Mill Sq PO33 . . . . .10 F4
Mill St PO30 . . . . .20 D7
Millstream Ct PO30 . . . . .20 C7
Millward Pl PO33 . . . . .12 C2
Millward Rd PO33 . . . . .12 C4
Millways PO40 . . . . .14 F2
Milne Ct PO30 . . . . .20 D8
Milner Ct SO15 . . . . .50 C8
Milne Way PO30 . . . . .20 E5
Milton Rd
  Cowes PO31 . . . . .3 B2
  Southampton SO15 . . . . . .50 F6
Milverton Ho PO5 . . . . .54 B2
Mimosa Cl PO30 . . . . .20 C7
Mimosa Rd PO37 . . . . .43 C8
Minerva Cres 20 PO1 . . . . . .53 A4
Minerva Ct 2 PO4 . . . . .53 E1
Minerva Dr 9 PO12 . . . . . . .52 C8
Minerva Rd PO12 . . . . .52 C9
Minnitt Rd PO12 . . . . .52 E5
Minstead Ct 17 SO17 . . . . . .51 A8
Minster Ct 9 SO15 . . . . .50 C6
Mirabella Cl SO19 . . . . .51 D2
Mistral 11 SO14 . . . . .51 B3
Mitchell Ave PO38 . . . . .47 A6
Mitchell Cl SO19 . . . . .51 D3
Mitchell's Rd PO33 . . . . .12 A3
Mitten Rd PO35 . . . . .25 D4
Moira Ho PO1 . . . . .3 B5
Molesworth Rd PO12 . . . . . .52 C4
Monastery Rd SO18 . . . . . . .51 E7
Monckton Rd PO2 . . . . .52 B2
Monks Brook PO30 . . . . .9 B2
Monks Ct 4 SO41 . . . . .48 F2
Monks La PO40 . . . . .14 E4
Monkton St PO33 . . . . .12 D5
Monmouth Ct SO41 . . . . .48 E3
Montagu Ct PO12 . . . . .52 C9
Montague Wallis Ct 40
PO1 . . . . .53 A5
Monterey Rd PO33 . . . . .12 A3
Montgomerie Rd PO5 . . . . . .54 C2
Monument Rd SO14 . . . . . . .51 A2
Monument La SO41 . . . . .49 A5
Moon Cl PO22 . . . . .3 D3
Moons Hill PO39, PO40 . . . .26 H6
Moorgreen Rd PO31 . . . . .3 A4
Moorhead Ct SO14 . . . . .51 C2
Moorings The PO31 . . . . .3 A3
Moor La PO30 . . . . .30 A3
Moorland Rd PO1 . . . . .53 E6
MOORTOWN 30 A3
Moortown La PO30 . . . . .30 A3
Moor View PO38 . . . . .33 D1
Moraunt Cl 1 PO12 . . . . . . .52 D9
Moraunt Rd PO12 . . . . .52 C9
Morant Rd SO14 . . . . .51 A7
Morecombe Ct 4 PO5 . . . . .54 C2
Moreland Rd PO12 . . . . .52 B6
Morey Cl PO33 . . . . .12 C4
Morley Cl SO19 . . . . .51 F6
Mornington Rd PO31 . . . . .2 F6
Morris Rd SO15 . . . . .50 E5
Mortimer Rd SO19 . . . . .51 E4
MORTON 24 B1
Mortonbrook PO36 . . . . .35 F7
Morton Comm PO36 . . . . . . .36 A5
Morton Lodge PO36 . . . . . . .36 A5
Morton Manor* PO36 . . . . . .24 A1
Morton Manor Rd PO36 . . . .24 A1
Morton Mews PO36 . . . . . . .24 A1
Morton Old Rd PO36 . . . . . .24 A1
Morton Rd PO36 . . . . .24 A1
Mosbach Pl 5 SO41 . . . . . . .48 E4
Moselle Ct SO15 . . . . .50 C5
Mottisfont Cl 1 SO15 . . . . . .50 A6
MOTTISTONE 29 C4
Mottistone Manor Gdn*
PO30 . . . . .29 D4
Moulin Ave PO5 . . . . .53 E2
Mound Ct PO12 . . . . .52 A4
Mountbatten Ave PO31 . . . . . .2 F5
Mountbatten Bsns Ctr
SO15 . . . . .50 E5
Mountbatten Dr
  Carisbrooke PO30 . . . . .20 B7
  Ryde PO33 . . . . .12 A4
Mountbatten Way
  Portsmouth PO1 . . . . .53 B7
  Southampton SO15 . . . . . .50 C5
Mountfield 8 PO40 . . . . .15 D6
Mountfield Rd PO38 . . . . . . .42 B3
Mountjoy Ct 4 PO1 . . . . . . .53 A3
Mount Pleasant Ho PO12 . . .52 B7
Mount Pleasant Ind Pk
SO14 . . . . .51 B7
Mount Pleasant Jun Sch
SO14 . . . . .51 B7
Mount Pleasant La SO41 . . .48 A7
Mount Pleasant Rd
  Gosport PO12 . . . . .52 A7
  Newport PO30 . . . . .20 D6
  Southampton SO14 . . . . . .51 B6
Mount Rd
  East Cowes PO32 . . . . .4 A1
  Wootton PO30 . . . . .10 A8
Mount St PO33 . . . . .12 C5
Mount The PO41 . . . . .15 D6
Mousehole La SO18 . . . . . . .51 F8
Muggleton La PO30 . . . . . . .30 E1
Muira Est SO14 . . . . .51 C5
Mulberry Cl
  Gosport PO12 . . . . .52 B5
  Newport PO30 . . . . .20 D5
Mulberry Way PO33 . . . . . . .12 F2

Mulberry Wlk SO15 . . . . . . .50 C8
Mullen Cl SO41 . . . . .51 E4
Mumby Rd PO12 . . . . .52 D6
Murefield Rd PO1 . . . . .54 C4
Murray's La PO1 . . . . .52 F7
Museum Rd PO1 . . . . .53 B4
Mus of Archaeology*
SO14 . . . . .51 A2
Mus of Island History*
PO30 . . . . .20 E7

N

Nancy Rd PO1 . . . . .54 D3
Nansen Cl PO35 . . . . .25 D5
Napier Rd PO5 . . . . .53 D2
Napier The PO37 . . . . .43 D3
Napoleons Landing PO36 . . .35 F4
Nat Gonella Sq 4 PO12 . . . .52 D5
Navy Rd PO1 . . . . .53 A6
Needles Battery Rd SO41 . . .50 E6
Needles Old Battery The*
PO39 . . . . .26 B4
Needles Pk The* PO39 . . . . .26 D5
Nelson Cl PO32 . . . . .3 D3
Nelson Cres PO33 . . . . .11 F4
Nelson Ct
  Cowes PO31 . . . . .3 B4
  8 Portsmouth PO1 . . . . . . .53 D2
Nelson Dr PO31 . . . . .3 B2
Nelson Rd 5 PO12 . . . . .52 E5
Nelson La PO33 . . . . .12 D6
Nelson Pl
  Lymington SO41 . . . . .48 F3
  Ryde PO33 . . . . .12 D6
Nelson Rd
  Gosport PO12 . . . . .52 B8
  Newport PO30 . . . . .20 C6
  Portsmouth, Landport PO1 . .53 D2
  Portsmouth PO5 . . . . .54 C4
  Southampton SO15 . . . . . .50 C6
Nelson's Quay PO33 . . . . . . .24 F7
Nelson St
  Ryde PO33 . . . . .12 C6
  12 Southampton SO14 . . . .51 B3
Nepean Ct PO12 . . . . .52 B2
Neptune Ct 14 PO1 . . . . . . .53 A4
Neptune Ho SO14 . . . . .51 B2
Neptune Way SO14 . . . . . . .51 B2
Nessus St PO2 . . . . .53 DE
Netley Ct 8 PO12 . . . . .52 C5
Netley Mans 10 PO5 . . . . . .53 D3
Netley Rd 13 PO5 . . . . .53 C2
Netley Terr PO5 . . . . .53 C2
NETTLECOMBE 41 D3
Nettlecombe Ave PO4 . . . . .53 E3
Nettlecombe La PO38 . . . . . .45 E7
NETTLESTONE 13 C3
Nettlestone Gn PO34 . . . . . .13 C2
Nettlestone Hill PO33,
PO34 . . . . .13 C3
Nettlestone Prim Sch
PO34 . . . . .13 C2
Neva Rd SO18 . . . . .51 F8
NEW BARN 3 E4
New Barn Bsns Pk PO30 . . .21 C3
New Barn Rd PO22 . . . . .31 C3
NEWBRIDGE 17 D3
Newbridge Jun Sch PO2 . . . .53 F7
Newbridge Way SO41 . . . . . .48 C1
NEWCHURCH 34 D7
Newchurch Prim Sch
PO36 . . . . .34 D7
New Cliff Ho SO19 . . . . .51 E1
Newcombe Rd SO15 . . . . . . .50 E6
Newcomen Rd PO2 . . . . .53 E6
Newcome Rd PO1 . . . . .53 E6
Newenham Rd SO41 . . . . . . .48 E2
Newland Ave PO21 . . . . .52 A5
Newlands
  Merstone PO30 . . . . .33 D5
  St Helens PO33 . . . . .25 B5
Newlands Ave SO15 . . . . . . .50 D7
Newman La PO30 . . . . .40 A3
Newman St 2 SO16 . . . . . . .50 B8
Newnham La PO33 . . . . .11 C3
Newnham Rd PO33 . . . . .11 E3
NEWPORT 20 B7
Newport CE Prim Sch
PO30 . . . . .20 C7
Newport Rd
  Cowes PO31 . . . . .8 F8
  Freshwater Bay PO40 . . . . .27 E7
  Godshill PO38 . . . . .33 C1
  Niton PO38 . . . . .45 B4
  Sandown PO36 . . . . .35 C4
  Ventnor PO38 . . . . .46 F6
Newport Roman Villa*
PO30 . . . . .20 E6
Newport St PO33 . . . . .12 C5
New Rd
  Brading PO36 . . . . .24 B2
  Brighstone PO30 . . . . .30 A1
  Porchfield PO30 . . . . .7 D2
  Portsmouth PO2 . . . . .53 F7
  Sandown PO36 . . . . .35 D4
  Southampton SO14 . . . . . .51 A5
  Wootton PO33 . . . . .10 F5
  Yalford PO30 . . . . .39 A7
New Road E PO2 . . . . .53 F8
New St
  Lymington SO41 . . . . .48 E4
  Newport PO30 . . . . .20 D6
  Sandown PO36 . . . . .35 E5
New Street Mews SO41 . . . .48 E4
New Theatre Royal* PO1 . . .54 A3

NEWTOWN
Gosport 52 D6
Newport 6 E2
Southampton 51 B6
Newtown CE Prim Sch
PO12 ....52 C6
Newtown Harbour National
Nature Reserve* PO30 ..6 D2
Newtown Marshes Nature
Reserve* PO30............6 F4
Newtown Old Town Hall*
PO30 ....6 E2
NEW VILLAGE 27 C8
Nicholas Cl PO36 ....3 D7
Nicholson Gdns ■ PO1 ..54 C3
Nicholson Rd PO33 ......12 D3
Nicholson St PO30 ....9 A3
Nickel St ■ PO5 ....54 A1
Nickleby Ho ■ PO1 ......53 D7
Nightingale Cl PO33 .....25 D5
Nightingale Gr SO15 .....50 C7
Nightingale Rd
Carisbrooke PO30 ....20 A6
Portsmouth PO5 ....53 B2
Southampton SO15 ....50 C7
Nine Acres Prim Sch
PO30 ....20 D6
NINGWOOD 17 C6
Ningwood Hill PO41 ......17 A7
Ninham Cl PO37 ....35 C2
Nippert Ct ■ PO30 ....20 D6
Nirvana Mans ■ PO5 ....53 D1
NITON 45 B3
Niton Prim Sch PO38 ....45 B4
Niton Rd PO38 ....32 F4
Niton Shute PO38 ....45 A4
Nobbs La PO1 ....53 A4
Node Cl PO33 ....12 B3
Nodehill Mid Sch PO30 ..20 D6
Nodes Rd PO31 ....8 F8
Nodgham La PO30 ....20 A6
Noke Comm PO30 ....8 E4
Norcliffe Rd SO17 ....51 A8
Norcott Dr PO35 ....25 D4
Norfolk Rd PO31 ....54 B2
Norfolk St PO5 ....54 B2
Norland Rd PO4 ....54 D1
NORLEYWOOD 49 F8
Norleywood Rd SO41 .....49 E8
Norman Ct
Camp Hill PO30 ....8 F1
■ Portsmouth PO4 ....53 D3
Normandy La SO41 ....49 A1
Normandy Way SO40 .....50 A1
Norman Ho ■ SO14 .....51 C6
Norman Rd
Gosport PO12 ....52 A6
Portsmouth PO4 ....53 E3
Southampton SO15 ......50 C6
Norman Way PO33 ....10 C5
Norrish Ct PO2 ....53 E7
NORTHAM 51 C6
Northam Bsns Ctr 21
SO14 ....51 C6
Northam Mews PO1 .....54 C3
Northam Rd SO14 ....51 B5
Northam St PO1 ....54 C3
Northbourne Ave PO37 ..43 B8
Northbrook Cl PO1 ....53 D7
Northbrook Rd SO14 .....51 B5
North Cl SO41 ....48 E4
Northcliff Gdns PO37 .....35 D1
Northcliff Hts PO37 ......35 D1
Northcote Rd PO4 ....53 E3
North Court Cl PO30 .....31 B2
North Cross St PO12 ....52 D5
North Ct PO1 ....53 E7
Northern Anchorage
SO19 ....51 F1
Northern Way PO1 ....52 F8
Northesk Ho PO1 ....54 C4
North Fairlee Rd PO30 ..9 E3
Northgate Ave PO2 ......53 E8
North Greenlands SO41 ..48 C2
Northlands Gdns SO15 ...50 E7
Northlands Rd SO15 .....50 E7
North Rd
Shanklin PO37 ....43 C4
Southampton SO17 ......51 C8
North St
Brighstone PO30 ....30 B2
Gosport PO12 ....52 D6
Lymington SO41 ....48 C2
Portsmouth PO1 ....53 A5
Portsmouth, Portsea PO1 .53 A5
Sandown PO36 ....36 A4
Ventnor PO38 ....47 B6
Northumberland Rd
Newport PO30 ....9 A1
Portsmouth PO5 ....54 D3
Southampton SO14 ......51 B6
North View
Newchurch PO36 ....34 D6
Thorley PO41 ....16 D6
North Wlk PO33 ....12 E6
NORTHWOOD 8 E8
Northwood Dr SO16 ......8 E8
Northwood Prim Sch PO31 .8 E7
NORTON 15 A5
Norton Cl SO19 ....51 E3
Norton Grange Village
PO41 ....15 A6
NORTON GREEN 15 A3

Norton Green Ind Pk
PO40 ....14 F3
Nostalgia Toy Mus*
PO38 ....41 D8
Nubia Cl PO31 ....2 F5
Nunnery La PO30 ....20 C4
Nunwell House & Gdns*
PO36 ....23 F3
Nunwell St PO36 ....35 E5
Nurseries The PO40 ......14 F1
Nursery Gdns PO32 ......3 C3
Nursery La PO33 ....12 A5
Nutfield Pl PO1 ....54 C4
Nyria Way PO12 ....52 D5

O

Oakbank Rd SO19 ....51 D3
Oak Ct SO41 ....48 C2
Oakfield CE Prim Sch
PO33 ....12 E4
Oakfield Rd PO33 ....12 D4
Oakhill Rd PO33, PO34 ..13 B8
Oak Hills PO37 ....43 A7
Oaklands SO41 ....48 F2
Oaklands Cl PO33 ....11 B5
Oakleigh Ct PO33 ....12 E5
Oakley Ct ■ SO16 ....50 B8
Oakley Ho
Portsmouth PO5 ....54 B1
■ Southampton, Banister's Pk
..........................50 F7
■ Southampton SO15 ...50 B8
Oakley Rd SO16 ....50 A8
OAKLYFIELD 12 D4
Oaklyn Gdns PO37 ....35 C1
Oak Rd
Newport PO30 ....20 F8
Southampton SO19 .....51 E2
Oaks Cl PO32 ....3 E4
Oakside Gdns PO35 ......25 C4
Oaks The SO19 ....51 F5
Oaktree Cl PO36 ....35 D3
Oak Tree Way PO32 .....3 D4
Oakville Mans ■ SO15 ..50 F6
Oakwood Cl PO30 ....12 B3
Oakwood Ct PO30 ....20 C7
Oakwood Rd PO30 ......12 B3
Oasis Acad Mayfield SO19 .51 F2
Obelisk Ct SO19 ....51 D2
Obelisk Rd SO19 ....51 D2
Oberland Ct SO40 ....48 D4
Oceana Ho PO1 ....54 B4
Oceana Way PO30 ....50 E5
Oceanic Way SO40 ......50 B3
Ocean Rd SO14 ....51 A1
Ocean View Rd PO38 ....46 F6
Ocean Way SO14 ....51 B2
Ochiltree Ho PO37 ......43 B7
Ockendon Cl PO5 ....54 B2
Officers Quarters The
PO12 ....52 D6
Ogle Rd ■ SO14 ....50 F5
Old Auction Ho 13 PO12 .52 E5
Old Bembridge Ho PO35 .25 C6
Old Blackgang Rd PO38 ..40 F2
Old Bridge Rd PO4 ......53 E2
Oldbury Ho ■ PO5 ......54 B2
Old Chapel La PO33 .....24 F7
Old Coastguard Cotts
PO40 ....27 D6
Old Commercial Rd PO1 .53 C7
Old Cricket Mews PO15 ..50 F8
Old Farmhouse Mews
SO41 ....48 E5
Old Farm Wlk SO41 .....48 D3
Old Forge Cl The PO33 ..11 F5
Old Forge Ct SO41 ......48 D3
Old Infirmary Ho 19 PO1 .53 A4
Old Maltings The SO41 ..48 C4
Old Oak View PO30 ......8 F1
Old Orchards SO41 ......48 E2
Old Park Rd PO38 ....46 A3
OLD PORTSMOUTH 53 A3
Old Rd
East Cowes PO32 ....3 D4
Gosport PO12 ....52 C4
Southampton SO14 ......51 C5
Old Reservoir La PO36 ..35 E4
Old Salterns Gate PO34 ..13 D4
Old School Ct PO38 ......42 B5
Old School La PO30 .....22 D1
Old Seaview La PO34 ....13 D5
Old Smithy & Gdns The*
PO38 ....41 D8
Old Star Pl ■ PO1 ....53 A4
Old Station Rd PO38 .....47 A6
Old Town Ct PO31 ....3 B5
Old Town Hall PO38 .....7 A1
Old Vicarage La PO30 ...7 A1
Old Westminster La ■
PO30 ....20 D7
Olinda St PO1 ....54 D3
Oliver Rd SO41 ....48 C3
Olivers Ct PO33 ....53 E8
Olivia Ct ■ PO30 ....20 D7
Omega Ho PO5 ....54 C3
Omega St PO5 ....54 C3
Ommanney Rd ■ PO41 ..15 D6
Onslow Rd
Portsmouth PO5 ....53 D1
Southampton SO14 ......51 A6
Orchard Cl
Freshwater PO40 ....15 A1
Wroxall PO38 ....42 B5
Orchard Ct PO30 ....35 C1

Orchard Ho ■ SO14 .....51 A3
Orchard La SO14 ....51 A3
Orchardleigh Rd PO37 ...43 C7
Orchard Mews PO30 .....20 E7
Orchard Pl
Cowes PO31 ....3 A4
Southampton SO14 ......51 A3
Orchard Rd
East Cowes PO32 ....3 D3
Portsmouth PO4 ....53 E4
Seaview PO34 ....13 D2
Shanklin PO37 ....43 B7
Orchard St PO30 ....20 D6
Orchards Way PO30 .....31 B2
Orchard The PO30 ....30 B2
Orchid Lodge PO37 ......35 D1
Ordnance Rd
Gosport PO12 ....52 D5
Southampton SO15 ......51 A6
Ordnance Row PO1 ......53 A5
Ordnance Way SO40 .....50 A3
Orion Ave PO12 ....52 C8
Ormsby Rd PO5 ....54 B1
Orwell Cl PO12 ....52 C8
Osborne Chase PO31 ....3 A3
Osborne Cl SO19 ....51 C4
Osborne Ct PO31 ....3 A3
Osborne Ho* PO32 ......3 F2
Osborne Hts PO32 ....3 E4
Osborne Mid Sch PO32 ..3 E1
Osborne Rd
East Cowes PO32 ....3 C3
Gosport PO12 ....52 C6
Portsmouth PO5 ....54 B1
Ryde PO33 ....12 B4
Shanklin PO37 ....43 C7
Osborne Road S SO17 ..51 C8
Osterley Rd SO19 ....51 E5
Our Lady & St Joseph RC
Prim Sch SO41 ....48 A4
Outram Rd PO5 ....54 C1
Overdell Ct ■ SO15 .....50 E7
Oxford Ave SO14 ....51 B6
Oxford Rd
Portsmouth PO5 ....54 D1
Southampton SO14 ......51 A7
Oxford St
Cowes PO31 ....8 F7
Southampton SO14 ......51 A3
Oyster Mews ■ PO1 ....53 A3
Oyster St PO1 ....53 A3

P

Pacific Cl SO14 ....51 C2
Packsfield La PO33 ......10 D3
Paddock Cl
Godshill PO38 ....41 D8
Shorwell PO30 ....31 B2
Paddock Dr PO33 ....25 F4
Paddock Gdns SO41 .....49 A5
Paddock Rd PO37 ....43 B7
Paddock The
Gosport PO12 ....52 A4
Winford PO36 ....34 F4
Padwell Rd SO14 ....51 A7
Paget Rd PO12 ....52 A3
Paget St SO14 ....51 B4
Pagham Pl PO38 ....33 B4
Pain's Rd PO5 ....54 C2
PALLANCEGATE 8 D5
Pallance La PO31 ....8 D7
Pallance Rd PO31 ....8 A7
Palm Ct 17 PO5 ....54 C2
Palmer's La PO36 ....34 E7
Palmers Rd PO33 ....10 D6
Palmerston Ct 28 PO5 ..54 C2
Palmerston Mans 3 PO5 .53 C2
Palmerston Rd
Portsmouth PO5 ....53 C2
Shanklin PO37 ....43 C7
Palmerston Road Prec ■
.........................53 C2
Palmyra Rd PO12 ....52 A8
Pamplyn Cl SO41 ....48 C4
Pan Cl PO30 ....20 E6
Pan La
Newport PO30 ....20 F6
Niton PO38 ....45 B4
Pannall Rd PO12 ....52 A8
Pan St PO1 ....54 B4
Parade The
Cowes PO31 ....3 B5
Portsmouth PO1 ....53 A6
Paradise Cotts PO38 ....45 D8
Paradise St PO1 ....54 B4
Parham Rd PO12 ....52 C7
Parish Ct SO41 ....48 E4
Park Ave
Lymington SO41 ....48 D4
Ventnor PO38 ....46 F5
Park Ct 17 PO5 ....19 F7
Park Court Flats ■ SO15 .50 C6
Park Cl
Cowes PO31 ....3 A5
Portsmouth PO5 ....54 B1
Parkers Hill PO40 ....14 F1
Park Gate PO32 ....3 E2
Park Ho Ro PO5 ....53 C2
PARKHURST 9 A3
Parkhurst Rd PO30 ......9 A2
Park La
Nettlestone PO34 ....13 C1
Shorwell PO30 ....39 B8
■ Southampton SO15 ..50 F5
Parkland Pl 15 SO17 ....51 A8

Parklands Ave PO31 .....2 F4
Parklands Cl PO12 ......52 B7
Parkmead Ct PO33 ......12 D5
Park Mews PO36 ....35 E6
Park Rd
Brading PO36 ....24 A3
Cowes PO31 ....2 F2
Gosport PO12 ....52 B4
Lymington SO41 ....48 D4
Portsmouth PO1 ....53 B5
Ryde PO33 ....12 D5
Shanklin PO37 ....43 D8
Wootton Bridge PO33 ...10 E3
Park Row PO36 ....35 E5
Parkside The SO16 ......50 A8
Park St
Gosport PO12 ....52 B6
Portsmouth PO5 ....54 A2
Southampton SO15 .....50 B8
Parkstone Ave PO4 .....53 E2
Park Terrs 11 PO12 .....52 C5
Park View PO33 ....10 C3
Park View Cl PO38 ......42 B5
Parkway
Freshwater PO40 ....15 A2
Ryde PO33 ....11 E4
Park Way PO36 ....34 F4
Park Wlk SO14 ....51 A5
Parsonage Rd
Southampton SO14 ......51 C6
Partlands Ave PO33 .....12 B4
Partlands Cl PO33 ......12 B4
Partridge Rd PO30 ......9 A2
Paulsgrove Rd PO2 .....53 F8
Pavilion Ct 14 SO15 ....50 E7
Pavilion Rise PO33 ......12 E5
Pavilion Way PO12 ......50 C6
Payne's Rd SO15 ....51 A6
Peacock Cl PO37 ....43 A7
Peacock Hill PO35 ......25 A1
Peacock La PO1 ....53 A3
Pearce Ct PO12 ....52 C6
Pearmain Dr ■ SO41 ...48 E2
Pearman Ct SO41 ....48 E2
Peartree Ave SO19 .....51 E5
Peartree Cl SO19 ....51 D4
Pear Tree Cl PO33 ......12 A3
Peartree Ct
7 Lymington SO41 .....48 E2
Southampton SO19 .....51 E4
Peartree Rd SO19 ......51 D4
Peel Pl PO5 ....54 B2
Peel Rd PO12 ....52 C5
Peggotty Ho 22 PO1 ....53 D7
Pelham Cl PO30 ....25 C4
PELHAMFIELD 12 B6
Pelham Rd
Cowes PO31 ....3 B3
Gosport PO12 ....52 B6
Portsmouth PO5 ....54 B1
Ventnor PO38 ....46 D5
Pellhurst Rd PO33 ......12 B4
Pell La PO33 ....11 F4
Pellview Cl PO33 ....11 F4
Pemberley Ct PO36 .....35 D4
Pembroke Cl PO1 ....53 A3
Pembroke Rd PO1 ......53 A3
Penhale Inf Sch PO1 ....53 E5
Penhale Rd PO1 ....53 E5
PENNINGTON 48 B1
Pennington Cl SO41 ....48 D2
Pennington Cross SO41 .48 D2
Pennington Inf Sch SO41 .48 C3
Pennington Jun Sch
SO41 ....48 C3
Pennington Oval SO41 ..48 B2
Penny Ct 7 PO12 ....52 C6
Penny St PO1 ....53 A3
Pepys Cl
Gosport PO12 ....52 B2
Portsmouth PO4 ....53 F3
Percival Rd PO4 ....53 F8
Percy Chandler St PO1 ..54 C4
Percy Rd
Gosport PO12 ....52 C5
Portsmouth PO5 ....53 E4
Sandown PO36 ....35 D4
Southampton SO16 .....50 A8
Perkins Ho 3 PO1 ......53 B5
Perowne Way PO36 .....35 E7
Perseus Terr 8 PO1 .....53 A4
Perth Ho PO1 ....53 B5
Peterborough Rd SO14 ..51 A7
Petersfield Ho PO1 .....54 C4
Petersham Ho 5 PO5 ...53 D1
Petticoat La PO30 ....20 D7
Pettinger Gdns SO17 ...51 D8
Peveril Rd SO19 ....51 E4
Phoenix Flats PO22 .....3 C3
Pickwick Ho 12 PO1 ....54 B2
Picton Ho 16 PO5 ......54 B2
Pierhead Rd PO2 ....53 A8
Pier Rd
East Cowes PO32 ....3 F3
Portsmouth PO1 ....53 B3
Seaview PO34 ....13 E3
Pierrellen Gdns PO37 ...35 C1
Pier St
Sandown PO36 ....35 F5
Ventnor PO38 ....47 A6
Yarmouth PO41 ....15 C6
Pilgrim Pl SO41 ....48 E3

Pinegrove Rd SO19 .....51 F4
Pine Ridge Ct PO39 .....14 C1
Pinetops Cl SO41 ....48 B3
Pine Tree Cl PO33 ......2 E5
Pineview Dr PO30 ....19 F6
Pink Rd PO2 ....53 E8
Pipit Cl PO12 ....52 B8
Pippin Cl 8 SO41 ....48 E2
Pippins Cl PO30 ....30 A2
Pippins The PO31 ....3 A3
Pirelli St SO15 ....50 F4
Pitt Place La PO30 ......29 E3
Pitt Rd SO15 ....50 C6
Pitts La PO33 ....11 F6
Pitt St PO33 ....12 B4
Pitts The PO38 ....47 D7
Pixley Hill PO40 ....15 A4
Place Rd PO31 ....2 F2
Place Side PO31 ....2 F2
Plaish La PO30 ....19 E3
Planet Ice PO33 ....12 D7
Plantation Ct SO41 .....48 D4
Platform Rd SO14 ......51 A2
Player St PO33 ....12 B4
Playfair Rd PO5 ....54 C2
Play La PO33 ....12 A4
Playstreet La PO33 .....12 A4
Plover Cl PO36 ....35 C3
Plymouth St PO5 ....54 B2
Poleclose La PO30 ......19 E7
Poles La SO41 ....48 B5
POLYGON 50 E6
Polygon Sch SO15 ......50 E6
Polygon The SO15 ......50 E6
Pomona Rd PO37 ....43 C7
Pompey Ctr PO4 ....53 F5
Pompey Ctr Trad Pk The
PO4 ....53 F5
Pondcast La PO33 ......11 C1
Pond La PO34 ....13 C3
PONDWELL 13 A3
Pondwell Cl PO33 ......13 B3
Pondwell Hill PO33 .....13 A3
Ponsonby Ho PO5 ......54 B2
Poole Rd SO19 ....51 E4
Popham Rd PO37 ....43 C6
Poplar Cl PO35 ....25 F4
Poplar Rd SO19 ....51 F6
Poplars The
Bembridge PO35 ....25 D4
Fishbourne PO33 ....11 B6
Porchester Rd SO19 ....51 E3
PORCHFIELD 7 D3
Porchfield Bsns Pk PO30 .7 B1
Portchester Rd PO2 .....53 E8
Porter Ave PO36 ....35 D3
Porter Ct PO36 ....35 D3
Porter's La SO14 ....50 F3
Portland Bldgs 5 PO12 ..52 C5
Portland Ho 7 PO12 ....52 D5
Portland Rd PO5 ....53 C2
Portland St
Newport PO30 ....20 D6
Portsmouth PO1 ....53 B5
Southampton SO14 ....50 F4
Portland Terr
2 Portsmouth PO5 .....53 C2
Southampton SO14 ....50 F4
Port La Salle PO41 .....15 F6
PORTMORE 49 A7
Port Royal St PO5 ......54 C4
PORTSEA 53 B6
PORTSEA ISLAND 53 F6
Portside Cl SO40 ....50 A3
PORTSMOUTH 54 A4
Portsmouth Cath* PO1 ..53 A3
Portsmouth City Mus &
Gallery* PO1 ....53 B3
Portsmouth Gram Sch ■
PO1 ....53 B3
Portsmouth Gram Sch 5
PO1 ....53 B3
Portsmouth Harbour Sta
PO1 ....52 F6
Portsmouth High Sch
26 Portsmouth PO5 ....53 C2
Portsmouth & Southsea Sta
PO1 ....54 B3
Portswood Ave SO17 ...51 B8
PORTSWOOD PARK 51 B8
Portswood Pk SO17 ....51 B8
Postern Cl SO14 ....51 B8
Postern Rd PO10 ....8 F1
POUND GREEN 27 B8
Pound La
Calbourne PO30 ....18 B5
Shorwell PO30 ....31 A1
Ventnor PO38 ....47 A6
Pound Mead PO33 ......22 A4
Pound Rd SO41 ....48 B2
Pounds Terr PO31 ......53 A6
Pound Tree Rd SO14 ...51 A4
Powell Cl PO30 ....21 B7
Powell Ho PO30 ....20 E7
Powell Sq 8 PO1 ....53 A5
Power Rd PO1 ....53 E6
Powerscourt Rd PO2 ...53 E8
Powlett Rd SO41 ....48 E3
Poynings Cl PO1 ....53 A3
Presidents Ct 12 PO12 ..52 C9
Preston Cl PO33 ....12 D3
Preston Rd
Bembridge PO35 ....25 D4

Preston Rd continued
Portsmouth PO2 . . . . .53 F8
Pretoria Rd PO4 . . . . .53 F3
PRIDDY'S HARD 52 C8
Priestlands La SO41 . . . . .48 C3
Priestlands Pl SO41 . . . . .48 D3
Priestlands Rd SO41 . . . . . . .48 C3
Priestlands St SO41 . . . . .48 D2
Prince Alfred St PO12 . . . . . .52 B4
Prince George St PO1 . . . . . .53 A5
Princelett Shute PO36 . . . . . .34 D3
Prince of Wales Ave SO15 . .50 A8
Prince of Wales Entrance
PO32 . . . . .3 E2
Prince of Wales Rd 3
PO12 .52 C5
Prince Regent Ct PO5 . . . . . .54 B2
Princes Ct 3 . . . . .14 E1
Princes Ct 2 SO14 . . . . .51 C6
Prince's Ct 4 PO1 . . . . .53 D7
Prince's Espl PO31 . . . . .2 D5
Princes Ho
Portsmouth PO5 . . . . .54 A1
3 Southampton SO14 . . . . . .51 C6
Prince's Pl 1 PO1 . . . . .53 D7
Princes Rd
Freshwater PO40 . . . . .14 E1
Southampton SO15 . . . . .50 D6
Princess Cl PO32 . . . . .3 D3
Princess Royal St SO41 . . . .48 D4
Princes St PO31 . . . . .3 A4
Prince's St
Portsmouth PO1 . . . . .53 D7
Southampton SO14 . . . . .51 C6
Prince St PO33 . . . . .12 C5
Princes Way PO37 . . . . .35 C2
Prior Cres PO30 . . . . .9 A3
Priors Wlk PO30 . . . . .20 B7
Priory Coll PO4 . . . . .54 D2
Priory Ct
Portsmouth PO5 . . . . .54 D2
Ventnor PO38 . . . . .46 F6
Priory Dr PO4 . . . . .13 D1
Priory Farm La PO30 . . . . . . .20 B5
Priory Ho 6 SO14 . . . . .51 A5
Priory Rd
Carisbrooke PO30 . . . . .20 A5
Gosport PO12 . . . . .52 B9
Gosport PO12 . . . . .52 C9
Shanklin PO37 . . . . .43 C6
Southampton, St Denys
SO17 .51 C8
Southampton, St Denys
SO17 .51 C8
Priors Dell PO37 . . . . .43 C5
Priory Wlk PO38 . . . . .46 F6
Pritchetts Way PO38 . . . . . . .33 A5
Private Rd SO41 . . . . .48 E5
Privett Ho PO1 . . . . .53 A6
Proctor La PO1 . . . . .53 F5
Prospect Bsns Ctr The
PO31 . . . . .2 F2
Prospect Cl
Cowes PO31 . . . . .2 F2
Newport PO30 . . . . .20 E6
Portsmouth PO1 . . . . .53 C7
Shanklin PO37 . . . . .43 C7
Providence Ct 2 PO1 . . . . . . .53 C7
Puckaster La PO38 . . . . .45 B2
Puckpool Cl PO33 . . . . .13 A4
Puckpool Hill PO33, PO34 . .13 A4
Puckwell La PO38 . . . . .45 B4
Pump House La PO32 . . . . . . .3 D2
Pump La PO35 . . . . .25 C6
Purbrook Rd PO1 . . . . .53 E5
Purdy Rd PO30 . . . . .20 B6
Pursley Cl PO36 . . . . .35 C5
Pycroft Cl SO19 . . . . .51 F5
Pye St PO1 . . . . .54 B4
PYLE 44 C7
Pyle Shute PO38 . . . . .39 F2
Pyle St PO30 . . . . .20 D7
Pylewell Park Gdns*
SO41 .49 E4
Pyramids La PO5 . . . . .53 D1
Pyrford Gdns 3 SO41 . . . . . .48 E2
Pyrford Mews SO41 . . . . .48 E2

Q

Quarr Abbey* PO33 . . . . .11 C6
Quarr Cl PO33 . . . . .11 E5
Quarr Hill PO33 . . . . .11 D5
Quarr Pl PO33 . . . . .11 E5
Quarr Rd PO33 . . . . .11 B6
Quarry La PO30 . . . . .17 F4
Quarry Rd PO33 . . . . .12 C4
Quarryside PO30 . . . . .20 D5
Quarry View PO30 . . . . .9 F1
Quarry View Ct PO30 . . . . .8 F1
Quarterdeck The PO1 . . . . . . .52 E6
Quay 2000 SO14 . . . . .51 C8
Quay Hill SO41 . . . . .48 F4
Quay La PO36 . . . . .24 B3
Quay Rd SO41 . . . . .48 F4
**Quays 'Eddie Read'
Swimming & Diving
Complex The** SO15 . . . . . . .50 F3
Quayside Rd SO18 . . . . .51 D7
Quay St
Lymington SO41 . . . . .48 F4
Newport PO30 . . . . .20 E7
5 Yarmouth PO41 . . . . .15 C6

Queen Elizabeth Ave
SO41 .48 D4
Queen Katherine Rd SO41 .48 F3
QUEEN'S BOWER 35 F1
Queens Cl PO40 . . . . .27 B8
Queen's Cres PO5 . . . . .54 B1
Queen's Ct
East Cowes PO32 . . . . .3 D2
Southampton SO15 . . . . .50 E6
Queen's Dr PO36 . . . . .24 A3
Queens Gate
East Cowes PO32 . . . . .3 D3
Portsmouth PO1 . . . . .53 B2
Queen's Gr PO5 . . . . .54 B1
Queens Ho 2 SO14 . . . . .51 A3
Queens Keep
2 Portsmouth PO5 . . . . .53 C2
4 Portsmouth SO15 . . . . . . .50 F5
QUEENSLAND 51 B5
Queen's Pl PO5 . . . . .54 B1
Queens Rd
Freshwater PO40 . . . . .27 B8
Newport PO30 . . . . .20 E5
Queen's Rd
Bembridge PO35 . . . . .25 D5
Cowes PO31 . . . . .3 A6
Gosport PO12 . . . . .52 C5
Portsmouth, Buckland PO2 . .53 E8
Portsmouth PO1 . . . . .52 F7
Ryde PO33 . . . . .12 B5
Sandown PO36 . . . . .35 F6
Shanklin PO37 . . . . .43 C7
Queen St
Lymington SO41 . . . . .48 D3
Portsmouth PO1 . . . . .53 A5
Queen's Terr
Portsmouth PO5 . . . . .54 B1
Southampton SO14 . . . . .51 A3
Queenstown Rd SO15 . . . . . . .50 D6
Queensway SO14 . . . . .51 A3
Queen's Way PO5 . . . . .54 B1
Queens Wlk PO12 . . . . .12 F4
Quinton Cl PO5 . . . . .54 C2

R

Racecourse PO32 . . . . .10 A4
Radcliffe Ct SO14 . . . . .51 B5
Radcliffe Rd SO14 . . . . .51 B6
Radnor St PO5 . . . . .54 B2
Radstock Rd SO19 . . . . .51 E3
Radway Cres SO15 . . . . .50 D8
Raglan Ct PO12 . . . . .52 A5
Raglan St PO5 . . . . .54 C3
Railway Flats PO1 . . . . .53 E5
Railway Ho SO14 . . . . .51 B2
Railway View Rd SO17 . . . . . .51 C8
Rainbow Pl SO15 . . . . .50 C6
Raleigh Ho 37 PO1 . . . . .53 A5
Ramillies Ho 16 PO12 . . . . . . .52 C5
Ramley Rd SO41 . . . . .48 B3
Rampart Rd SO18 . . . . .51 D7
Rampart Row SO41 . . . . .48 E5
Rampart The SO41 . . . . .48 D5
Ranalagh Dr PO33 . . . . .11 B6
Randolph St SO15 . . . . .50 C7
Ranelagh Ct 9 SO17 . . . . . . .51 A8
Ranelagh Gdns SO15 . . . . . . .50 E7
Ranelagh Rd PO36 . . . . .35 E4
Ranger Cl SO14 . . . . .51 B2
Rashley Mews SO41 . . . . .48 E3
Ratcliffe Ave PO33 . . . . .12 B4
Raven Croft PO5 . . . . .54 B1
Raven Rd SO14 . . . . .51 B6
Ravenscourt Rd SO41 . . . . . .48 D2
Ravenswood Gdns 12
PO5 . . . . .53 D2
Rawlinson Terr PO1 . . . . .53 A6
Raymond Rd SO15 . . . . .50 D7
Rayners PO38 . . . . .46 E7
Rebecca Ct 16 PO30 . . . . .20 D6
Recreation Ground Rd
PO30 .20 C6
Rectory Cl
Gosport PO12 . . . . .52 A3
Wootton PO33 . . . . .10 E5
Rectory Dr PO33 . . . . .10 E5
Rectory La
Brighstone PO30 . . . . .30 B2
Gatcombe PO30 . . . . .32 C8
Niton PO38 . . . . .45 B4
Rectory Rd
Niton PO38 . . . . .45 B4
Shanklin PO37 . . . . .43 C6
Redan The PO12 . . . . .52 C2
Redcliff Cl PO36 . . . . .36 C5
Redhill Ho PO1 . . . . .54 C4
Redhill La PO38 . . . . .42 A6
Red House Mews SO41 . . . . .48 E3
Redlake Rd PO40 . . . . .14 B2
Redlands Dr SO19 . . . . .51 F6
Redmoor Cl SO19 . . . . .51 F6
Rednal Ho PO5 . . . . .54 C3
Red Rd PO33 . . . . .10 F5
Redshank Way PO30 . . . . .9 E4
Redstart Cl PO30 . . . . .9 E4
Redstone Bsns Ctr PO36 . . . .36 A4
Redver Gdns PO30 . . . . .20 D8
Redvers Cl SO41 . . . . .48 D2
Redwing Cl PO30 . . . . .20 B6
Redwing Quay PO35 . . . . .25 C5
Redwood Cl
Carisbrooke PO30 . . . . .20 B7
Lymington SO41 . . . . .48 D5
Reed's Pl PO12 . . . . .52 B7
Reeds Rd PO12 . . . . .52 B8
Reed St PO33 . . . . .12 D4

Reeth Flats PO38 . . . . .45 B2
Regency Ct 15 PO1 . . . . .53 A4
Regency Ct 2 PO1 . . . . .53 D7
Regent Pl PO5 . . . . .54 A1
Regents Ct 8 SO16 . . . . .50 B8
Regent's Gr 1 SO16 . . . . .50 B8
Regents Park Com Coll 3
SO16 .50 A8
Regent's Park Gdns SO15 . .50 A8
Regent's Park Rd SO15 . . . . .50 A7
Regents Pl PO12 . . . . .52 D7
Regent St
Portsmouth PO1 . . . . .53 C7
Shanklin PO37 . . . . .43 C8
Southampton SO14 . . . . .50 F4
Regina Rd PO40 . . . . .15 A1
Reigate Ho PO1 . . . . .54 B4
Reldas The 2 PO1 . . . . .53 A3
Renny Rd PO1 . . . . .53 F5
Renouf Cl SO41 . . . . .48 C3
Renown Ho 18 PO12 . . . . .52 C5
Resolution Ho 14 PO12 . . . . .52 C5
Retreat The PO5 . . . . .54 B1
Revenge Ho 3 PO12 . . . . .52 C5
Rew Cl PO38 . . . . .44 D4
Rew Down Nature Reserve*
PO38 .46 E5
Rew La PO38 . . . . .46 D7
Rew St
Cowes PO31 . . . . .2 D2
Gurnard PO31 . . . . .2 D2
REW STREET 2 C1
Rew Valley Sp Ctr PO38 . . . .46 E7
Reynolds Cl PO31 . . . . .2 F4
Reynolds Rd
Gosport PO12 . . . . .52 C3
Southampton SO15 . . . . .50 C8
Rhododendron Wlk PO42 . . . .4 B2
Riboleau St PO33 . . . . .12 C5
Ricardo Way SO41 . . . . .48 D7
Richmond Ho 1 SO16 . . . . . .50 E4
Richmond Meade PO40 . . . . .14 E1
Richmond Pl
Portsmouth, Portsea PO1 . . . .53 B5
Portsmouth, Southsea PO5 . .53 C2
Richmond Rd
Gosport PO12 . . . . .52 A5
Portsmouth PO5 . . . . .53 D2
Southampton SO15 . . . . .50 C6
Southampton SO14 . . . . .51 B3
Richmond Terr 17 PO5 . . . . . .53 C2
Richville Rd SO16 . . . . .50 A8
Ridge The PO31 . . . . .9 B8
Ridget La PO30 . . . . .29 C3
Ridgeway La SO41 . . . . .48 D1
Ridgeway The PO36 . . . . .35 F7
Rigby Rd SO17 . . . . .51 B8
Ringbury SO41 . . . . .48 C6
Ringwood Rd PO33 . . . . .11 F5
Rink Rd PO33 . . . . .12 D5
Rink Rd Ind Est PO33 . . . . . . .12 E5
Ripplewood SO40 . . . . .50 A1
Riverbourne Ct SO18 . . . . . . .51 D8
River Ct SO41 . . . . .48 F4
Riverdene Rd SO18 . . . . .51 D8
River Rd PO41 . . . . .15 C6
Riverside Bsns Pk SO41 . . . .48 F4
Riverside Ct
Southampton, Bitterne Manor
SO18 .51 C7
Southampton, Bitterne
SO18 .51 D8
Rivers Reach SO41 . . . . .48 F3
River's St PO5 . . . . .54 C2
River View PO32 . . . . .9 F8
River View Ho SO19 . . . . .51 D3
Riverview Pk PO30 . . . . .9 C3
River Way PO30 . . . . .20 D8
**RN Submarine Mus & HMS
Alliance*** PO12 . . . . .52 E4
Road View PO2 . . . . .53 C8
Robere Ho SO19 . . . . .51 D3
Robert Mack Ct 39 PO1 . . . . .53 A5
Roberts Rd SO15 . . . . .50 E5
Robin Ct SO15 . . . . .50 F8
**Robin Hill Countryside
Adventure Pk*** PO30 . . . . .21 F4
Robin Hood St PO30 . . . . .20 E7
Rochester Rd PO4 . . . . .53 F3
Rochester St SO14 . . . . .51 C5
ROCK 30 A4
Rockstone Ct 2 SO14 . . . . . . .51 A6
Rockstone La SO14 . . . . .51 A6
Rockstone Pl SO15 . . . . .50 F6
Rodney Ho 10 PO12 . . . . .52 D5
Roebuck Dr PO12 . . . . .52 C8
Rogate Ho 1 PO1 . . . . .54 C4
Rogers Ct PO37 . . . . .52 B7
Rogerson Cl PO37 . . . . .2 F2
Rogers The PO37 . . . . .35 C2
Rolfs Cl PO35 . . . . .25 C5
Rolla Ct PO30 . . . . .20 D6
Rollesbrook Gdns SO15 . . . .50 E6
Rolls Hill PO31 . . . . .8 A6
Rolls Hill Rd PO31 . . . . .8 B7
Roman Ho SO14 . . . . .51 C7
Romsey Ct SO15 . . . . .50 D6
Ronsons Ct PO31 . . . . .3 A3
Ronstan Gdns PO40 . . . . .15 B2
Rooke Ho 17 PO1 . . . . .53 A5
Rookes La SO41 . . . . .48 E2
Rooke St PO30 . . . . .9 A3
ROOKLEY 32 F5
Rookley Ctry Pk* PO38 . . . .33 A4
ROOKLEY GREEN 32 F4
Rope Quays PO12 . . . . .52 D6
Rope Walk 4 PO31 . . . . .3 A4
Rope Wlk PO34 . . . . .13 D4

Rosalind Ct PO33 . . . . .12 C4
Roseberry Ct PO36 . . . . .35 E5
Rosebrook Ct 4 SO18 . . . . . .51 E7
Rose Cl PO36 . . . . .24 A3
Rose Ct PO30 . . . . .34 E4
Rosemary La
29 Portsmouth PO1 . . . . .53 A5
Ryde PO33 . . . . .12 C3
Rosemary Vineyard*
PO33 .12 C2
Rosemead PO36 . . . . .35 D3
Rosemount PO36 . . . . .35 E4
Rose Rd SO14 . . . . .51 A8
Rosery The PO12 . . . . .52 B2
Rosetta Dr PO32 . . . . .3 C3
Roseway PO36 . . . . .35 D5
Rosewood Gdns SO40 . . . . . .50 A1
Rosida Gdns SO16 . . . . .50 E6
ROSLIN .32 C1
Roslyn Ho PO5 . . . . .54 B1
Rosoman Ct SO19 . . . . .51 F4
Rosoman Ho SO19 . . . . .51 F4
Rosoman Rd SO19 . . . . .51 F4
Rossington Ave SO18 . . . . . .51 E8
Rossington Way SO18 . . . . . .51 F7
Rostrevor La 8 PO4 . . . . .53 E1
Rostrevor Mans 8 PO4 . . . . . .53 E1
Rosyth Rd SO19 . . . . .51 F7
Rotary Ct PO33 . . . . .12 B3
Rotary Ho SO15 . . . . .50 D8
Rothesay Rd PO12 . . . . .52 B4
Rothschild Cl SO19 . . . . .51 E1
ROUD 41 B5
Roud La PO38 . . . . .41 B5
Rougemont PO33 . . . . .12 E4
Roundhouse Ct SO41 . . . . . . .48 D3
Rowan Ct
Portsmouth PO4 . . . . .53 F4
Southampton SO19 . . . . .51 F3
Rowan Gdns PO30 . . . . .20 C7
Rowans Pk SO41 . . . . .48 D3
Rowans The PO33 . . . . .12 D4
Rowantree Dr PO34 . . . . .13 D2
Rowborough La PO36 . . . . . . .24 B4
Rowborough Rd SO18 . . . . . . .51 F8
Rowena Ct PO5 . . . . .54 C2
Rowlands Cross PO33 . . . . . .11 D2
Rowlands La PO33 . . . . .22 E6
Rowridge La PO30 . . . . .19 A2
Roxan Ct 5 SO15 . . . . .50 F7
Royal Cl PO37 . . . . .35 C2
Royal Cres PO36 . . . . .35 F5
Royal Crescent Rd 10
SO14 .51 B3
Royal Entrance PO32 . . . . .3 E3
Royal Exchange PO1 . . . . .20 F7
Royal Mews PO5 . . . . .53 D2
Royal Naval Mus* PO1 . . . . .52 F7
Royal South Hants Hospl
SO14 .51 A6
Royal St PO36 . . . . .35 F5
Royal Wlk PO33 . . . . .12 F5
Rudd Way 15 SO14 . . . . .51 B3
Rudmore Rd PO2 . . . . .53 C8
Rudmore Sq PO2 . . . . .53 B8
Rufflers Way PO33 . . . . .11 F5
Rugby Rd PO5 . . . . .54 C2
Ruskins The PO35 . . . . .25 C5
Russell Ho PO30 . . . . .20 F8
Russell Rd PO30 . . . . .31 B2
Russell St
Gosport PO12 . . . . .52 A7
5 Southampton SO14 . . . . . .51 A3
Russet Cl 3 SO41 . . . . .48 F2
Rustington Ho 3 PO1 . . . . . . .54 B3
Rychris Ct PO37 . . . . .43 C7
Rydal Rd PO12 . . . . .52 A9
RYDE 12 E6
Ryde Bsns Pk PO33 . . . . .12 D3
Ryde Ct 8 PO33 . . . . .12 C5
Ryde Esplanade Sta PO33 . .12 C6
Ryde High Sch PO33 . . . . .12 A4
Ryde House Dr PO33 . . . . .12 C5
Ryde Pier Head Sta PO33 . . .12 C8
Ryde Rd PO34 . . . . .13 D4
Ryde Sch with Upper Chine
PO33 .12 B5
Ryde Terr SO14 . . . . .51 B3

S

Sackville St PO5 . . . . .54 B2
Sadlers Cl PO33 . . . . .12 E4
Sainsbury Lodge PO4 . . . . . . .54 D3
St Agathas Way PO1 . . . . .54 B4
St Alban's Gdns PO38 . . . . . .46 F6
St Albans Rd PO4 . . . . .53 F3
St Alban's Rd
Southampton SO14 . . . . .51 B5
Ventnor PO38 . . . . .46 F6
St Andrews Ho 3 SO17 . . . . .51 B8
St Andrews Rd SO14 . . . . .51 A5
St Andrew's Rd
Gosport PO12 . . . . .52 B5
Portsmouth PO5 . . . . .54 C2
St Andrew's Rd 7 PO31 . . . . . .3 B4
St Andrews Way PO40 . . . . . .14 F2
St Annes Gdns SO41 . . . . .48 D3
St Anne's Gdns SO19 . . . . . . .51 F2
St Annes Mews SO14 . . . . . . .51 A8
St Anne's RC Sch SO19 . . . . .51 F2
St Anne's Rd SO19 . . . . .51 F2
St Ann's Cres PO12 . . . . .52 A7
St Augustine Rd PO4 . . . . .53 F3
St Augustines Rd PO30 . . . . .20 B7
St Barbara PO40 . . . . .14 E3

St Barbe Mus & Art Gall*
SO41 .48 E
St Bartholomew's Sch
PO5 . . . . .54 C
St Bernard Ho 15 SO14 . . . . .51 A
St Boniface CE Prim Sch
PO38 .47 B
St Boniface Cliff Rd PO37 . .37 D
St Boniface Down PO38 . . . . .47 B
St Boniface Rd PO38 . . . . .47 B
St Boniface Terr PO38 . . . . . . .47 B
St Catherine's Lighthouse*
PO38 .44 D
St Catherine's Oratory*
PO38 .44 E
St Catherines Pl PO38 . . . . . . .47 B
St Catherines Rd PO38 . . . . . .51 E
St Catherine's Rd PO38 . . . . .45 A
St Catherine's Sch PO38 . . . .47 A
St Catherine St
Portsmouth PO5 . . . . .53 D
Ventnor PO38 . . . . .47 B
St Catherines View
Godshill PO38 . . . . .41 C
Ventnor PO38 . . . . .47 B
St Christopher Ct 1 PO5 . . . .53 E
St Cross Bsns Pk PO30 . . . . . .9 B
St Cross Ct 1 PO30 . . . . .20 D
St Cross La PO30 . . . . .20 C
St Cyres Memorial Cotts
SO41 .48 F
St David's Rd
East Cowes PO32 . . . . .3 C
Portsmouth PO5 . . . . .54 C
ST DENYS . . . . .51 C
St Denys' Sta SO17 . . . . .51 C
St Edmunds Cl PO38 . . . . .40 A
St Edmunds Cotts PO33 . . . . .10 E
St Edmunds RC Sec Sch
PO1 . . . . .54 C
St Edmund's Rd SO16 . . . . . . .50 B
St Edmund's Wlk PO33 . . . . . .10 E
St Edward's Rd
Gosport PO12 . . . . .52 B
Portsmouth PO5 . . . . .54 B
St Edward's Terr 6 PO12 . . . .52 A
St Faith's Cl PO12 . . . . .52 A
St Faith's Rd
Cowes PO31 . . . . .3 A
Portsmouth PO1 . . . . .54 B
St Francis Rd PO30 . . . . .52 C
St Georges App PO30 . . . . . . .20 E
**St George's Beneficial CE
Prim Sch** 15 PO1 . . . . .53 A
St George's Bsns Ctr 14
PO1 . . . . .53 A
St George's Cl PO33 . . . . .12 C
St George's Dr 1 PO5 . . . . . . .54 A
St George's Ho 2 SO17 . . . . .51 B
St Georges La PO30 . . . . .20 F
St George's Rd
Portsmouth, Old Portsmouth
PO1 . . . . .53 A
Ryde PO33 . . . . .12 B
Shanklin PO37 . . . . .43 C
St Georges Sq PO1 . . . . .53 A
St Georges St SO14 . . . . .51 A
St George's Way SO14 . . . . . .51 A
St Georges Wlk PO12 . . . . . . .52 D
ST HELENS . . . . .24 F
St Helens Cl PO4 . . . . .54 E
St Helen's Mans 7 PO4 . . . . .53 E
St Helen's Par PO4 . . . . .53 E
St Helen's Prim Sch PO33 . .24 F
St Helier Rd PO12 . . . . .52 C
St James Cl
East Cowes PO32 . . . . .3 D
Yarmouth PO41 . . . . .15 C
St James Ct 4 PO30 . . . . .20 D
St James Ho 4 SO14 . . . . .51 A
St James's Rd PO30 . . . . .20 D
St James' Sq 2 PO41 . . . . . . .15 C
St James's Rd
Portsmouth PO5 . . . . .54 B
Southampton SO15 . . . . .50 D
St James' St
Newport PO30 . . . . .20 D
Portsmouth PO1 . . . . .53 B
St James' St
Newport PO30 . . . . .20 D
8 Ryde PO33 . . . . .12 C
Yarmouth PO41 . . . . .15 C
St John's Ave PO33 . . . . .12 D
St John's CE Prim Sch
Gosport PO12 . . . . .52 C
Sandwn PO36 . . . . .35 F
St John's Cl PO30 . . . . .20 D
St John's Cl PO12 . . . . .52 B
St John's Coll PO5 . . . . .54 C
St John's Cres PO30 . . . . .36 A
St John's Hill PO30 . . . . .20 D
St Johns Inf Sch 3 SO14 . . . .50 F
St Johns Mews PO5 . . . . .54 C
ST JOHN'S PARK . . . . .12 E
St John's Pl 9 PO38 . . . . .47 B
St John's RC Cath* PO1 . . . .54 A
St John RC Prim Sch
PO1 . . . . .54 C
St John's Rd
Newport PO30 . . . . .20 D
Ryde PO33 . . . . .12 C
Sandown PO36 . . . . .35 F
Shanklin PO37 . . . . .43 C
Wroxall PO38 . . . . .42 C
St John's Road Sta PO33 . . . .12 D
St John's Sq 8 PO12 . . . . .52 B
St John's Wood Rd PO33 . . . .12 D

t Joseph's Cl P032 . . . . 3 E2
t Josephs Mews P05 . . . . . . 54 C1
t Jude's CE (Controlled)
  Prim Sch P01 . . . . 53 B3
t Judes Ct P05 . . . . 54 B1
t Julien's Hospl
  (Almhouses) S014 . . . . 51 A2
t LAWRENCE 46 A3
t Lawrence Rd 2 S014 . . . 51 B3
t Lawrence Shute P035 . . 46 B4
t Luke's CE Sec Sch P05 54 B3
t Lukes Dr P035 . . . . 25 D4
t Luke's Rd P012 . . . . 52 A7
t Margarets P038 . . . . 46 E7
t Margarets CE Prim Sch
  P038 . . . . 46 E7
t Margarets Gdns P038. .46 E7
t Mark's CE Jun Sch
  S011 . . . . 50 D7
t Mark's Cl P012 . . . . 52 B2
t Marks Ct 1 P012 . . . . . . 52 A6
t Mark's Pl P012 . . . . 52 B3
t Marks Rd
  Lymington S041 . . . . 48 A3
  Southampton S014 . . . . 51 B5
t Mark's Rd P033 . . . . 51 B4
t Mark's Coll S016 . . . . 51 F8
t Mark's Ct P036 . . . . 24 B3
t Mary's Ho P01 . . . . 53 F6
t Mary's Hospl (Newport)
  P030 . . . . 9 A1
t Mary's Hospl
  (Portsmouth) P01 . . . . 53 F6
t Mary's L Ctr S011 . . . . . . 50 C8
t Mary's Pas 5 P033 . . . . 12 C5
t Mary's RC Prim Sch
  Gosport P012 . . . . 52 A6
  Ryde P033 . . . . 12 E5
t Mary's Rd
  Brading P036 . . . . 24 A3
  Cowes P031 . . . . 3 A4
  Portsmouth P01 . . . . 53 F6
  Southampton S014 . . . . 51 A4
t Mary's Stadium
  (Southampton FC) S014 . 51 B5
t Mary St S014 . . . . 51 A5
t Matthews Cl 2 S014 . . 51 A5
t Matthews P012 . . . . 52 D6
2 Michael's Ave P033 . . . 12 B3
t Michaels Cl P030 . . . . 17 F7
t Michaels Rd P033 . . . . . . 51 A4
t Michael's Rd P01 . . . . 54 A2
t Michael's Sq 11 S014 . . 50 F1
t Michael's St 13 S014 . . 50 F1
t Nicholas Cl P030 . . . . 20 D5
t Nicholas St P01 . . . . 53 A2
t Patrick's RC Prim Sch
  S019 . . . . 51 E3
t Paul's Ave P037 . . . . 43 C8
t Paul's Cres P037 . . . . 54 A2
t Paul's Rd P01 . . . . 54 A2
t Paul's Sq P05 . . . . 54 A2
t Paul's View Rd P030 . . 20 E8
t Peter's Gr P05 . . . . 35 F6
t Ronan's Ave P04 . . . . 53 E2
t Ronan's Rd P04 . . . . 53 E2
t Saviors RC Prim Sch
  P039 . . . . 26 H7
t Saviour's Rd 2 P030 . 26 H8
t Simons Rd P05 . . . . 53 D2
t Stephens Rd P02 . . . . 42 B8
t Swithins Cl P041 . . . . . . 15 F6
t Swithins Ct 8 S014 . . 51 A6
t Swithun's RC Prim Sch 10
  P05 . . . . 54 A2
t Thomas of Canterbury RC
  Prim Sch P030 . . . . 20 B5
t Thomas Pk S041 . . . . 48 D3
t Thomas Rd P02 . . . . 3 D4
t Thomas's Cl 1 P01 . . . 53 A4
t Thomas's Sq P033 . . . 12 C6
t Thomas's Rd P012 . . . . . 52 B9
t Thomas's St 6 P030. .20 D7
t Thomas's St
  Lymington S041 . . . . 48 E3
  Portsmouth P01 . . . . 53 A4
t Urians P036 . . . . 13 D6
t Ursula Gr P05 . . . . 54 C1
t Valerie Rd P012 . . . . 52 B4
t Vincent Coll P012 . . . . . . 52 B6
t Vincent Rd
  Gosport P012 . . . . 52 B7
  Portsmouth P05 . . . . 53 D2
t Vincents Cotts P033 . . 12 A5
t Vincent's Rd P033 . . . . . . 12 A5
t Vincent St P05 . . . . 54 A2
t Wilfrids Prim Sch
  P038 . . . . 47 B6
alcombe Rd S015 . . . . 50 C7
alem Rd P012 . . . . 52 A7
alisbury Rd
  Portsmouth P04 . . . . 53 F2
  Ryde P033 . . . . 12 E3
alisbury St 6 S015 . . . . 50 F6
alisbury Way S015 . . . . . 35 F6
alsette Ct P033 . . . . 12 E6
alterne Ho 2 S041 . . . . 48 E3
altern's Rd P034 . . . . 13 D4

Salter's Rd P033. . . . . 12 A3
Saltmarsh Rd S014 . . . . . . 51 B3
Samantha Ct P037 . . . . . . 43 D8
Samber Cl S041 . . . . 48 C4
Samber Hill P030 . . . . 39 A8
Samphire Cl S041 . . . . 48 E5
Sampson Rd P01 . . . . 52 F7
Samuel Rd P01 . . . . 53 F6
Sandcove Rise P034 . . . . . 13 D3
Sandford Barns P038 . . . 41 F8
Sandford Cotts P038 . . . . 41 F8
Sandham Ct P036 . . . . 35 E7
Sandham Gdns P036. . . . 35 C3
Sandham Mid Sch P036. . 35 D6
Sandhurst Cl S041 . . . . . . 54 C1
Sandhurst Rd S015 . . . . . 50 E6
San Diego Rd P012 . . . . . . 52 B7
Sandlands P034 . . . . 13 D3
Sandon Ct P05 . . . . 35 E5
SANDOWN 35 E5
Sandown CE Prim Sch
  P036 . . . . 35 F6
Sandown High School
  P036 . . . . 35 D6
Sandown Rd
  Bembridge P035 . . . . 25 B2
  Brading P035 . . . . 24 D1
  Sandown P036 . . . . 35 D2
  Sandown Sta P036 . . . . . . 35 E5
Sandpath P033 . . . . 11 E5
Sandpiper P04 . . . . 53 E4
Sandpipers P035 . . . . 25 E4
Sandringham Ct
  12 Gosport P012 . . . . 52 D6
  5 Southampton, Millbrook
  S015 . . . . 50 A6
Sandringham La P01 . . . . 54 D3
Sandringham Rd S014 . . 54 D3
Sandringham Rd P038 . . 45 A2
Sandy Cl P030 . . . . 20 F1
Sandy La
  Blackwater P030 . . . . 20 D1
  Cowes P031 . . . . 3 A6
Sandy Way P030 . . . . 31 C1
Sapphire Cl 1 P012 . . . . 52 C8
Saracen Cl S041 . . . . 48 C1
Sarah Robinson Ho 22
  P01 . . . . 53 A5
Sarum Wlk S041 . . . . 48 A5
Saunders Dr P031 . . . . 3 B4
Savoy Country Club P041 .15 A5
Savoy Ct
  Newport P030 . . . . 20 E7
  Sandown P036 . . . . 36 A3
  Shanklin P037 . . . . 43 C7
Saxon Ho 17 S014 . . . . . . 51 C6
Saxon Pl S041 . . . . 48 D6
Saxon Rd S015 . . . . 50 D8
Scarrots La P030 . . . . 20 D7
School Cl P036 . . . . 34 E7
School Cres P038 . . . . 33 D1
SCHOOL GREEN 14 F1
School Green Rd P040 . . 14 F1
School Hill Rd P032 . . . . . 3 C3
School La
  Arreton P030 . . . . 21 F2
  Calbourne P030 . . . . 18 A2
  Carisbrooke P030 . . . . 20 A5
  Lymington S041 . . . . 48 E4
  Lymington, Warborne S041 .48 F8
  Newchurch P036 . . . . 34 E7
  Newport P030 . . . . 20 D7
  Niton P038 . . . . 45 B4
  Wootton P033 . . . . 10 F5
School Pl S019 . . . . 51 E4
School Rd P038 . . . . 41 D8
School Rd P033 . . . . 12 D4
Scinde Cres P037 . . . . 43 C8
Sconce Rd P041 . . . . 15 A6
Scotchells Brook La P036 35 B4
Scotchell's Cl P037 . . . . . . 35 C2
Scott Rd
  Portsmouth, Portsea Island
  P01 . . . . 52 F7
  Southampton S019 . . . . . . 51 F1
Scotts Cl S017 . . . . 17 E7
Scout La 6 S014 . . . . 50 F4
Sea Breeze Cotts P030 . . 29 F1
Sea Cl
  Ryde P033 . . . . 12 B6
  Sandown P036 . . . . 35 D2
SEAFIELD 52 D4
Seafield Rd P034 . . . . 13 D4
Seafield Terr P012 . . . . . . 52 D5
Seager's Ct P01 . . . . 52 F4
Seagrove Ct P034 . . . . 13 D3
Seagrove Dr P036 . . . . 35 F6
Seagrove Farm Rd P034 .13 D3
Seagrove Manor P034 . . . 13 D3
Seagrove Manor Rd P034 13 D3
Seahorse Wlk P012 . . . . . . 52 D6
Sealark Rd P012 . . . . 52 B8
Sea Mill Gdns 59 P033 . . 53 A5
Sea Rd S019 . . . . 51 D4
Searle Ct P033 . . . . 12 D4
Sea St P030 . . . . 20 E7
Seaton Cl S041 . . . . 48 E5
SEAVIEW 13 E5
Seaview Cotts 2 P039. .14 F1
Seaview Ho P033 . . . . 13 E3
Seaview La P034 . . . . 13 D3
Seaview Rd P031 . . . . 3 A3
Sea View Rd
  Cranmore P041 . . . . 5 E2
  Totland P040 . . . . 14 D2

Seaview Wildlife Encounter*
  P034 . . . . 13 B4
Seaward Gdns S019 . . . . . 51 E4
Seaward Rd S019 . . . . 51 E4
Seaward Twr 8 P012 . . . 52 E5
Sedgeley Gr P012 . . . . 52 A8
Sedgley Cl P05 . . . . 54 C2
Selborne Gdns P012 . . . . . 52 A5
Selbourne Terr S014 . . . . 54 D3
Seldon Ave P033 . . . . 12 F4
Selhurst Ho P01 . . . . 54 C4
Sellwood Rd P040 . . . . 27 E7
Selma Cl 11 P05 . . . . 53 D2
Selman Gdns P012 . . . . . . 8 F8
Selsey Ave P012 . . . . 52 A9
Selsey View P037 . . . . 35 D1
Selwyn Ct P033 . . . . 25 A6
Senator Ind Est P036 . . . 36 A5
Serpentine Rd 7 P05. .53 D2
Settle Cl 3 S016 . . . . . . 50 B8
Settlers Cl P01 . . . . 54 C4
Seven Sisters Cl P038. . 46 A3
Seven Sisters Rd P038 . . 46 A4
Seymour Cl P02 . . . . 53 D7
Seymour Cl 1 P012 . . . . . 3 C4
Seymour Pl P035 . . . . 25 C6
Shaftesbury Rd
  Gosport P012 . . . . 52 C4
  Portsmouth, Southsea P05. 53 C2
Shaftsbury Rd P012 . . . . . 52 C4
Shakespeare Ave P037 . . 51 B8
Shakespeare Rd P01 . . . . 53 E7
Shakespeare Terr 12 P01. 53 A3
Shalbourne Rd P012 . . . . 52 A8
SHALCOMBE 29 A8
SHALFLEET 17 D7
Shalfleet CE Prim Sch
  P041 . . . . 17 B7
Shallow La S041 . . . . 48 A5
Shamblers Rd P031 . . . . . . 3 B3
Shamrock Cl P012 . . . . 52 D5
Shamrock Quay S014 . . . 51 C5
Shamrock Rd S019 . . . . . . 51 D3
SHANKLIN 43 D7
Shanklin CE Prim Sch
  P037 . . . . 43 B7
Shanklin Chine* P037 . . 43 C7
Shanklin Rd
  Godshill P038 . . . . 41 F8
  Shanklin P04 . . . . 53 E4
  Shanklin P037 . . . . 42 F7
Shanklin Sta P037 . . . . . . 43 C8
Shanklin Theatre* P037 .43 C7
Shanklin Twrs P037 . . . . . 43 C7
Shannon Ct 7 P012 . . . . 53 D3
Shannon Ho 9 S014 . . . 51 C5
Shaplands 5 P033 . . . . . 12 A6
Sharon Ct
  Cowes P031 . . . . 3 A6
  4 Gosport P012 . . . . 52 C6
Sharon Orchard* P033 . . 12 C1
Shearer Rd P01 . . . . 54 D4
Sheat Farm Ind Est P030 .32 C6
Sheffield Rd P01 . . . . 54 D3
Sheilings The P040 . . . . . . 14 E2
Shelley Ct S015 . . . . 50 C8
Shepheard's Way P01 . . . 52 C3
Shepherd Mews 2 P033 .12 C6
Shepherds' La P030 . . . . . 38 B8
Sherborne St P035 . . . . . . 25 C5
Sherbourne Ave P033 . . . 12 A5
Sherfield Ho 10 S015 . . . 50 E7
Sherwin Wlk P012 . . . . . . 52 A4
Sherwood Rd
  Gosport P012 . . . . 52 A5
  Newport P030 . . . . 9 A1
Shide Chalk Pit Nature
  Reserve* P030. . . . . 20 F5
Shide Cross P030 . . . . 20 D5
Shide Ct P030 . . . . 20 E5
Shide Rd P030 . . . . 20 E5
Shide Villa P030 . . . . 20 E5
Shiner Ct P034 . . . . 13 C2
Shipbuilding Rd P01 . . . . . 52 F8
Ship Leopard St 12 P01. 53 A5
Shippards Rd P030 . . . . . . 30 A2
SHIRLEY 50 C8
Shirley Ave S015 . . . . 50 C8
Shirley Bsns Pk S015 . . . 50 C8
Shirley High St S015,
  S016 . . . . 50 B8
Shirley Park Rd S016 . . . 50 B8
Shirley Rd
  Portsmouth P05 . . . . 54 C2
  Southampton S015 . . . . . . 50 C7
Shirley Twrs S015 . . . . . . 50 C8
Sholing Rd S019 . . . . 51 E4
Sholing Sta S019 . . . . 51 F2
Shooters Hill P031 . . . . 3 B4
Shore Hill P038 . . . . 47 A5
Shore Path P031 . . . . 2 E4
Shore Rd
  Grand P031 . . . . 2 D4
  Ventnor P038 . . . . 47 D6
Short Row P01 . . . . 53 A6
SHORWELL 31 B3
Shorwell Shute P030 . . . . 31 B4
Shotts La S041 . . . . 49 C4
Shrewsbury Ct P034 . . . . 13 D3
Shrubbery Dr P033 . . . . . . 11 E5
Shrub's Ave S041 . . . . 48 E4
Shute The P036 . . . . 34 E8
Sibden Hill & Batts Copse
  Nature Reserve* P037 .43 A7
Sibden Mews P037 . . . . . . 43 A7
Sibden Rd P037 . . . . 43 B7
Sidings The P037 . . . . 43 A7
Silcombe La P040 . . . . 14 E1

Silver Birch Dr P030 . . . . . 20 B7
Silverdale Cl S015 . . . . . . 50 E7
Silverdale Rd S015 . . . . . . 50 E7
Silver St 1 P05 . . . . 54 A1
Silver Trees P037 . . . . 43 A7
Simeon St P033 . . . . 12 D6
Simmonds Cl P040 . . . . . . 27 C7
Simnel St 8 S014 . . . . . . 50 F3
Sirenia Cl P030 . . . . 30 A2
Sir George's Rd S015 . . . 50 D6
Sirius Cl P034 . . . . 13 D2
Sirius Ct P034 . . . . 13 D2
Sirius Ho 10 P05 . . . . 54 A1
Sir Max Aitken Mus* P031 . 3 B5
Six Cotts P032 . . . . 10 A7
Six Dials S014 . . . . 51 A5
Skinner's Hill P036 . . . . . . 34 F6
Skipper Cl S040 . . . . 50 A3
Slade Rd P033 . . . . 12 A4
Slay La P038 . . . . 45 D7
Slindon St P01 . . . . 54 B3
Slingsby Cl P01 . . . . 54 A1
Slipway The P031 . . . . 2 F3
Sloane Stanley Ct P012 . 52 B7
Slocum Ho 18 P012 . . . . 52 C5
Sloop La S015 . . . . 10 F5
Smallbrook Junction*
  P033 . . . . 12 D2
Smallbrook La P033 . . . . . 12 D2
Smallbrook Stadium
  P033 . . . . 12 C1
Smart's Cross P038 . . . . . . 41 C4
Smithards La P033 . . . . 3 B3
Smith St P012 . . . . 52 A6
Snook's Hill P030 . . . . 20 E7
Snooks La S041 . . . . 49 B6
Snowberry Rd P030 . . . . . 20 C7
Snowdrop La P030 . . . . . . 32 A8
Soberton Ho P01 . . . . 54 C4
Solent Ave S041 . . . . 49 A3
Solent Bsns Ctr S015 . . . 50 B6
Solent Cl
  Lymington S041 . . . . 48 F3
  Ryde P033 . . . . 12 F5
Solent Ct
  82 Portsmouth P05 . . . . . . 53 C2
  Southampton S019 . . . . . . 51 E1
  Totland P040 . . . . 14 D2
Solent Gate 12 P05 . . . . . 53 E1
Solent Gdns
  Freshwater P040 . . . . 14 E2
  Ryde P033 . . . . 11 F5
Solent Hill P030 . . . . 14 F3
Solent Ind Ctr S015 . . . . 50 C6
Solent Landing P035 . . . . 25 C6
Solent Mead S041 . . . . . . 48 E3
Solent Mid Sch P031 . . . . 2 E4
Solent Rd
  Cranmore P041 . . . . 5 E1
  Southampton S015 . . . . . . 50 E4
Solent View
  Bembridge P035 . . . . 25 D5
  Totland P040 . . . . 14 D2
  Walhampton S041 . . . . 49 B3
Solent View Cl P034 . . . . 13 D3
Solent View Rd
  Gurnard P031 . . . . 2 D3
  Seaview P034 . . . . 13 D2
Solihull Ho P05 . . . . 54 A2
Solway Ho 10 S014 . . . . 51 C6
Somborne Ho S019 . . . . . 51 F1
Somerset Cl 6 S015. . . . 50 C6
Somerset Rd
  Portsmouth P05 . . . . 53 D1
  Ryde P033 . . . . 12 E3
  Seaview P034 . . . . 13 D3
Somerset Terr S015 . . . . . 50 C6
Somers Park Prim Sch
  P05 . . . . 54 C2
Somers Rd
  Portsmouth P05 . . . . 54 C3
  Portsmouth P05 . . . . 54 C3
Somers Road N P01 . . . . 54 C3
Somerton Ind Pk P031 . . 3 A2
Somerton Mid Sch P031 . 3 A2
Somervell Cl P012 . . . . . . 52 A3
Somers Ct S017 . . . . 51 C3
SOUTHAMPTON 51 A5
Southampton Central Sta
  S015 . . . . 50 E5
Southampton City Art Gall*
  S014 . . . . 51 A5
Southampton City Coll
  S014 . . . . 51 B4
Southampton Maritime
  Mus* S014 . . . . 50 F3
Southampton Oceanography
  Ctr S014 . . . . 51 B2
Southampton Rd S041 . . 48 D5
Southampton Solent Univ 10
  S014 . . . . 50 F4
Southampton Solent Univ
  Marine Operations Ctr
  S040 . . . . 50 A2
Southampton St 3 S015. 50 E4
Southampton Wr Activity Ctr
  S014 . . . . 51 C3
SOUTH BADDESLEY 49 B4
South Baddesley Prim Sch
  S041 . . . . 49 E6
South Bank Rd P032 . . . . . 3 D2
Southbourne Rd S041. . . 48 C3
Southbrook Rd S015 . . . . 50 B6
Southcliffe Ho 1 S014. . 51 A6
Southcliff Rd S014. . . . . . 51 A7
South Cross St P012 . . . . 52 D5

Southdown P038 . . . . 39 E2
Southdown Mews P040 . . 27 E7
Southdown Rd P040 . . . . . 27 E7
Southern Rd
  Lymington S041 . . . . 48 D3
  Southampton S015 . . . . . . 50 E4
Southfield Gdns P033. . . 12 B3
SOUTHFORD 41 B2
Southford La P038 . . . . . . 45 C8
South Front S014 . . . . 51 A5
South Gr S041 . . . . 48 F3
Southgrove Rd P038 . . . . 47 A6
Southgrove Terr P038 . . . 47 A6
Southlands S041 . . . . 48 C2
Southlands Sch & The Wing
  Ctr S041 . . . . 48 C2
South Mill Rd S015 . . . . . 50 C7
South Normandy 4 P01 . 53 A4
South Parade P05 . . . . 54 A1
South Parade Pier* P04. 53 E1
South Quay P033 . . . . 25 A6
South Rd
  Cowes P031 . . . . 3 B3
  Portsmouth, Portsea Island
  P01 . . . . 53 E7
  Southampton S017 . . . . . . 51 C8
SOUTHSEA 53 C1
Southsea Castle* P05 . . . 53 C1
Southsea Inf Sch 7 P05. 53 E2
Southsea Model Village*
  P04 . . . . 53 F1
Southsea Terr P05 . . . . . . 54 A1
South St
  Gosport P012 . . . . 52 D5
  Lymington S041 . . . . 48 C2
  Newport P030 . . . . 20 E7
  Portsmouth P05 . . . . 54 A1
  10 Ryde P033 . . . . 12 C5
  Ventnor P038 . . . . 47 B6
  Yarmouth P041 . . . . 15 D6
South Terr P01 . . . . 53 A5
South View 4 P04 . . . . . . 53 E2
South View P030 . . . . 20 D6
South View Cotts P038. . 40 A4
South View Rd S015 . . . . 50 D8
Southwick Ho 5 P01 . . . 54 C4
South Wight Sports Ctr
  P036 . . . . 35 D5
Sovereign Ave P012 . . . . . 52 C8
Sovereign Way P033 . . . . 12 B4
Spanners Cl P031 . . . . 3 A2
Spartina Dr S041 . . . . 48 E5
Spear Rd S014 . . . . 51 A8
Speeds La P033 . . . . 11 B1
Spencer Cl P033 . . . . 12 A6
Spencer Ct 2 P05 . . . . . . 53 D2
Spencer Glade P033 . . . . 12 A6
Spencer Rd
  Portsmouth P04 . . . . 53 F2
  Ryde P033 . . . . 12 B6
Spenlow Cl P02 . . . . 53 D8
Spice Quay 1 P01. . . . . . 53 A3
Spicer Ho P01 . . . . 54 A1
Spicer St P01 . . . . 54 B4
Spindleberry Cl P030 . . . . 20 C7
Spindlers Rd P038 . . . . . . 46 A3
Spinnaker Ct 21 P01 . . . 53 A5
Spinnaker Quay P012 . . . 52 F4
Spinnaker Twr* P01 . . . . 52 F5
Spitfire Ct S019 . . . . 51 D3
Spitfire Gr S019 . . . . 51 C4
Spithead Ave P012 . . . . . . 52 C4
Spithead Bsns Ctr P036. 35 C3
Spithead Cl P034 . . . . 13 D3
Spring Cl S019 . . . . 51 F4
Spring Cres S017 . . . . 51 B8
Springfield Cl S041 . . . . . . 49 A3
Springfield Ct S019 . . . . . 51 F2
Springfield Mews P035 . . 35 F5
Spring Firs S019 . . . . 51 E3
Spring Garden La P012 . 52 C6
Spring Gdns
  Portsmouth P01 . . . . 54 A3
  Shanklin P037 . . . . 43 C8
  Ventnor P038 . . . . 47 C6
Springhead P038 . . . . 45 A4
SPRINGHILL 3 E4
Spring Hill P030 . . . . 47 B6
Spring Hill Rd P030 . . . . . 47 B6
Springhill RC Prim Sch
  S015 . . . . 50 D6
Spring La P030 . . . . 20 B5
Spring Rd
  Lymington S041 . . . . 48 D3
  Southampton, Itchen S019 . 51 F4
  Southampton, Merry Oak
  S019 . . . . 51 E4
Spring St P01 . . . . 54 B3
SPRING VALE 13 B4
Springvale Rd P034 . . . . . 13 B5
Spring Wlk
  Newport P030 . . . . 19 F6
  Portsmouth P01 . . . . 54 B4
Square The
  Freshwater Bay P040 . . . . 27 C2
  Gosport P012 . . . . 52 C9
  Lymington S041 . . . . 48 C3
Squires Wlk S019 . . . . 51 E1
Stacey Ct P05 . . . . 53 C1
Stafford Rd
  Portsmouth P05 . . . . 54 C1
  Southampton S015 . . . . . . 50 D6
Stag La P030 . . . . 9 B4

Stag Rd PO36............35 E3
Stainers Cl PO33...........12 C5
Stamford St PO1...........54 D4
Stamford St SO14..........51 B4
Stamford Gdns SO41.......48 D2
Stanford Hill SO41..........48 D3
Stanford Rd SO41..........48 D3
Stanhope Dr PO31............3 A6
Stanhope Gate **1** PO5 ....53 C2
Stanhope Lodge PO41........2 F5
Stanhope Rd PO1..........54 B3
Stanley La PO5...........53 C2
Stanley Rd
    Cowes PO31.............3 B3
    Lymington SO41........49 A2
Stanley St PO5...........53 C2
Stansted Rd PO5...........54 D2
Stanton Bldgs SO15........50 A7
Stanton Rd SO15..........50 A7
Stanton Rd Ind Est SO15 ..50 A7
STAPLERS.................21 A7
Staplers Ct PO30..........20 F7
Staplers Rd PO30..........21 B7
Starkes Ho PO40..........27 C7
Starks Cl PO30............31 B2
Star St PO33.............12 C5
Station App
    25 Portsmouth PO1......53 A5
    Sandown PO36..........35 E5
Station Ave PO36..........35 E5
Station Gdns PO36.........24 B2
Station La PO36...........35 E5
Station Rd
    Ashey PO33............23 B7
    Bembridge PO35........25 C6
    Brading PO36..........24 B3
    Newbridge PO41........17 C4
    Ningwood PO30, PO41 ...17 C4
    Sandown PO36..........35 E5
    Southampton, Sholing SO19 .51 F3
    St Helens PO33........24 F6
    Wootton Bridge PO33 ...10 D3
    Wroxall PO38...........42 C4
Yarmouth PO41............15 D5
Station St
    Lymington SO41........48 F4
    Portsmouth PO1........54 B3
    Ryde PO33.............12 C5
Staunton St PO1...........54 B4
Steel St PO5..............54 A1
STEEPHILL................46 E5
Steephill Court Rd PO38 ..46 D5
Steephill Down Rd PO38 ..46 F6
Steephill Rd
    Shanklin PO37.........43 C4
    Ventnor PO38..........46 E5
Steerforth Cl PO2.........53 D8
Stenbury View PO38.......42 C3
Stephen Lodge PO5........54 B1
Stephenson Cl PO12........52 A3
Stephenson Rd PO31.........3 A3
Steuart Rd SO18...........51 D7
Stewart Cl PO40..........15 A1
Stewart Pl PO1............53 E7
Steyne Cross PO35.........25 C3
Steyne Rd
    Bembridge PO35........25 D4
    Seaview PO34..........13 D3
Stickworth Hall PO30.......33 F7
Stirling St PO2............53 D8
Stoddart Ave SO19.........51 F6
Stoke Gdns PO12..........52 C2
Stoke Rd PO12............52 C5
Stokes Ct **2** SO15.......50 E6
Stokeway **4** PO12........52 C5
Stonechat Ct PO30.........20 B6
Stoneham Cotts PO33......11 E5
Stone La
    Gosport PO12..........52 B4
    5 Gosport PO12.......52 B5
Stonelands Orch PO33.....11 F5
Stonelands Pk PO33.......11 F5
Stonepitts Cl PO33........12 A6
Stones Cl PO31.............3 A4
Stone St PO5.............54 A1
Stony La PO1.............53 A6
Stower Pl PO36...........35 F7
Strand SO14..............51 A4
Strand The PO33..........12 D6
Stratford Ho PO5...........54 B2
Stratford Pl SO41.........48 D5
Strathmore Rd PO12.......52 C5
Strathwell Cres PO38......45 D6
Strawberry La PO30........29 E5
Stroud Rd PO40...........27 C8
Stroud Wood Rd PO33.....11 E2
Suffolk Ave SO15.........50 D7
Sultan Rd PO1............53 D7
Summerfields Prim Sch
    PO30.................20 F8
Summers Ct PO40.........27 A8
Summers La PO39.........26 H7
Summers St SO14.........51 C6
Sunbeam Way PO12.......52 B4
Sun Ct PO5..............54 C2
Sundowner SO14..........51 B2
Sun Hill
    Calbourne PO30........18 B2
    Cowes PO31............3 B5
Sunningdale Rd PO30......20 C6
Sunnyhill Cl PO30.........35 C3
Sunnyside Gdns PO36......35 E4
Sunnyvale PO37..........43 C8
Sunny Wlk PO1...........53 A6
Sun Pl PO33..............12 C5

Sunset Bgwls PO40.........14 D2
Sunset Cl PO40...........14 F1
Sunset Dr PO36...........35 F6
Sun St PO1..............53 A5
Surbiton Gr PO33..........12 D4
Surrey Cl SO15...........50 C6
Surrey Rd SO19...........51 D2
Surrey St
    Portsmouth PO1........54 B3
    Ryde PO33.............12 C4
Sussex Ct
    6 Gosport PO12.......52 C9
    Portsmouth PO5........54 B1
Sussex Pl
    Portsmouth, Landport PO1 .54 B4
    Portsmouth PO5........54 B1
SUSSEX PLACE............51 A4
Sussex Rd
    Portsmouth PO5........54 B1
    Southampton SO14......51 A4
Sussex Terr PO5...........54 B1
Sutherland Rd PO4........53 E4
Sutton Cl PO33...........12 D3
Suvretta Ho PO37..........43 C7
Swains La PO35...........25 D5
Swains Rd PO35...........25 D5
Swallow Cl PO30..........20 A6
Swanage Cl PO30.........20 A6
SWANMORE...............12 C4
Swanmore Mid Sch PO33 .12 B3
Swanmore Rd PO33........12 B4
Swan Quay SO18..........51 D8
Sway Rd SO41.............48 B6
Swedish Hos SO41.........49 E8
Swift Gdns SO31..........51 D1
Swift Hollow SO19.........51 D1
Swift Rd SO19............51 D1
Swiss Cottage Mus* PO32 .4 B2
Swiss Cottage Rd PO32 ....4 A2
Sycamore Gdns PO30......20 C7
Sycamores The PO33.......12 D4
Sydenham Ct PO1.........54 D3
Sydenham Terr PO1........54 D3
Sydney Cl PO30...........20 E5
Sydney Cotts PO36........24 B3
Sydney Ho PO1...........54 B4
Sydney Rd PO12..........52 B5
Sylvan Ave PO32...........3 D3
Sylvan Dr
    Carisbrooke PO30......20 B7
    Newport PO30..........20 C7
Synor Ho **12** SO15.......51 A6

T

Tadhurst Ho **4** PO1......54 C3
Talbot Ct **21** SO14.......51 A4
Talbot Rd
    Portsmouth PO4........53 E4
    Southampton SO15......50 D8
Tamar Cl PO36............35 F7
Tamarisk Gdns SO18......51 E8
Tamworth Ct **3** PO12....52 B4
Tandy Cl PO33............12 A4
Tanglewood SO41.........50 A1
Tankerville Rd SO19.......51 D3
Tapnell Cotts PO41.........16 C1
Tasman Cl SO14..........51 B2
Tasman Ct SO14..........51 B2
Tattels La PO41...........16 C6
Taylor Cl SO15............51 D1
Taylor Rd PO12...........52 C3
Tebourba Dr PO12.........52 A4
Ted Bates Ct **7** SO15 ...51 B3
Ted Bates Rd **8** SO14 ...51 B3
Ted Kelly Ct **43** PO1.....53 A5
Telephone Rd PO4.........53 E4
Temeraire **11** SO15.......50 F8
Templar Ct **2** SO14......51 A7
Temple Gdns SO19.........51 F2
Temple Rd SO19...........51 F2
Temple St PO1............54 B4
Tennyson Cl
    Ryde PO33.............12 A5
    Yarmouth PO41.........15 D6
Tennyson Ho **6** PO33 ....12 C6
Tennyson Mon The*
    PO39.................26 H5
Tennyson Rd
    Cowes PO31.............3 B3
    Freshwater PO40.......14 E1
    Portsmouth PO2........53 F8
    Yarmouth PO41.........15 E6
Tennysons View PO40......27 D6
Tennyson View PO30.......18 A3
Terence Gdns PO40........27 C6
Terminus Rd PO31..........3 A5
Terminus Terr SO14........51 B3
Ternal Mead PO38.........33 D1
Terrace La PO40...........27 C6
Terrace Rd PO30..........20 D6
Terrace The PO38.........44 C5
Testcombe Rd PO12.......52 A4
Testwood Rd SO15........50 B6
Teviot Ho **9** SO14........51 C6
Tewkesbury Ave PO12......52 B8
Thackeray Rd SO17........51 B8
Thatchers La SO41.........49 F8
Theatre Mews **17** PO5...53 D7
Thetis Rd PO31.............3 B4
Thicket The PO5...........54 C1
Thomas Grant Ave PO42 ...52 D7
THORLEY.................16 C6
Thorley Rd PO41..........15 E6
THORLEY STREET..........16 D5
Thornbrake Rd PO12.......52 C4

Thornbrough Cl PO33.......12 A5
Thornbury Ave SO15.......50 E7
Thorncroft Rd PO1.........53 E5
THORNCROSS.............38 F8
Thorncross La PO30........38 G7
Thorners Ct **8** SO15......50 F6
Thorner's Homes, Centre Ct
    15 SO15..............50 B8
Thorner's Homes, North Ct
    14 SO15..............50 B8
Thorner's Homes, South Ct
    16 SO15..............50 B8
Thorner's Homes, West Ct **13**
    SO15.................50 B8
Thorness La PO41..........50 B8
Thorngate Ct **5** PO12....52 A7
Thorngate Way **5** PO12 ..52 D5
Thornhill Flats...............3 A5
Thornleigh Rd SO19.......51 E2
Thornton Cl PO33..........12 F4
Thornton Manor Dr PO33 .12 F4
Thornton St PO2...........52 B9
Thornycroft Ave SO19......51 D2
Threefield La SO14.........51 A3
Three Gates Rd PO31........2 F2
Three Tun Cl PO38..........53 A5
Thruxton Ct SO19..........51 E5
Ticonderoga Gdns SO19...51 E1
Tides Reach
    Cowes PO31.............3 B4
    Southampton SO18......51 D8
    Yarmouth PO41.........15 D5
Tiger Rd PO1..............52 F8
Tilbrook Rd SO15..........50 A8
Tilbury Rd PO31............2 D3
Timberley Rd **2** PO1.....54 C3
Timpson Ho PO34..........13 D3
Timpson Rd PO1...........54 D4
Timsbury Ct SO15.........51 F4
Tinkers Hill PO30..........20 F7
Tintern Gr **2** SO15.......50 E5
Tintern Rd PO12...........52 A5
Tipton Ho PO5............54 B2
Tithe Barn SO41..........48 E5
Tivoli Ct PO7.............53 F8
Toby St PO1..............54 B4
Tonbridge St PO5..........53 C2
Torcross Cl SO19..........51 E2
Toronto Pl PO12...........52 B6
Toronto Rd PO2...........53 E7
Torquay Ave
    Gosport PO12..........52 A9
    Southampton SO15......50 D8
TOTLAND................26 H8
Tottenham Rd PO1........54 D4
Tower Ho SO19............51 E1
Tower Rd PO4............53 F3
Tower St PO1.............52 F4
Tower The **3** PO12.......52 B6
Town End PO38...........45 B4
Towngate Ret Pk PO30.....20 D7
Town La
    Chale Green PO30......40 A5
    Newport PO30..........20 E7
    Sandown PO36.........35 F5
Town Mews PO36..........35 F5
Town Quay
    Cowes PO31.............3 B5
    Portsmouth PO1........52 F4
    Southampton SO15......50 F2
Trafalgar Ct
    Cowes PO31.............3 A5
    12 Newport PO30......20 D6
    6 Portsmouth PO5.....53 D2
Trafalgar Dr PO33.........11 F4
Trafalgar Pl
    Lymington SO41........48 F4
    Portsmouth PO1........54 D4
Trafalgar Rd
    Newport PO30..........20 D6
    Southampton, Freemantle
        SO15...............50 C6
    Southampton SO14......51 A2
Trafalgar Sq PO12.........52 B6
Tranby Rd SO19............51 E4
Tranmere Cl SO41.........48 F2
Treefields SO15...........12 A5
Treeside Rd SO15.........50 C8
Tregantle Mews PO12.....52 A5
Trelawny Way PO35........25 D5
Trent Ho **8** SO14.........51 C5
Trevanians Way PO39......27 A8
Trevor Rd
    Newport PO30..........20 C6
    Portsmouth PO4........53 E3
Tribe Rd PO12.............52 A6
Trimmer's Ct PO1.........52 F5
Trinity Church La PO31......3 A6
Trinity Ct PO12............52 E5
Trinity Ct
    Ryde PO33.............12 D6
    8 Southampton SO15 ..50 C6
Trinity Gn PO12...........52 E5
Trinity Rd
    Southampton SO14......51 A5
    Ventnor PO38..........47 B6
Trinity St PO33............12 D5
Troubridge Ct **7** PO1....53 D7
Troughton Ct PO36.........35 F5
Tudor Ct **3** PO5..........53 D1
Tulse Hill PO38............47 A6
Tupman Ho **1** PO1.......53 D7
Turf Wlk PO31.............14 C1
Turner Rd PO1............53 D7
Tuttons Hill PO30...........2 E3
Tweed La SO41...........48 D8
Twining Rd PO38...........46 B4
Twin Oaks SO19...........51 F3

Two Firs PO36............34 D6
Twyford Ho SO15..........50 F7
Tylers Cl SO41............48 D5
Tyne Wlk PO35............25 D5
Tyseley Rd PO5...........54 B2

U

Uffa Fox Pl PO31............3 B3
Ulster Cres PO30...........9 A1
Undercliff Dr PO38.........45 D3
Undercliff Gdns PO38......46 E5
Underwood PO38..........47 D7
Undershore SO41..........48 B6
Undershore Rd SO41.......49 A4
Unicorn Rd PO1...........54 B4
Unicorn Training Ctr The
    PO1..................54 A4
Union Pl
    7 Lymington SO41.....48 E4
    Portsmouth PO5........54 C4
Union Rd
    Cowes PO31.............3 A5
    Ryde PO33.............12 C6
    Sandown PO36.........35 F5
    Southampton SO14......51 C6
Union St
    Newport PO30..........20 D6
    10 Portsmouth PO1....53 A5
    Ryde PO33.............12 C6
University of Portsmouth **5**
    PO1..................54 A2
Univ of Portsmouth (Eldon
    Bldg) PO1.............54 B2
Unwin Cl SO19............51 D1
Uplands Rd
    Cowes PO31.............8 F8
    Totland PO39...........14 D1
Upper Adgestone Rd
    PO36.................23 E1
Upper Arundel St **3** SO15 54 B3
Upper Ash Dr PO38........45 E6
Upper Banister St **1**
    SO15.................50 F6
UPPER BONCHURCH.......47 D2
Upper Bugle St SO14.......50 F3
Upper Comm Rd SO41......48 A3
Upper Green Rd PO33......24 F7
Upper Highland Rd PO33 ..12 D4
Upper Horn Hill PO31.......2 C3
Upper House La PO38......44 D6
UPPER HYDE..............42 F7
Upper Hyde Farm La
    PO37.................43 A8
Upper Hyde La PO37.......43 A8
Upper La PO30............30 B2
Upper Moorgreen Rd PO31 .2 D5
UPPER PENNINGTON.......48 A3
Upper Rd PO36............23 D1
Upper Woodside Rd PO33 .10 F7
Upper Yarborough Rd
    PO32..................3 D3
UPTON...................12 A2
Upton Rd PO33............12 A3

V

Vadne Gdns PO12.........52 B7
Vale Gr PO12.............52 A8
Vale The PO5.............53 C2
Valley Wlk PO32............4 A3
Vancouver Wharf SO19.....51 C4
Vanguard Rd **5** PO12.....52 C9
Varna Rd SO15...........50 C6
Varos Cl PO12............52 A7
Vaughan Way PO37........43 C6
Vectis Cotts PO30...........9 B4
Vectis Rd PO12............3 D2
Velsheda Ct PO39.........14 D1
Velsheda View PO31.........2 F3
Venner Ave PO31...........8 F8
VENTNOR................47 B5
Ventnor Botanic Gdn*
    PO38.................46 D4
Ventnor Heritage Mus*
    PO38.................47 A6
Ventnor Ind Est PO38.......47 A6
Ventnor Middle Sch PO38 .46 E7
Ventnor Rd
    Portsmouth PO4........53 E4
    Shanklin PO36.........34 E2
    Whitwell PO38.........45 E5
Vereker Dr PO32...........3 D4
Verlands Cl PO38..........45 B3
Vernon Cl PO12...........52 A6
Vernon Rd PO12...........52 A6
Vernon Sq PO30...........20 C5
Vernon Wlk **5** SO15......50 F6
Verulam Rd SO14..........51 B7
Verwood Dr PO33..........11 E4
Vespasian Ct SO18.........51 D7
Vespasian Rd SO18........51 D7
Vicarage La PO36..........44 C5
Vicarage Wlk PO30........20 D7
Victoria & Albert Almshouses
    PO32...................9 E8
Victoria Ave
    Portsmouth PO1........53 B3
    Shanklin PO37.........43 B7
Victoria Cotts PO33.......12 E3
Victoria Ct
    East Cowes PO32........3 D3
    Freshwater Bay PO40 ...27 C2
    Newport PO30..........20 D6
    6 Portsmouth PO1.....53 D7

Victoria Ct continued
    Shanklin PO37..........43 C
Victoria Gr
    East Cowes PO32........3 D
    Portsmouth PO5........54 C
Victoria Mews PO31........3 A
Victoria Pl
    6 Gosport PO12.......52 B
    4 Lymington SO41.....48 E
    Ryde PO33.............12 C
Victoria Rd
    Bouldnor PO41.........16 C
    Cowes PO31.............3 A
    Freshwater Bay PO40 ...27 C
    Newport PO30..........20 D
    Portsmouth PO1........53 A
    Sandown PO36.........36 A
    Southampton SO19......51 D
    Yarmouth PO41.........15 D
Victoria Road N PO5.......54 C
Victoria Road S PO5.......53 D
Victoria St
    Gosport PO12..........52 C
    Newport PO30..........20 D
    Ryde PO33.............12 C
    Shanklin PO37.........43 C
    Ventnor PO38..........47 B
Victory Cl PO33...........11 F
Victory Cres PO5..........50 B
Victory Rd
    27 Portsmouth PO1....53 A
    Southampton SO15......50 B
    Ventnor PO38..........46 C
Victory Ret Pk PO2........53 C
Village Rd PO12...........52 A
Villiers Ct **18** PO5.......53 C
Villiers Rd
    Portsmouth PO5........54 C
    Southampton SO15......50 C
Vincent Rd SO15..........50 C
Vincent's Gr SO15.........50 B
Vincent St SO15...........50 C
Vincent's Wlk SO14........51 A
Vineyard Cl SO19..........51 D
Viney Rd SO41............48 F
Vinings Gdns PO36........35 F
Vinings Rd PO36...........35 F
Vinyard The PO41..........15 F
Vitre Gdns SO41...........48 E
Vittlefield Cross PO30......19 C
Vittlefields Ind Est PO30 ..19 B.
Vivash Rd PO1............54 D
Vulcan The **19** PO1.......53 A
Vyse La **18** SO14........50 F

W

WACKLAND................34 C.
Wackland La PO36.........34 D
Wainsford Cl SO41.........48 B.
Wainsford Ct SO41.........48 C
Wakefield Pl PO12.........52 A.
Waldegrave Cl SO19.......51 D
WALHAMPTON............49 A.
Walhampton Hill SO41.....48 F
Walker's La PO30..........31 B.
Wallace Ct PO30..........20 F
Wallace Rd
    Portsmouth PO2........53 F
    Southampton SO19......51 F
Wallis Cl PO33............42 C
Walls Rd PO35............25 E.
Walmer Rd PO1...........53 E
Walpole Rd PO12..........52 D
Walpole Terr **21** PO12 ..52 D
Waltham St PO5...........54 A
Walton Cl PO12...........52 A
Walton Ct **10** PO1.......53 A
Walton Lodge PO33........12 E.
Walton Rd PO12...........52 A
Waltzing Waters Aqua
    Theatre* PO33.........12 F
Warblington Cl **3** PO1...53 A
Warblington St PO1........53 A
WARBORNE..............48 F
Warborne La SO41.........48 F
Ward Ave PO31............3 A
Ward Cl PO30.............20 B
Warden Ct **2** PO12......52 B
Ward Ho PO1.............53 A
Ward Rd PO39............14 C
Wards Cotts PO33..........3 B
Warlands La PO30..........17 D
Warnes La PO30...........30 B
Warnford Cr PO12.........52 A
Warnford Ct SO15.........51 F
Warren Cr PO36...........35 D
Warren Point PO31.........9 B
Warren The PO36..........35 F
Warrior Ave PO5...........54 B
Warwick Cres PO5.........54 B
Warwick La SO41..........51 C
Warwick Pl **4** SO41......51 C
Warwick St PO5...........54 C
Washington Rd PO2........53 F
WATERFORD..............49 B
Waterford Cl SO41.........48 F
Waterford La SO41.........48 E
Watergate **12** PO12......52 B
Waterhouse La SO15.......50 D
Waterhouse Way SO15 ....50 D
Water La **2** SO15........50 F
Waterloo Cres PO33.......11 F

Waterloo Rd
Gosport PO12 . . . . .52 C2
Lymington SO41. . . . . .48 F4
Southampton SO15 . . . . . . .50 D6
Waterloo St PO5. . . . . .54 B2
Waterloo Terr SO15 . . . . . .50 F6
Waterman Terr PO5 . . . . . .54 D1
Waters Edge PO41 . . . . . . .15 F6
Watersider Pool PO33 . . . . .12 D6
Watery La PO36. . . . . .34 D5
Watts Rd PO1. . . . . .53 D7
Wavecrest Cl SO40. . . . . . .50 A3
Waverley Ct PO37. . . . . . . .43 D7
Waverley Gr PO4. . . . . .53 E2
Waverley Rd
Portsmouth PO4 . . . . .53 E2
Southampton SO15 . . . . . .50 D5
Wavesound Cl PO35. . . . . . .25 E4
Wayside Dr PO30 . . . . .20 D8
Weavers Yd PO35 . . . . .25 E4
Webbers Way PO12 . . . . . . .52 C3
Webster Way PO36. . . . . . . .35 A8
WEEKE 54 B8
Week La PO38 . . . . .46 A6
WEEKS 12 C4
Weeks Rd
Ryde, Swanmore PO33 . . . . .12 C3
Ryde, Weeks PO33. . . . . . . .12 C4
Weevil La PO12. . . . . .52 D7
Welch Rd
Gosport PO12 . . . . .52 A8
Portsmouth PO4 . . . . .53 E2
Weller Ho St PO1 . . . . .53 D7
Wellington Rd
East Cowes PO32 . . . . .3 E2
Gosport PO12. . . . . .52 C9
Ryde PO33. . . . . .12 B6
Southampton SO15 . . . . . .50 B8
Wellington Lodge PO33 . . . .12 B6
Wellington Rd
Carisbrooke PO30 . . . . . . .20 B6
Ryde PO33. . . . . .11 F4
Wellington Sq PO41. . . . . . .15 D5
Wellington St PO5 . . . . .54 B2
WELLOW 16 F5
Wellow Ct PO30 . . . . .20 D6
Wellow Top Rd PO41 . . . . . .17 B4
Well Rd PO32. . . . . .3 C4
Well St PO33 . . . . .12 C4
Wellworth Rd PO33 . . . . . . .11 E5
Wellworthy Rd SO41 . . . . . .48 D6
Wentworth Cl PO37 . . . . . . .43 A7
Wesley Ct
Portsmouth PO1 . . . . .54 D3
Ventnor PO38 . . . . .48 F6
Wessex Ct St SO17. . . . . . . .51 A8
Wessex Gate St SO15 . . . . . .50 E7
West Ashey Farm Cotts
PO33 . . . . .23 A5
West Ave PO36 . . . . .35 D3
West Bargate St SO14. . . . . .50 F4
West Bay Rd SO15 . . . . .50 C5
Westbourne Rd PO2 . . . . . . .53 F8
West Cl
Cranmore PO41. . . . . .5 D7
Lymington SO41. . . . . .48 B2
Westcliff Mews SO19. . . . . . .51 D3
Westcourt Cl PO30. . . . . . . .31 B2
West Ct
Portsmouth, Buckland
PO1. . . . . .53 E7
Southampton SO19 . . . . . . .51 F1
Western District Cut
SO15 . . . . .50 D7
Western Esplanade SO14,
SO15 . . . . .50 F3
Western Par PO5 . . . . .53 B2
Western Rd
Lymington SO41. . . . . .48 D4
Shanklin PO37. . . . . .43 C7
Western Way PO1. . . . . .52 F8
Westfield Bglws PO38. . . . . .47 C6
Westfield Ind Est PO12. . . . .52 A5
Westfield Mews PO38 . . . . . .47 C6
Westfield Pk PO33 . . . . .12 B6
Westfield Rd
Lymington SO41. . . . . .49 A2
Southampton SO15 . . . . . .50 A7
St Helens PO33 . . . . .24 F7
Westgate St St SO14 . . . . . . .50 F3
West Gn PO33 . . . . .24 E7
West Hayes SO41 . . . . .48 F3
West Hill Ct SO15. . . . . .50 E5
West Hill Dr PO37. . . . . .43 B7
West Hill Gr St PO31 . . . . .3 B4
Westhill La PO41. . . . . .15 A6
Westhill Rd
Cowes PO31 . . . . .3 B4
Shanklin PO37. . . . . .43 B6
West Hill Rd PO33 . . . . .12 E5

West La PO33, PO36 . . . . . . .23 F5
Westlake Ave PO36. . . . . . . .35 D2
Westland Gdns PO12. . . . . . .52 A4
Westlands PO39 . . . . .14 E1
West Marlands St SO14. . . . .50 F5
Westmill PO30. . . . . .20 C6
Westmill Rd PO30. . . . . .20 B7
Westminster La PO30 . . . . . .20 C7
Westminster Pl PO1. . . . . . . .53 D7
WESTON. 51 F1
Weston Cl SO19. . . . . .51 F1
Weston Com Sch PO39. . . . . .26 G8
Weston Grove Rd SO19. . . . .51 D2
Weston La
Southampton SO19 . . . . . . .51 F1
Totland PO39. . . . . .26 G7
Weston Rd
Cowes PO31 . . . . .3 A4
Totland PO39. . . . . .26 G8
West Park Rd SO15 . . . . .50 F5
West Pl PO33. . . . . .12 B5
West Quay La SO14 . . . . .50 F4
West Quay Rd SO15. . . . . . . .50 E4
West St SO19 . . . . .51 E2
Westridge Cross PO33 . . . . . .12 E2
Westridge Ctr PO33 . . . . . . .12 F1
Westridge Rd SO17. . . . . . . .51 B8
Westrow Gdns SO15 . . . . . . .50 E7
Westrow Rd SO15. . . . . .50 E7
West Side PO36. . . . . .24 A3
Westside La PO38. . . . . .39 F2
West St
Brading PO36. . . . . .24 B3
Godshill PO38 . . . . .41 C8
Newport PO30 . . . . .20 D6
Portsmouth PO1. . . . . .54 F4
Ryde PO33. . . . . .12 B6
Seaview PO34 . . . . .13 D4
Southampton SO14 . . . . . .50 F3
Ventnor PO38 . . . . .47 B6
Wroxall PO38. . . . . .42 B4
West View PO30. . . . . .20 D6
Westview Cotts PO38 . . . . . .44 C7
Westview Rd PO31. . . . . .2 C1
Westview Terr PO33 . . . . . . .12 D5
Westway PO31. . . . . .8 E8
West Way SO41 . . . . .48 C2
West Wight Mid Sch
PO40 . . . . .27 B8
West Wight Sp Ctr PO40 . . . .27 B8
Westwood Cl PO31. . . . . .2 F7
Westwood Ct St SO17. . . . . . .51 A8
Westwood Dr PO33 . . . . .12 B5
Westwood Rd
Ryde PO33. . . . . .12 B5
Southampton SO17 . . . . . . .51 A8
Wharf Rd
Portsmouth PO2 . . . . .53 C8
Southampton SO19 . . . . . . .51 D3
Wharncliffe Ho SO19. . . . . . .51 D3
Wharncliffe Rd SO19. . . . . . .51 D3
Wheatear Cl PO30 . . . . .20 A6
Wheatstone Rd PO4 . . . . .53 F3
Wheeler Cl PO12 . . . . .52 B7
Wheelers Bay Rd PO38. . . . . .47 B5
Wheeler Way PO37 . . . . .35 D2
Whinscot Cl PO38. . . . . .45 D7
WHIPPINGHAM. 9 E8
Whippingham Cty Prim Sch
PO32 . . . . .9 F7
Whippingham Rd PO32. . . . . . .9 F7
Whitaker Cres SO41. . . . . . . .48 C3
Whitchurch Ct SO19 . . . . . . .51 F3
Whitcombe Cross PO30 . . . . .20 B3
Whitcombe Gdns PO1. . . . . . .53 F6
Whiteacres Cl St PO12. . . . . . .52 B6
Whitecliff Cl PO36 . . . . .36 C5
White Cloud Pk PO4. . . . . . . .53 F3
White Cloud Pl PO4. . . . . . . .53 F3
WHITECROSS 35 D3
Whitecross Ave PO37 . . . . . . .35 C2
Whitecross Farm La PO36 . . . .35 C2
Whitecross La
Apse Heath PO37 . . . . .34 F2
Shanklin SO36, SO37. . . . . .35 C2
Whitefield Terr PO33 . . . . . . .12 D4
White Hart Rd
St PO12. . . . . .52 B5
Portsmouth PO1. . . . . .53 A3
Whitehead Cres PO33. . . . . . .10 E5
Whitehouse Gdns SO15 . . . . .50 A6
Whitehouse Rd PO30. . . . . . . .7 F3
Whitelaw Rd SO15. . . . . .50 B7
WHITELEY BANK 42 C8
White Lion Wlk PO12 . . . . . . .52 D6
White Oaks Cl St SO16. . . . . .50 B8
Whitepit La PO30. . . . . .20 C5
Whiterails Rd PO33 . . . . .10 C2

White's Mead PO36. . . . . . . .35 D4
Whitesmith Rd PO30 . . . . .9 A1
Whitestar Pl St SO14 . . . . . . .51 B3
White Swan Rd PO1 . . . . .54 A3
Whitethorns Ct PO36. . . . . . .35 F5
Whithedwood Ave SO15. . . . .50 D8
WHITWELL. 45 E6
Whitwell Farm Maisonettes
PO38 . . . . .45 E6
Whitwell Rd
Godshill PO38 . . . . .41 C6
Portsmouth PO4 . . . . .53 E1
Ventnor PO38 . . . . .46 C5
Whitworth Cl PO12 . . . . .52 B5
Whitworth Cres SO18 . . . . . .51 D8
Whitworth Ct SO18 . . . . .51 D7
Whitworth Rd
Gosport PO12 . . . . .52 A6
Portsmouth PO2 . . . . .53 F8
Southampton SO18 . . . . . .51 D8
Wicken Hill La PO30 . . . . . . .38 E8
Wickham St PO1. . . . . .53 A5
Wicks Cl PO33. . . . . .12 D4
Widbury Rd SO41. . . . . .48 C2
Widgeon Cl PO12. . . . . .52 B8
Wight Hall Ct PO33 . . . . .12 E6
Wigmore Ho PO1. . . . . .54 C4
Wilberforce Rd
Brighstone PO30 . . . . .30 B2
Gosport PO12 . . . . .52 C2
Portsmouth PO5 . . . . .54 B1
Wilkes Rd PO36. . . . . .35 F5
Willet's Cross PO30. . . . . . . .31 B1
William Booth Ho St PO1. . . . .53 B5
William Rd SO41. . . . . .48 E5
William St
Ryde PO33. . . . . .12 B3
Southampton SO14 . . . . . .51 C5
Willis Rd
Gosport PO12 . . . . .52 C5
Portsmouth PO1. . . . . .54 C4
Withey Cl PO30. . . . . .20 B6
Withgood Cl PO30. . . . . .17 E7
Withyfields PO30 . . . . .17 F7
Wolfe Cl PO30 . . . . .20 B6
Wolseley Rd SO15 . . . . .50 C7
Wolverton Rd SO14 . . . . .51 B5
Woodbine Cl PO30. . . . . .20 D6
Woodbine Cotts PO36 . . . . . .24 B2
Woodhall Dr PO36 . . . . .35 C3
Woodhill Cl PO33. . . . . .12 D4
Woodland Cl PO40. . . . . .15 A1
Woodland Dr PO37 . . . . .43 B7
Woodland Gr PO35. . . . . .25 C4
Woodland Mews PO33 . . . . . .12 C5
Woodland Pl St SO15 . . . . . . .50 E7
Woodlands PO35 . . . . .25 D4
Woodlands Cres PO33. . . . . . .10 E5
Woodland St PO1. . . . . .54 D4
Woodlands Way SO15 . . . . . .50 F8
Woodland View PO33. . . . . . .12 B3
Woodley Gdns SO41. . . . . . . .48 D5
Woolley Rd
Gosport PO12 . . . . .52 C5
Southampton SO19 . . . . . .51 D3
Woodmoor Cl SO41. . . . . . . .50 A1
Woodnutt Cl PO35 . . . . .25 D5
Woodpath PO5 . . . . .54 B1
Woodpath Ho PO5. . . . . .54 B1
Woods Dr PO30. . . . . .34 E4
WOODSIDE 48 E1
Woodside Ave
Alverstone Garden Village
PO36. . . . . .35 A7
Lymington SO41. . . . . .48 E1
Woodside Cl
Cowes PO31 . . . . .8 E8
Lymington SO41 . . . . .48 E2
Woodside Ct St SO17 . . . . . . .51 B8
Woodside La SO41 . . . . .48 E1
WOODSIDE (NR
WOOTTON). 11 A7
Woodside Rd
Southampton SO17 . . . . . . .51 B8
Wootton PO33 . . . . .11 A7
Wood St PO33 . . . . .12 D5
Woodvale Cl PO31 . . . . .2 E4
Woodvale Ho PO31. . . . . .2 E4
Woodwale Rd PO31. . . . . .2 E4
Woodville Dr St PO31. . . . . . .53 B3
Woolcombe Rd PO30. . . . . .9 A2
Woolley Ho St SO14 . . . . . . .51 A5
WOOLSTON 51 E2
Woolston Inf Sch SO19 . . . . .51 E2
Woolston Sta SO19 . . . . .51 D3
Wooton Lodge PO33 . . . . . . .10 E5
WOOTTON 10 D5
WOOTTON BRIDGE 10 E4

Windsor Ct continued
St Southampton, Westwood Pk
SO17. . . . . .51 A8
Windsor Dr PO37. . . . . .43 A7
Windsor Ho St PO1 . . . . .54 C3
Windsor La St PO5 . . . . .54 B2
Windsor Mews St PO33 . . . . .12 C5
Windsor Rd PO12. . . . . .52 A5
Windward St St PO12. . . . . . .52 C5
WINFORD. 34 E5
Winford Cross PO36. . . . . . . .34 D5
Winford Ct PO36. . . . . .34 E4
Winford Rd
Newchurch PO36. . . . . .34 D7
Winford PO36 . . . . .34 D4
Winford Way PO36. . . . . .34 F5
Wingfield St PO1 . . . . .53 D7
Winkle St
Calbourne PO30. . . . . .18 A2
Southampton SO14 . . . . . .51 A2
Winn Ct SO17. . . . . .50 E7
Winston Ave PO33 . . . . .12 A4
Winston Churchill Ave
PO5 . . . . .54 B2
Winston Rd
Cowes PO31 . . . . .2 F4
Newport PO30 . . . . .20 C5
Winton Cl SO41. . . . . .48 F3
Winton Ct PO33. . . . . .12 D5
Winton St
Ryde PO33. . . . . .12 D5
St Southampton SO14. . . . . .51 A5
Wisborough Rd PO5 . . . . .53 E2
Wises Ct St PO12 . . . . .52 E5
Wish Pl PO5 . . . . .54 D1
Witbank Cl PO37 . . . . .35 C1
Witbank Gdns PO37. . . . . . . .35 C1
Withers Rd PO38. . . . . .40 A4
Withewood Mans St 50 C7
Wootton Bsns Pk PO33. . . . .10 B2
Wootton Prim Sch PO33 . . .10 D5
Wootton Sta* PO33. . . . . . .10 D3
Worcester Cl
St Portsmouth PO5. . . . . . .54 C2
Sandown PO36 . . . . .35 E6
St Southsea PO5. . . . . .54 B2
Worcester Pl St SO41 . . . . .48 F2
Worcester Rd PO30 . . . . . . .8 F1
Worsley Cl PO38. . . . . .42 C4
Worsley Dr PO38. . . . . .42 B5
Worsley La PO31. . . . . .2 D4
Worsley Rd
Godshill PO38 . . . . .33 D1
Gurnard PO31. . . . . .2 D1
Newport PO30. . . . . .20 C8
Norton PO41. . . . . .15 A6
Worth Apts PO5 . . . . .53 D1
Worthing Rd PO5 . . . . .53 D2
Wrax Rd PO36. . . . . .24 B2
Wray St PO33. . . . . .12 B3
Wrexham Ave PO33 . . . . . .12 A3
WROXALL. 42 C4
Wroxall Cl PO33 . . . . .11 F8
Wroxall Ho PO38. . . . . . . .42 C4
Wroxall Prim Sch PO38 . . .42 C4
Wyatts Cl PO31 . . . . .8 E8
Wyatts La PO31. . . . . .8 F8
Wychwood Cl PO34 . . . . . .13 D2
Wykeham Cl SO41 . . . . . . .48 B3
Wykeham Rd PO30. . . . . . .20 E6
Wymering Rd PO2 . . . . . . .53 E8
Wyndcliffe Rd PO4. . . . . . .53 E3
Wyndham Ct SO15 . . . . . .50 E5
Wyndham Mews PO1 . . . . .53 A3
Wyndham Pl St SO15 . . . . .50 E5

Wat–Zil 67

Y

YAFFORD 38 H8
Yaldhurst La SO41 . . . . . . .48 B3
Yapton St PO1. . . . . .54 B3
Yarborough Cl PO38 . . . . . .33 C1
Yarborough Ho PO33 . . . . .47 A5
Yarborough Ho PO36. . . . . .36 A4
Yarborough Rd
East Cowes PO32 . . . . .3 C3
Portsmouth PO5 . . . . .54 B1
Wroxall PO38. . . . . .42 C4
Yarborough Terr PO38. . . . . .42 C4
YARBRIDGE 24 A1
YARMOUTH 15 D6
Yarmouth Castle* PO41. . . .15 C6
Yarmouth CE Prim Sch
PO41. . . . . .15 C5
Yarmouth Rd PO30. . . . . . . .19 B7
Yar Quay PO33. . . . . .25 A6
Yarrell Croft SO41. . . . . . . .48 B3
Yarrell Mead SO41 . . . . . . .48 B3
YAVERLAND. 36 C6
Yaverland Cl PO36 . . . . . . .36 C5
Yaverland Rd PO36. . . . . . .36 C5
Yelfs Rd St PO33. . . . . .12 C6
York Ave PO32. . . . . .3 D3
York Bldgs SO14. . . . . .51 A4
York Cl SO14 . . . . .51 C6
Yorke St PO5 . . . . .54 A2
York Ho
St Gosport PO12. . . . . .52 D5
St Southampton SO14. . . . .51 C6
York La PO39 . . . . .26 G7
York Pl PO1 . . . . .53 B6
York Rd
Newport PO30. . . . . .20 E6
Sandown PO36 . . . . .35 F5
Southampton SO15 . . . . . .50 C7
Totland PO39 . . . . .26 F6
Ventnor PO38 . . . . .46 F6
York St PO31 . . . . .3 B4
York Villas PO38 . . . . .46 E6
York Wlk St SO14 . . . . .51 A4
Youngwoods Copse PO36 . .35 A7
Youngwoods Way PO36 . . .35 A7
Yves Mews PO5. . . . . .53 D2

Z

Zetland Rd PO12. . . . . . . .52 B6
Zig Zag Rd PO38. . . . . . . .46 F6
Zille Est PO33 . . . . .12 D6

Willment Marine & Bsns Pk
SO19 . . . . .51 D5
Willments Ind Est SO19 . . . . .51 D4
Willow Cl PO38 . . . . .46 E7
Willow Ct St PO30 . . . . .20 D6
Willowdene Ct PO35 . . . . . . .25 E4
Willow Pl PO12 . . . . .52 B6
Willows The
Newport PO30 . . . . .20 C7
Ryde PO33. . . . . .12 D4
Willowtree Dr PO34. . . . . . . .13 D2
Willow Tree Dr PO31 . . . . .8 F7
Willow Tree Ho SO41. . . . . . .48 C2
Willow Way PO30 . . . . .35 D3
Wilmar Lodge PO36. . . . . . . .35 D3
Wilmcote Gdns St PO5. . . . . .54 C3
Wilmcote Ho PO5 . . . . .54 C3
Wilmingham La PO41 . . . . . .15 E2
Wilson Gr PO5. . . . . .54 C1
Wilson St SO14 . . . . .51 C5
Wilton Ave SO15 . . . . .50 D8
Wilton Cl SO15 . . . . .50 D8
Wilton Park Rd PO37. . . . . . .35 C1
Wilton Pl PO5 . . . . .53 D2
Wilton Rd PO37. . . . . .35 C1
Wilton Terr PO5. . . . . .53 D2
Wiltshire St PO5 . . . . .54 A2
Wiverley Cl SO41. . . . . .48 B2
Wilver Rd PO30. . . . . .20 C6
Wimbledon Park Rd PO5. . . . .53 C2
Wimpole Ct PO1 . . . . .54 C4
Wimpole St PO1 . . . . .54 C4
Winchat Cl PO30. . . . . .20 B6
Winchester Cl
Newport PO30 . . . . .20 C5
Sandown PO36 . . . . .35 E6
Winchester Cnr PO30 . . . . . .17 F7
Winchester Mews
Ryde PO33. . . . . .12 D5
St Southampton SO17. . . . . .51 A8
Winchester Park Ct PO36 . . . .35 F5
Winchester Park Rd PO36 . . . .35 F6
Winchester Rd PO30 . . . . . . .20 C5
Winchester St St SO23 . . . . . .53 E8
Winchfield Cl St PO15. . . . . . .50 F6
Winchfield Ho St PO12. . . . . .52 E5
Windemere Ct PO37 . . . . .35 D1
Winding Way PO31. . . . . .2 D4
Windmill Cl
Cowes PO31 . . . . .3 A3
Newport PO30 . . . . .12 A2
Windmill Cotts PO35 . . . . . . .25 D4
Windmill La PO29. . . . . .26 H8
Windsor Ct
St Portsmouth PO5. . . . . . . .53 C2
St Southampton, Bevois Mount
SO17. . . . . .51 A8
St Southampton, Bitterne
SO19. . . . . .51 E7
St Southampton, Millbrook
SO15. . . . . .50 A6